NEW TESTAMENT GREEK

NEW TESTAMENT GREEK

A Beginning and Intermediate Grammar

by

JAMES ALLEN HEWETT
B.A., B.D., M.A., Ph.D.

 HENDRICKSON PUBLISHERS

Copyright © 1986 Hendrickson Publishers, Inc.
P.O. Box 3473
Peabody, MA 01961-3473
All rights reserved
Printed in the United States of America

ISBN: 0-913573-32-9

Third Printing —August 1995

The Greek text used herein is the United Bible
Societies' 3rd edition of the *Greek New Testament.*
Copyright © 1966, 1968, 1975. American Bible Society.
Used with permission.

Library of Congress Cataloging-in-Publication Data

Hewett, James Allen.
   New Testament Greek : a beginning and intermediate grammar / by
James Allen Hewett.
      p. cm..
   Includes bibliographical references and index.
   "The Greek text used herein is the United Bible Societies' 3rd
edition of the Greek New Testament."
   ISBN 0-913573-32-9
   1. Greek language. Biblical —Grammar.   2. Bible. N.T.—Language,
style. I. Title
PA817.H4 1989
487'.4—dc20   89-11123
                                           CIP

To
Barbara,
Gregory, Kara,
Lisa, and Matthew

TABLE OF CONTENTS

PREFACE   xiii

CHAPTER

1. ALPHABET, ORTHOGRAPHY, AND PUNCTUATION   1
   The Alphabet   1
   Vowels, Diphthongs   2
   Iota Subscript, Formation of Lower-Case Letters,
      Breathing Marks   3
   Syllabification, Accents   4
   Punctuation, Other Marks, A Textual Criticism Note   7
   Exercises   8

2. VERB SYSTEM. I: PRIMARY, ACTIVE ENDINGS AND TENSES,
   INDICATIVE MOOD   9
   Definition of Verb, Methodology in Verb Formation   9
   Two Categories of Verb Tenses: Primary and Secondary
      Set I: Primary Tenses, Active Voice   10
   Time and Kind of Action, Movable ν   13
   Exercises   14

3. NOUN SYSTEM. I: SECOND DECLENSION. THE VERB "TO BE"   15
   Vocabulary   15
   Nouns and Adjectives: Their Declensions and
      Characteristics   16
   Functions of Greek Inflectional Forms   17
   Formation of Second Declension   19
   Function of Adjectives   21
   The Verb "To Be"   22
   Exercises   24

4. NOUN SYSTEM. II: FIRST DECLENSION. CONDITIONAL
   SENTENCES   27
   Vocabulary   27
   Formation of First Declension Nouns and Adjectives   28
   Formation of the First Declension Article   31
   Second Declension Feminines, Nouns in the Attributive
      Position, Conditional Sentences   32
   Exercises   33

5. NOUN SYSTEM. III: PERSONAL AND RELATIVE PRONOUNS   35
    Vocabulary   35
    Personal Pronouns   36
    The Relative Pronoun   39
    Exercises   40

6. NOUN SYSTEM. III (CONT.): DEMONSTRATIVE AND REFLEXIVE
    PRONOUNS   43
    Vocabulary   43
    Demonstrative Pronouns   44
    Reflexive Pronouns   45
    Exercises   46

7. PREPOSITIONS, COMPOUND VERBS, ὅτι   49
    Vocabulary   49
    Definitions and Purpose of Prepositions, Compound
    Verbs   50
    Prepositions in Attributive Position and as Substantives,
    ὅτι   51
    Exercises   52

8. VERB SYSTEM. II: SECONDARY ACTIVE ENDINGS AND TENSES:
    IMPERFECT TENSE. IMPERFECT OF εἰμί. CONDITIONAL
    SENTENCES. ADVERBS   55
    Vocabulary   55
    Secondary Active Endings and Tenses   56
    Imperfect Tense Active Voice   57
    Imperfect of εἰμί. Conditional Sentences   59
    Adverbs   60
    Exercises   61

9. VERB SYSTEM. II (CONT.): SECONDARY ACTIVE ENDINGS.
    AORIST TENSES   63
    Vocabulary   63
    Aorist Tense Active Voice   66
    Aorist Tense Passive Voice   70
    Exercises   72

10. VERB SYSTEM. II (CONT.): SECONDARY ACTIVE ENDINGS.
    PERFECT ACTIVE: PLUPERFECT ACTIVE. CONDITIONAL
    SENTENCES   73
    Vocabulary   73
    Perfect Tense Active Voice   74
    Pluperfect Tense Active Voice   76

Aorist Tense in Contrary-to-Fact Conditional Sentences　　78
Exercises　　78

11. VERB SYSTEM. III: PRIMARY MIDDLE ENDINGS AND TENSES, INDICATIVE MOOD. DEPONENT VERBS. FUTURE OF εἰμί. RECIPROCAL PRONOUN　　81
Vocabulary　　81
Significance of Middle and Passive Voices　　82
Formation and Translation of Primary Middle Tenses　　83
Instrumental Dative of Impersonal Means　　87
Deponent Verbs, εἰμί: Future Tense, Reciprocal Pronoun　　88
Exercises　　89

12. VERB SYSTEM. IV: SECONDARY MIDDLE ENDINGS AND TENSES, INDICATIVE MOOD: IMPERFECT MIDDLE/PASSIVE TENSE; FIRST AND SECOND AORIST MIDDLE TENSES; PLUPERFECT MIDDLE/PASSIVE TENSE　　91
Formation and Translation of Secondary Middle Tenses　　91
The Indicative Mood: A Review　　93
Exercises　　96

13. NOUN SYSTEM. III: THIRD DECLENSION MASCULINE AND FEMININE NOUNS　　97
Vocabulary　　97
Formation of Third Declension Masculine and Feminine Nouns: Stems Ending with a Consonant　　98
Formation of Third Declension Feminine and Masculine Nouns: Stems Ending with a Vowel　　102
Neuter Plural Subjects with Singular Verbs, Exercises　　103

14. NOUN SYSTEM. III (CONT.): THIRD DECLENSION NEUTER NOUNS, ADJECTIVES AND NUMERALS; INDEFINITE/INTERROGATIVE PRONOUNS　　105
Vocabulary　　105
Formation of Third Declension Neuter Nouns　　106
Third Declension Nouns Presented in This Text: A Summary　　108
Adjectives and Numerals　　108
Indefinite and Interrogative Pronouns　　111
Exercises　　112

15. CONTRACT VERBS; LIQUID VERBS; NOMINATIVE TO NAME SOMEONE; NOMINATIVE ABSOLUTE; COMPARATIVE AND SUPERLATIVE OF ADVERBS AND ADJECTIVES　　115

Vocabulary   115
Formation of Contract Verbs   116
Formation of Liquid Verbs   121
The Nominative to Name Someone; Nominative Abso-
  lute; Comparative and Superlative Degrees of Adverbs
  and Adjectives   122
Exercises   123

16. -μι VERBS   125
Vocabulary   125
Conjugation of -μι Verbs   126
Exercises   131

17. PARTICIPLES: THEIR FORMATION   133
Vocabulary: More -εω Contract Verbs   133
Participles: A Definition   134
Formation of Participles   134
Exercises   144

18. FUNCTION OF PARTICIPLES: ADJECTIVAL AND SUPPLEMENTARY   145
Vocabulary   145
A Word About Translating Participles   145
Temporal Value   146
The Adjectival Participle   148
The Supplementary Participle   150
Exercises   152

19. FUNCTION OF PARTICIPLES (CONT.): ADVERBIAL-CIRCUMSTAN-
  TIAL. ADVERBS   155
Vocabulary   155
Adverbial-Circumstantial Participles, Definition of Cir-
  cumstantial Participle   156
Types of Circumstantial Participles   156
Genitive Absolute   158
Exercises   159

20. THE SUBJUNCTIVE MOOD   161
Vocabulary   161
English and the Subjunctive Mood   162
Tenses in the Subjunctive Mood   162
Formation of the Subjunctive Mood Tenses   163
Uses of the Subjunctive Mood   166
Anticipated Answers to Questions, Exercises   171

21. INFINITIVES, INDIRECT DISCOURSE   173
    Vocabulary   173
    Infinitives: A Definition   174
    Formation of Infinitives   176
    Functions of the Infinitive   177
    Use of ὥστε, Indirect Discourse   182
    Exercises   184

22. THE IMPERATIVE MOOD. THE OPTATIVE MOOD. FOURTH CLASS
    CONDITIONS   187
    Vocabulary   187
    The Imperative Mood in English, The Imperative Mood
       and Tenses in Greek   188
    Formation of the Imperative Mood Tenses   188
    Functions of the Imperative Mood   191
    Formation of the Optative Mood   193
    Functions of the Optative Mood   194
    Exercises   195

23. USES OF THE GENITIVE, DATIVE, AND ACCUSATIVE CASES   197
    Vocabulary, The Genitive Case   197
    The Dative Case   201
    The Accusative Case   203
    Exercises   203

    TABLES   205

    GREEK-ENGLISH VOCABULARY   209

    ENGLISH-GREEK VOCABULARY   215

    INDEX OF SUBJECTS   223

    INDEX OF SCRIPTURES   229

    LIST OF SCRIPTURES USED WITH EXERCISES   233

    λύω CONJUGATION CHART

PREFACE

This text is written for the person who seriously wishes to learn Greek and to read intelligibly a Greek New Testament. Whereas it is expected that the volume will be primarily used in classroom settings, the text was written with the intention that a person, using the Translation Key to evaluate his or her exercises, could readily progress to competent exegetical studies without professorial help.

Experience has shown that the most significant stumbling block to learning Greek is an inadequate knowledge of English grammar. Hence, while the text assumes that a person does know English grammar, it also includes explanations and illustrations of each English grammatical counterpart as new Greek materials are introduced.

The text proceeds from the basic structures of the verb and noun to the more complex constructions. Forms and vocabulary are introduced at a rate such that by the end of two semesters (30 weeks) or an intensive summer program (e.g., eight 40-hour weeks) the student will have covered all the grammar and vocabulary necessary to enter basic Greek exegesis courses.

My goal, preparing students for basic Greek exegesis, determined the scope of the text. In exegetical studies one wishes to move along to matters of interpretation, employing grammatical skills already learned. With this in mind materials have been included that are not found in most beginning grammars, but which are essential if one is to comprehend the significance of the variety of forms that Greek writers used. One will find minimal information that is simply "interesting"; the materials herein are functional and relevant to exegesis. For these reasons students who have already studied Greek for a year or so will find this to be an excellent tool for refurbishing and synthesizing prior knowledge and for acquiring materials ordinarily presented at the intermediate level of language study.

The approach to the noun system is traditional. Nouns of the second and first declensions are introduced in early chapters, together with the other nominal items—adjective, pronoun, article—that are of like formation. Always, the determinative factor for presentation has been to show repetition and similarity so as to facilitate learning.

The verb system has been presented differently from most texts. Although the principal parts are given in the vocabularies, the conjugations are introduced according to the formative endings. For example, when learning the primary active endings, the student is able to see the two tenses that use these endings and he or she can simply note that a sigma between the stem and endings differentiates the two tenses. Persons using this text for review purposes who began Greek study from the principal part approach will find tables illustrating this perspective.

The first twelve chapters contain all words of the first and second declensions, the omega conjugation, and the particles that occur more than fifty times in a Greek New Testament. The remainder of the text presents all other words occurring more than thirty times (for an approximate total of 475 items). The vocabularies are presented with exercises that use the words in the same or immediately preceding chapters. In addition the exercises from Chapter 13 forward will have terms marked with an asterisk that do not occur in the vocabularies of this text, but are encountered infrequently in a Greek New Testament. These may be readily identified by consulting a standard Greek lexicon. Accents are treated as a separate section in the early chapters; elaborations are provided as different grammatical forms are introduced.

The exercises illustrate and give practice in using the grammatical matters being learned. I have chosen not to include English to Greek translations because my goal is exclusively to immerse students in Koine Greek and to have them reading it. On the basis of this text a student will not be able to buy an admission ticket for the Acropolis tour. She or he will be able, however, to understand and explain the nuance of meaning when a writer shifts from an aorist imperative to an aorist subjunctive; from a present to an aorist participle; or chooses to use the simple genitive or dative case.

In keeping with this intent I begin exclusively using verses from the Greek New Testament for the exercises after Chapter 12. Students often have a familiarity with some of the verses and may be tempted to rely upon memory for "translation." A few class recitations and attempts at explaining the "translation" in the light of a literal or precise translation usually correct any such temptation. By using the New Testament itself for exercises the student is soon rewarded in terms of reaching the goal of this language study. Moreover, there is opportunity at this early stage of learning to determine what the student is doing with various published translations. This fosters an appreciation that often translation of these texts involves interpretation. Hence, it is all the more critical that one learn whatever rules there may be so as to have at one's disposal what controls do exist.

Persons coming to the study of Greek may be helped if they understand that the task, finally, is one of becoming so conversant with the Greek idiom that they can comprehend what is being said *in Greek*—not in translation. One then moves from Greek into one's own vernacular and expresses the original thought in comprehendable ways, faithfully presenting to the listener or reader the message of the original statement. That is true translation; that is the goal toward which this text is directed.

This is neither a text in hermeneutics nor in linguistics. Nor is it a general Greek grammar. It consciously presents the grammar of *New Testament* Greek. As such, it introduces and familiarizes the reader with the idiosyncrasies encountered in the various New Testament documents. The relevance of this text to the study of any Koine Greek text is obvious, but the student should be aware of the specific focus.

It is my distinct pleasure to thank a number of people for the part they have played in preparing me for the production of this text. Little did I realize some 28 years ago that Dr. James N. Truesdale of Duke University, in beginning classical Greek—or even four years later when I was the only member of a senior Greek composition class, was introducing me to one aspect of my life's work. Dr. James L. Price, Jr., of Duke's graduate religion program introduced me to Koine Greek in Romans and Matthew. At Wheaton, Dr. A. Berkeley Mickelsen and Merrill C. Tenney spent a year saturating me in the grammar and thought of the Gospels, Acts, the Pauline letters and Hebrews; since then, I have not been the same. Professor F. F. Bruce, my doctoral supervisor, always encouraged me and lived before me the model of excellence in handling the original texts. Dr. Robert Lyon of Asbury Theological Seminary gave me the opportunity to teach beginning and intermediate Greek grammar when I was seeking vocational direction. Each of these men I value and salute with gratitude, appreciation, and admiration.

I thank Drs. James M. Efird, Duke Divinity School; Robert Lyon; Berkeley Mickelsen, now retiring from Bethel Seminary; Professor F. F. Bruce, formerly Rylands Professor of Biblical Criticism and Exegesis at the University of Manchester, England; my former colleagues in the undergraduate college and the seminary at Oral Roberts University—Arden Autry, James Shelton, Siegfried Schatzmann, Linda Pattillo, Trevor Grizzle, and Robert Mansfield; Lynn M. Nichols, University Editor; and all my students these past ten years for the reading and re-reading of manuscript portions. It is a particular pleasure to recognize Edna Fassett, one of those who has used the text to teach herself, passed all the tests at an A level, frequently offered helpful critiques, and proofed galleys—all this at seventy years of age. Many errors are gone because of their perceptive eyes. Many things are clearer due to their suggestions. The lacks are mine and I invite you the reader to share any oversights you may note.

Throughout this endeavor Barbara, my wife, has continued to teach me new, positive meanings for that loveliest of Greek words. To her and four more, who were youngsters when it began and may be found in some of the illustrations, this volume is affectionately dedicated.

When all has been said and done, I am acutely aware that I have only touched a part of the whole. Much more could have been said. Nevertheless, my goal will have been reached if by the work which you hold the Gospel is better comprehended. καὶ τῷ ὑπὲρ ἡμῶν ἀποθανόντι καὶ ἐγερθέντι ἡ δόξα εἰς τοὺς αἰῶνας.

Tulsa, Oklahoma   *James Allen Hewett*
Easter, Birthday, 1986

CHAPTER 1

ALPHABET, ORTHOGRAPHY, AND PUNCTUATION

The Alphabet

The Greek alphabet consists of 24 characters, many of which correspond to their Latin equivalents and will, thus, be easily recognized. Capitals, known as uncials,[1] are used infrequently in the United Bible Societies' third edition of the *Greek New Testament*. When they occur, it is usually under one of the following circumstances:[2]

1. Beginning of a paragraph (Mt. 1:1, 2, 6b, 12);

2. Proper names (Mt. 1:1ff.);

3. Quotations and direct speech (Mt. 1:20, 23);

4. Beginning of a sentence which, in the editors' opinions, starts a new thought—rather like a subparagraph (Mt. 1:19, 22).

The small characters (minuscules) are those that are commonly used in contemporary texts. The student must carefully memorize both their names and their formations.

Name	Uncial	Minuscule	English equivalent	Pronunciation
Alpha	A	α	a	*a* as in *father*[3]
Beta	B	β	b	*b* as in *boy*
Gamma	Γ	γ	g	*g* as in *go*[4]
Delta	Δ	δ	d	*d* as in *dawn*

---

[1] The student will recognize many of the Greek uncials at the outset. Learn all the forms, noting that they sit on the line.

[2] Kurt Aland, Matthew Black, Carlo M. Martini, Bruce M. Metzger, and Allen Wikgren, *The Greek New Testament*, 3d ed., (New York: United Bible Societies, 1966, 1968, 1975, 1983), p. xii. Hereafter cited as *GNT*.

[3] Greek has no short *a* sound as in *pad*. Alpha is always as here indicated.

[4] Double gamma is sounded *ng* as in *sing*; e.g., ἄγγελος is *an-ge-los*.

Epsilon	E	ε	e	*e* as in *bed*[5]
Zeta	Z	ζ	z or dz	*z* as in *zero* or *dz* as in *adze*[6]
Eta	H	η	e	*e* as in *they*
Theta	Θ	θ	th	*th* as in *theology*
Iota	I	ι	i	*i* as in *machine*[7]
				i as in *bit*
				y as in *yellow*
Kappa	K	κ	k	*k* as in *keep*
Lambda	Λ	λ	l	*l* as in *letter*
Mu	M	μ	m	*m* as in *moor*
Nu	N	ν	n	*n* as in *now*
Xi	Ξ	ξ	x	*x* as in *axe*
Omicron	O	ο	o	*o* as in *omlet*
Pi	Π	π	p	*p* as in *put*
Rho	P	ρ	r	*r* as in *row*
Sigma	Σ	σ, ς	s	*s* as in *single*[8]
Tau	T	τ	t	*t* as in *top*
Upsilon	Y	υ	u	French *u*, German *ü*
Phi	Φ	φ	ph	*f* as in *foot*
Chi	X	χ	chi	*ch* as in *loch*[9]
Psi	Ψ	ψ	ps	*ps* as in *hips*
Omega	Ω	ω	o	*o* as in *wrote*

Vowels

There are seven vowels: α, ε, η, ι, ο, υ, ω. E and o are always short; η and ω are always long; α, ι, and υ may be either. They can be identified as long only by consulting a lexicon or by certain rules of accentuation that will be introduced in later sections.

Diphthongs

Certain vowels combine into two-letter units called diphthongs to produce a distinct sound (the quantity of these is long by nature). As a unit they form part of one syllable.

---

[5]This is always short *e*. Eta is long *e*.

[6]When initial, zeta is *z*; when internal, it is *dz*.

[7]Iota is used in Hebrew terms beginning with *yod* as a consonant with an English equivalent of *y*; e.g., Ἰακώβ is *ya-kob*. In such words the iota will be followed by a vowel. If no vowel follows, iota itself is a vowel. Iota with a circumflex accent (˜) is long; otherwise short.

[8]Initial or internal sigma is formed σ; final sigma is ς (Ἰησοῦς).

[9]Chi has a rough, guttural sound, whereas kappa has a smooth guttural sound. By aspirating the *ch* (as the *k* in *kitchen*, but with more accentuation of the *k*), one can help to distinguish the two letters.

αι as in *aisle*, e.g., παῖς

ει as in *freight*, e.g., προσκυνεῖ

οι as in *boil*, e.g., πλοῖον

υι as in *queen*, e.g., υἱός

αυ as in *now*, e.g., κλαυθμός

ευ, ηυ as in *feud*, e.g., θεραπεύω

ου as in *soup*, e.g., δαιμονιζομένους

Iota Subscript

Iota may also occur beneath a final α, η, or ω, in which case it is called "iota subscript"; e.g., λάθρᾳ or πληρωθῇ. It does not affect the pronunciation, but it *is* part of the spelling. These two-letter combinations are considered diphthongs and, therefore, are long.

Formation of Lower-case Letters

Certain letters extend above or below the lines.

α β γ δ ε ζ η θ ι κ λ μ ν ξ ο π ρ σ (ς) τ υ φ χ ψ ω

Note well the following:

1. Never dot an iota.

2. Carefully form a point at the base of nu to distinguish it from upsilon.

3. Let phi's circle, chi's cross-point, and psi's arc each sit on the line. The vertical bars of phi and psi do not sit on the line, nor do the arms of chi.

Breathing Marks

Above initial vowels (as ἐγέννησεν), the second vowel of a diphthong (as οὕτως), preceding an initial uncial vowel or rho (as Ἀράμ, Ῥαχάβ), one observes small marks similar to single quotation marks. These are breathing marks. The first and third Greek words above have a smooth breathing mark, indicating that the first vowels will be sounded as *eh* as in *bed* and *ah* as in *arm* respectively. The second example had a rough breathing mark (note the reversed direction of the sign), indicating omicron upsilon is to be preceded by an *h* sound, thus *hoo-tōs*. Initial rho always has a rough breathing mark and is sounded as though one were slightly panting, thus *hra-chab*.

Syllabification

Diphthongs, since they make one sound unit, are considered as a single unit when determining syllables. A word has as many syllables as it has vowels and/or diphthongs. Beginning at the extreme left part of a word, divide immediately after each vowel unit, e.g., γε-νέ-σε-ως. If two consonants that may begin a word occur in succession (consult the lists of a lexicon to determine which these are), they are not divided, but together begin another syllable, e.g., in με-τα-σχη-μα-τί-ζω, σχ may begin a word (e.g., σχολή = school), so it does not divide. This rule also applies to consonants followed by μ or ν: they do not divide, e.g., πνεῦμα = πνεῦ-μα (spirit); μνημονεύω = μνη-μο-νεύ-ω (I remember).

When two consonants that cannot begin a word occur together internally, they usually divide so that one closes the first syllable, while the other is the initial consonant of a subsequent syllable. Observe the following: ἀ-δελ-φούς, ἐ-γέν-νη-σεν, but Χρι-στοῦ, 'Α-βρα-άμ. When three consonants occur in succession, the first will close one syllable; the other two will be pronounced together as the beginning of the next syllable, e.g., γασ-τρί. By practice and observation the student will discover which consonants blend euphonically. Through experience, an aural sensitivity to the language will develop that will assist in the task of syllabification.

Accents[10]

Written accentuation of Greek texts began to occur in the fourth century B.C.,[11] but it was not systematically practiced until around 200 B.C. Accents are not included in the oldest uncial manuscripts of the *GNT*. The earliest of these to have any accents is the Cambridge manuscript D, dated in the sixth century A.D.

Only the last three syllables of a word may have an accent mark: the final, called the *ultima* (e.g., ἀ-γα-θός); the next-to-last, called the *penult* (e.g., δι-καί-α); the second from last, called the *antepenult* (e.g., ἄν-θρω-πος). Three accent marks are employed: the acute (´), grave (`), and the circumflex (˜). When a diphthong is accented the second of the two letters receives the accent mark. In the earliest use accents indicated changes in pitch. However, the different accents have come to signify no difference in sound value; they indicate only that one is to *stress* the accented syllable.

---

[10]This discussion may be delayed until after or during Chapter 3 when labels such as nominative will have meaning.

[11]A. T. Robertson, *A Grammar of the Greek New Testament in the Light of Historical Research* (Nashville: Broadman Press, 1934), pp. 446–543, esp. pp. 447f., 453–56. (Hereafter cited as *Robertson.*)

The following rules are normally observed:

1. Final -αι or -οι is short.

2. The antepenult may have the acute if the ultima is short (e.g., ἄνθρωπος).

3. The penult may have the acute if it is short or long (a long vowel or diphthong indicates a long syllable) and the ultima is long (e.g., λόγου, οἴκῳ).

4. The penult may have the circumflex only if it is long and the ultima short (e.g., οἶκος, δοῦλος).

5. The ultima may have any of the three accents so long as it is remembered that the circumflex will only stand on a long syllable (e.g., υἱός, υἱοῦ, υἱὸν).

6. The grave accent is only used when the accented ultima (e.g., ὁ υἱὸς τοῦ ἀνθρώπου) is immediately followed by another word that is of the same sentence. The grave does not occur immediately prior to the period or colon. This change also does not occur if the next word is an enclitic (see p. 23) or the interrogative pronoun τίς, (see p. 112).

Rules of accentuation are pertinent only in the areas of the verb (and verbals) and the nominal forms (noun, pronoun, adjective). The other parts of speech have fixed accents that do not change except for the alternation of an acute to a grave on an ultima.

These general rules are graphically presented in the following chart where a short or long ultima is postulated on the far right and the potential places of accentuation are presented moving to the left.

Accented Antepenult	Accented Penult	Accented Ultima	
´ ἄνθρωπος	Long Penult = ˜ δοῦλος Short Penult = ´ λόγος	´ or ` υἱός or υἱὸς	Short Ultima
No Accent Possible	Long Penult = ´ δούλου Short Penult = ´ λόγου	´ or ` or ˜ πολλή πολλὴ πολλῆς	Long Ultima

Refinements and application of these general rules must now be explored.

Verb Accent

The fundamental rule of verb accentuation is that the accent is *recessive*. The accent will normally go as far toward the antepenult as the length of the ultima will allow. The antepenult receives the acute accent if the ultima is short. When the ultima is long, the antepenult cannot be accented; it must fall on the penult. So, one finds λαμβάνομεν and λαμβάνει. Since the penult may have either a circumflex or acute accent, a question arises concerning which to use. The matter is resolved simply: when the ultima is long (and it must be for the penult to be accented), the penult refuses to accept a circumflex; hence, the acute will be normally used. So, λαμβάνω, λαμβάνεις.

Noun Accent

The fundamental rule of noun accent is that the accent *remains* on the syllable accented in the nominative so long as the ultima will allow. One must learn the accent of the nominative by observation.

Some words of elaboration are in order. ἄνθρωπος may have an accented antepenult because the ultima is short. In the genitive and dative the accent must shift to the penult because the ultima is long. Since both the penult and the ultima are long the accent will be acute. λόγος, though, retains the acute on the penult throughout the declension, since the acute *may* stand on a short penult (a long ultima will not pull an accent from the penult). Furthermore, it must *remain* acute because λογ- is a short syllable. οἶκος will have the circumflex since the penult is long and the ultima short, but that must change to an acute when the ultima lengthens, thus οἴκου, οἴκῳ, etc. When the accent falls on the ultima in the nominative, it is acute in both the nominative, accusative, and vocative. But the genitive and dative in both the first and second declensions have the circumflex; thus, one reads υἱοῦ, υἱῷ, φωνῶν, φωναῖς.

Let the student be aware of two admissions concerning accents that were made by scholars of great stature in the field of Greek grammar.

> The accent often shows the quantity of its own vowel, or of vowels in following syllables.
> Thus the circumflex on κνῖσα *savor* shows that ι is long and α is short; the acute on χώρα *land* shows that α is long; on τίνες *who?* that ι is short. On βασιλεία *kingdom* the acute shows that the final α is long; on βασίλεια *queen* that final α is short.[12]

This observation pinpoints what lies at the heart of the issue concerning requiring students to learn rules of accent. To place the accents one must

---

[12]William Watson Goodwin, *Greek Grammar*, rev. Charles B. Gulick (New York: Ginn and Company, 1930), ¶125c. (Hereafter cited as *G.G.*) His italics.

first know the quantity of vowels in question, but vowels are not all of fixed value. Often only as the accents are observed in place upon a given word can one *deduce* the quantity of the vowel in question. Hence, the uninitiated student is often times left in a quandary regardless of the rules committed to memory.

The second comment is from J. Gresham Machen who observes:

> What the accent actually is, within these limits [of rules he has given that are essentially of the same content as I have given], can be determined in part by the special rules which follow [which I have also indicated], but *in very many cases must be learned by observation of the individual words.*[13]

The student must be observant, note the presence of the accent in the text, and learn that pronunciation. Then, forge ahead to more significant matters of exegesis!

Punctuation

The period (.) and the comma (,) correspond to the English forms. The semicolon or colon (·) is a dot above the line. The question mark (;) must not be confused with the English symbol of like form.

Other Marks

Two other marks the student will encounter are the apostrophe (') and the diaeresis (¨). The apostrophe occurs at the end of words that end with a short vowel when that final vowel is deleted before a subsequent initial vowel, a process called elision. For example, in μεθ᾽ ἡμῶν the α of μετά has been deleted, and for euphony (i.e., greater ease of pronunciation) the τ has been replaced by the corresponding rough sound θ. This latter phenomenon occurs when the second word begins with a rough breathing mark. Contrast μεθ᾽ ἡμῶν and μετ᾽ αὐτοῦ; ἐφ᾽ ὑμᾶς and ἐπ᾽ αὐτόν.

The diaeresis occurs infrequently and, when it does, is over the second of two vowels that would otherwise be a diphthong. The two vowels are to be divided into separate syllables (e.g., Ἡσαῒου is Ἡ-σα-ῒ-ου).

A Textual Criticism Note

In verse 7 of the Exercises Key for this chapter, the student will notice one ῾Ροβοαμ has been deleted. It was not intentional—originally. The eye of the typist overlooked one of them. Compare the key copy with your *GNT* and determine which has been deleted. (Note the accent marks.) This type of error also occurred in the transmission of early manuscripts, as scribes' eyes, too, overlooked duplications. This type of error is called haplography.

---

[13] My italics. *New Testament Greek for Beginners* (Toronto: Macmillan, 1923), p. 15.

Exercises

1. The student's first task is committing to memory the sound values for the alphabet. This will be done in conjunction with learning the names of the letters. However, the names are not so critical to learn as the sound values. Therefore, learn the Greek symbol α is *a* as Jud*a*h; β is *b* as *B*oaz; γ is *g* as *G*ehenna, etc.

2. Learn all the diphthongs and their sound values. Do not simply learn to recognize visually the vowel formation that is designated as a diphthong. Instead, learn the sound values of each. E.g., αι is *i* as in *ai*sle.

3. Mt. 1:1–8. Using your *GNT* practice the formation of the Greek letters by copying this text. Ξ and ψ do not occur here. They may be practiced by copying Mt. 12:18a and 20a.

4. Continuing with Mt. 1:1–8, divide each word into its component syllables. Deliberately, distinctly, sound aloud each syllable. Now seek to run the syllables together into a euphonic whole, carefully putting emphasis on the accented syllable.

CHAPTER 2

VERB SYSTEM. I: PRIMARY, ACTIVE ENDINGS AND TENSES, INDICATIVE MOOD

Vocabulary

ἄγω; ἄξω	I lead; I shall lead
ἀκούω; ἀκούσω	I hear; I shall hear (cf. acoustical)
ἀνοίγω; ἀνοίξω	I open; I shall open
βαπτίζω; [βαπτιδ-*]; βαπτίσω	I baptize; I shall baptize
βλέπω; βλέψω	I see; I shall see
γινώσκω; [Irregular]	I know; learn; perceive
γράφω; γράψω	I write; I shall write (cf. graphics)
διδάσκω; διδάξω	I teach; I shall teach (cf. didactic)
εὑρίσκω; εὑρήσω	I find; I shall find (cf. Eureka, California's motto, "I have found it!")
ἔχω; ἕξω	I have; I shall have
κηρύσσω [κηρυκ-*]; κηρύξω	I preach; I shall preach (cf. kerygmatic)
λέγω; [Irregular]	I say; utter; express with words
λύω; λύσω	I loose; I shall loose
πέμπω; πέμψω	I send; I shall send
πιστεύω; πιστεύσω	I believe; I shall believe
σῴζω; σώσω	I save; I shall save

Definition of Verb

A verb is a word that expresses action or a state of being, e.g., he *talks*, she *is* a teacher.

Methodology in Verb Formation

Verbs may consist of two or three segments. All verbs have a basic segment called the stem, which identifies the word in terms of its lexical meaning

---

*See p. 12 for a discussion of this stem.

and provides the basic building block on which one forms a tense or group of tenses. To identify the stem, simply remove the final ω from the first form given in the vocabulary list.[1] Thus, the stem of λύω is λυ-; the stem of πέμπω is πεμπ-, etc. In regular verbs this stem will remain the same[2] throughout the (possibly) six principal parts[3] in which the stem is used to express the various Greek verb tenses.

The second segment of all verbs is the sufformative. Sufformatives are letters that may be added to the right side of the stem in a variety of combinations so as to express the following information:

1. Person: first, second, or third

2. Number: singular or plural

3. Tense: past (In Greek there are four past tenses: imperfect, aorist, perfect, plurperfect), present, future

4. Voice: active, middle, or passive

5. Mood: indicative, subjunctive, imperative, or optative

The third segment that may occur as a part of a verb is the preformative. It is either a letter or letters prefixed to the stem in conjunction with certain sufformatives in order to indicate tense.

In summary, by joining preformatives and sufformatives to the stems, Greek verbs convey person, number, tense, voice and mood. To *parse* a verb is to identify these five elements.

Two Categories of Verb Tenses: Primary and Secondary

The beginner is often bewildered and discouraged by the many forms of the Greek verb. Rote memorization of these becomes an unnecessarily frustrating experience. If the student will organize the task of memorization according to the sets within the following categories of the verb, the task should be greatly simplified.

The verb tenses are divided into two basic categories: (1) primary tenses and (2) secondary tenses. This schema has nothing to do with either

---

[1] The student will be introduced later to a class of verbs called -μι verbs. For now all verbs encountered except the irregular verb *to be* will be of the ω class.

[2] This consistency is what constitutes the verb as regular. Irregular verbs, by contrast, have differing stems in some or all the basic tenses.

[3] Principal part refers to the first person singular form of a verb in any one of the following tenses (N.B. not all verbs will occur in all these tenses): present active, future active, aorist active, perfect active, perfect middle, and aorist passive. See p. 63 where verbs are introduced according to this scheme.

frequency or importance. The criterion is time of action. Primary tenses are the present, future, and perfect. Secondary tenses are the imperfect, aorist, and pluperfect. Primary tenses are oriented to the present or future, whereas secondary tenses are oriented to the past. One might object that the perfect tense expresses past action. True though that may be, the distinct aspect of the Greek perfect is its abiding effect in the present time.

Set I: Primary Tenses, Active Voice

In the active voice,[4] indicative mood,[5] the present and future tenses both use the primary active endings.[6]

	Singular			Plural	
first person	-ω		first person	-ομεν	
second person	-εις		second person	-ετε	
third person	-ει		third person	-ουσι	

A single letter—σ—suffixed to the stem before adding the primary endings distinguishes the two tenses.

PRESENT ACTIVE INDICATIVE: λύω

	Singular		Plural	
1. λύ ω[7]	I loose/am loosing	λύ ομεν	we loose/are loosing
2. λύ εις	you loose/are loosing	λύ ετε	you loose/are loosing
3. λύ ει	he, she, it looses/is loosing	λύ ουσι	they loose/are loosing

FUTURE ACTIVE INDICATIVE: λύω

	Singular		Plural	
1. λύ σ ω	I shall loose/be loosing	λύ σ ομεν	we shall loose/be loosing

---

[4]Voice expresses the relation between the subject of a verb and the action that the verb expresses. A verb is said to be in the active voice when the subject performs the activity. Thus, in "I throw the ball," *I*, being the actor, is subject of an active voice verb *throw*.

[5]Mood (sometimes called mode) refers to the manner in which an action is conceived by the speaker. "I speak," a simple declaration of action, is in the indicative mood. Indicative mood may be couched as either a statement of fact or as a question. Three other moods, the subjunctive, imperative, and the optative, will be introduced later.

[6]Although the perfect tense is a primary tense, in the active voice it does not use these endings. Its forms will, therefore, be presented later.

[7]Spacing between the stem and the personal ending is for emphasis only. Printed texts will not be so spaced.

2. λύ σ εις   you will loose/be   λύ σ ετε   you will loose/be
                 loosing   loosing

3. λύ σ ει   he, she, it will loose/   λύ σ ουσι   they will loose/
                 be loosing   be loosing

Changes in Final Consonant of Stem

If the verb stem ends in certain consonants a change will occur in that final consonant when the primary active suffix is attached. This change is for euphony; it has no other grammatical basis. When a stem ends in a labial (so named because of the particular use of the lips in forming the sounds of π, β, φ), the addition of σ produces the consonantal blend ψ. A stem ending in a palatal (note the use of the palate in forming κ, γ, χ) joined to a σ produces the consonantal blend ξ. A stem ending in a dental (note the placement of the tongue behind the teeth in forming τ, δ, θ and internal ζ[8]) will delete the dental and simply add the σ as a suffix.

In chart form these changes are as follows:

Labials (π, β, φ) + σ = ψ (e.g., γραφ + σω = γράψω)

Palatals (κ, γ, χ) + σ =ξ (e.g., αγ + σω = ἄξω)

Dentals (τ, δ, θ [or internal ζ]) + σ = σ (e.g., βαπτιδ + σω = βαπτίσω)

A few variations need to be noted. In some verbs the final stem letter which is used in forming the principal parts is hidden. For example, in the above illustration of a dental, βαπτίζω, the final consonant in the present active indicative is ζ. When one identifies the stem, however, the ζ is not said to be the final consonant. Rather, a δ is considered final (recall zeta was said to be equivalent to *z* when initial, but *dz* when internal). This δ deletes before σ to form the future active indicative βαπτίσω.

In a verb like διδάσκω, κ combines with σ according to normal patterns. The σ preceding the resultant ξ is deleted as redundant. Note that the verb κηρύσσω has as a stem κηρυκ-, so that the future is κηρύξω.

Irregular verbs.   Numerous verbs simply add the primary active personal endings to the present stem, interposing the future tense indicator σ (or its consonantal blend) and thereby form the future tense. These are called regular verbs. However, many verbs, called irregular, have future tense stems (and other tense stems yet-to-be introduced) that differ significantly

---

[8]Though ζ is, strictly speaking, not a dental (it is a double consonant), when internal it functions as a dental.

from the present. Ἐυρίσκω is illustrative. Its future principal part is εὑρήσω. Once the first person singular is known, the forms are quite regular: εὑρήσω, εὑρήσεις, εὑρήσει, etc. Simply learn by rote the principal parts and then the conjugation follows easily.

Time and Kind of Action

When analyzing a Greek verb one must consider two perspectives: (1) the time of the action and (2) the kind of action. Time of action is regularly associated with tense per se in the indicative mood only. "He is loosing" is present time/tense. "He loosed" is past time/tense. "He will loose" is future time/tense.

Of much greater significance to the Greek mind than "When did the action occur?" was "What kind of action occurred?" Kind of action (often referred to by grammarians with the German equivalent *Aktionsart*; pl. *Aktionsarten*) crosses temporal boundaries in order to describe all tenses. The basic kinds of action are linear, unitary, and completed with continuing result.[9]

John 15:12a well illustrates linear action: "This is my commandment, that you continue loving one another." Jesus intended to evoke neither a single experience nor a repetitive one, but rather, an ongoing lifestyle characterized by loving one another in an unceasing fashion. The present tense is basically linear or durative, ongoing in its kind of action. The durative notion may be expressed graphically by an unbroken line (_____), since the action is simply continuous. This is known as the progressive present. Refinements of this general rule will be encountered; however, the fundamental distinction will not be negated.

The *Aktionsart* of the future tense is basically unitary. Something will occur in a yet-to-be experienced time frame, but no reference to that action's continuation is implicit in the verb tense. If Greek wishes to emphasize an ongoing nature of the future action, the future of the verb "to be" and the present participle will be used.

Movable ν

The third person plural primary active ending often has added a final ν, called the movable ν, e.g., καλέσουσιν (Mt. 1:23). Movable ν is for euphony and does not affect the meaning of the verb. It may occur when the initial letter of the following word is a vowel or when the word is the last in a sentence.

---

[9]Unitary *Aktionsart*, expressed by the aorist, and completed with continuing results, expressd by the perfect, are treated later.

Exercises

A. Translate the following.

1. ἄξεις, ἄξουσιν, ἄξει
2. λέγω, λέγετε, λέγομεν
3. κηρύξεις, κηρύσσεις, κηρύξουσιν
4. ἕξει, ἔχει, γράφω
5. εὑρίσκω, ἄγεις, βαπτίσουσιν
6. ἀνοίξετε, διδάξω, πιστεύσομεν
7. σώσεις, λέγει, εὑρήσουσιν
8. βλέψομεν, πέμψετε, σῴζω

B. Provide the requested information.

1. εὑρισκ + ομεν = _____.
2. ἐχ + σετε = _____.
3. πεμπ + σω = _____.
4. γραφ + ετε = _____.
5. ἀγ + σομεν = _____.
6. ἀκου + σει = _____.
7. εὑρισκ + σεις = _____.
8. ἀνοιγ + σετε = _____.
9. σῳζ + σομεν = _____.
10. Tense designates _____.
11. *Aktionsart* designates _____.
12. Voice expresses _____.
13. Mood expresses _____.
14. The primary tenses are _____, _____, _____.
15. The secondary tenses are _____, _____, _____.
16. The primary active endings are _____.
17. To identify the verb stem of the first principal part, one should
    _____
18. Movable ν occurs where for what reason? _____.
19. List the labials, palatals, and dentals: _____.
20. What consonantal blends result as each of the above groups combine with σ? _____.

CHAPTER 3

NOUN SYSTEM. I: SECOND DECLENSION.
THE VERB "TO BE"

Vocabulary

Second Declension Masculine Nouns

ἄγγελος, -ου, ὁ[1]	angel, messenger (cf. angel)
ἀδελφός, -οῦ ὁ	brother (cf. Philadelphia)
ἄνθρωπος, -ου, ὁ	human being, man (cf. anthropology)
θεός, -οῦ, ὁ	God (cf. theology)
κόσμος, -ου, ὁ	world (cf. cosmic)
κύριος, -ου, ὁ	Lord (cf. Kyrie)
λόγος, -ου, ὁ	word (cf. logical)
νόμος, -ου, ὁ	law (cf. antinomian)
οὐρανός, -οῦ, ὁ	heaven (cf. Uranus)
υἱός, -οῦ, ὁ	son

Second Declension Neuter Nouns

ἔργον, -ου, τό	work (cf. energy)
εὐαγγέλιον, -ου, τό	gospel (cf. evangelize)
ἱερόν, -οῦ, τό	temple (cf. hierarchy)
πρόσωπον, -ου, τό	face, presence
τέκνον, -ου, τό	child

Second Declension Adjectives:
Masculine and Neuter Forms

ἀγαθός, -όν[1]	good[2] (cf. Agatha = "A Good One")
ἅγιος, -ον	holy (cf. hagiography)

---

[1]The following information is given in the noun vocabulary list: the noun itself in the nominative singular of the given word, followed by the genitive singular ending. These are then followed by the nominative article in the appropriate gender—which article would, in normal speech, precede the nominative form of the noun. See pp. 16–18 for a discussion of the inflectional forms and cases.

[2]The adjective is listed in this vocabulary in the masculine nominative singular form, followed by the neuter nominative singular ending for that word. Beginning with Chapter 4

15

ἄλλος, -ο	other (cf. allonym = another name a writer may assume)
καλός, -όν	beautiful (cf. calligraphy)
νεκρός, -όν	dead (cf. necrosis)
πιστός, -όν	faithful

Article

ὁ, τό   the (masculine and neuter)

Irregular Verb

εἰμί   I am, exist

Nouns and Adjectives:
Their Declensions and Characteristics

A noun is a word that designates a person, place, or thing, e.g., Jesus, Nazareth, angel. An adjective is a word that describes or limits a noun or a noun substitute, e.g., good, evil, strong.

In English a noun may be used as either the subject (i.e., the actor or that about which something is said) or the object of the verb (i.e., the recipient of the action) without altering its form. One may say "The *angel* is beautiful" or "I see the beautiful *angel*." In Greek the form of *angel* ἄγγελος must be changed depending upon its function in the given sentence or clause in which it occurs. Thus, one writes ὁ ἄγγελός ἐστιν καλός, but βλέπω τὸν καλὸν ἄγγελον. This variation in the ending of the terms ἄγγελος and καλός (and the preceding articles ὁ and τὸν) so as to indicate function is called inflection. Most Greek nouns, pronouns, and adjectives, and all articles and participles, may be inflected. As is illustrated in the above example, inflecting a term, first of all, involves adding a suffix to the stem.

A declension is the orderly arrangement of the inflected nominal forms with their various suffixes so as to indicate the different basic grammatical functions. In English when an inflection occurs, there are three categories as the following table of English pronouns illustrates.

	Singular	*Plural*
Subjective	I	we
Possessive	my, mine	our, ours
Objective	me	us

---

the pattern of presentation for adjectives in the vocabulary lists will be the adjective in the masculine nominative singular, followed by the nominative singular endings for the feminine and neuter genders.

By contrast, in Greek there are five inflectional forms: nominative, genitive, dative, accusative, and vocative.

In addition to inflectional forms, Greek nominal terms have gender and number. Greek gender may be masculine, feminine or neuter. It is indicated by the inflectional endings or the article, but it should not be viewed as determined by sex. The ideal method of learning gender is by careful observation when memorizing the vocabulary. *Sea* is feminine, but *river* is masculine. *House* may be feminine or masculine, but *door* is feminine. None of these is ever neuter. In Koine Greek there are two numbers: singular and plural.

These inflectional forms occur in three declensions which differ in form, but not in significance: the first, which is almost totally composed of feminine terms; the second, which is mostly masculine or neuter; and the third, which is composed of all three genders. Students usually find the second declension the easiest. Hence, we begin with it.

Functions of Greek Inflectional Forms

Thus far, care has been exercised to refer to "inflectional forms" rather than "case endings." Numerous grammars, including the authoritative work by F. Blass, A. Debrunner, and R. Funk,[3] present the nominal system as having only five cases: nominative, genitive, dative, accusative, and vocative. In contrast, others, including A. T. Robertson,[4] opt for eight cases: the above five, plus ablative, instrumental, and locative. Ablative shares the same form as genitive; while instrumental and locative share the dative form. Hence, one will encounter grammarians who speak of an ablatival genitive and an instrumental or locative dative.

I am not convinced one should follow Robertson and others in setting forth eight discrete cases. I do, nonetheless, clearly recognize various functions of the genitive and dative which cause these grammarians to make the divisions. Following the pattern of Classical Greek as set forth in Goodwin and Gulick's *Grammar* (see esp. the comment of ¶1040) and that of Blass, Debrunner, and Funk I make no divisions into eight separate cases, but will gradually present the various functions.

Even when one grants that Greek has descended from a language that had eight cases, in the development of the language the genitive and dative forms have assumed the functions of the ablative, instrumental, and locative. It should suffice for the beginning–intermediate student, then, simply to note carefully the more frequent usages of these inflectional forms.

---

[3] *A Greek Grammar of the New Testament and Other Early Christian Literature* (Chicago: The University of Chicago Press, 1961), pp. 79–109. (Hereafter cited as *BDF*.)

[4] *Robertson*, pp. 447f., 453–56.

nominative =
subject of
the verb

genitive =
possession
or
descriptor

The nominative case is used with words when one names explicitly the subject of a verb, the predicate noun, the predicate adjective, or adjectival modifiers of any of these. For example, in the earlier illustration, "The angel is beautiful," *angel* is subject nominative (it is that about which we speak) and *beautiful* is the predicate adjective (it describes the subject).

The genitive case expresses kind or specification; most frequently it is used to express possession or description. Often the preposition *of* effectively translates the Greek genitive. In "the cross of Christ" and "the crown of thorns," *of Christ* tells whose cross; *of thorns* describes the crown. Although either thought may be expressed in Greek by the simple genitive ending without a preposition, the student must carefully discriminate between the two meanings. *Christ* does not describe the cross; *thorns* do not own the crown.

dative =
personal
interest

The dative case may express personal interest, instrumentality or location. The most common expression of personal interest occurs as the indirect object, i.e., the one to or for whom an action occurs. In "He preaches to the people" *to the people* indicates the personal interest involved, those for whom *he preaches*. The preposition *to* is not essential for an indirect object. "He gives *me* a book" illustrates another format of indirect object.

The accusative case indicates the extent to which an action occurs, or it may express the referent about which an assertion is made. This is most frequently encountered as direct object.[5] In "I see the beautiful angel," the act of seeing extends to *angel*. In "I read the book," reading has reference only to *book*. Note that the noun in the objective (accusative) case is following a transitive verb, i.e., a verb whose action transfers from the subject actor to another noun.

Certain Greek transitive verbs and their objects sound strange in English without some modification. This is due to differences in Greek and English idioms. Note the italicized direct objects in the following literal translations: "Do not swear either the *heaven* or the *earth*" (Jas. 5:12); "Work not the *food* which perishes" (Jn. 6:27); "For we are not ignorant the *designs* of him" (2 Cor. 2:11b). English idiom would supply "by," "for," and "of" respectively.

The vocative case is the form that expresses direct address. Its form will sometimes be distinct from and sometimes identical to that of the nominative. It may occur with or without the article—which will be nominative in form since there is no discrete vocative article. The vocative is grammatically independent from the rest of the sentence. Illustrative are Acts 17:22, "Athenian men!" and Rev. 11:17, "Lord God Almighty."

---

[5]Often the accusative is described simply as the case of the direct object. "Extent" is a more basic description that should facilitate the student's subsequent appreciation of this form in the Greek language.

Formation of Second Declension

Masculine Nouns and Adjectives in Masculine Gender

Any masculine noun of the second declension, as well as many adjectives used in the masculine gender, will be declined by using the endings of the following chart.

MASCULINE ENDINGS

	Singular	Plural
the N.	-ος	-οι
of G.	-ου	-ων
to for D.	-ῳ	-οις
A.	-ον	-ους
V.	-ε	-οι

The noun or adjective stem in the second declension (or first—see Chapter 4) is the nominative singular vocabulary form without the case ending. To that stem attach the appropriate declensional endings. The declension of ὁ ἄγγελος is representative.

ἄγγελος, ἀγγέλου, ὁ: angel

	Singular			Plural	
N.	ἄγγελ-ος	angel	N.V.	ἄγγελ-οι	angels
G.	ἀγγέλ-ου	of an angel		ἀγγέλ-ων	of angels
D.	ἀγγέλ-ῳ	to/for an angel		ἀγγέλ-οις	to/for angels
A.	ἄγγελ-ον	angel		ἀγγέλ-ους	angels
V.	ἄγγελ-ε	angel			

καλός, καλοῦ: beautiful

	Singular		Plural
N.	καλ-ός	N./V.	καλ-οί
G.	καλ-οῦ		καλ-ῶν
D.	καλ-ῷ		καλ-οῖς
A.	καλ-όν		καλ-ούς
V.	καλ-έ		

Neuter Nouns and Adjectives in Neuter Gender

These nouns and adjectives in the neuter gender use the same genitive and dative endings as the masculine in the singular and plural. The other forms vary slightly. Note the nominative, vocative, and accusative forms are identical in the singular and then in the plural.

NEUTER ENDINGS

	Singular	Plural
N./A./V.	-ov	-α
G.	-ου	-ων
D.	-ῳ	-οις

τέκνον, -ου, τό: child

	Singular	Plural
N./A./V.	τέκν-ον	τέκν-α
G.	τέκν-ου	τέκν-ων
D.	τέκν-ῳ	τέκν-οις

καλόν, καλοῦ: beautiful

	Singular	Plural
N./A./V.	καλ-όν	καλ-ά
G.	καλ-οῦ	καλ-ῶν
D.	καλ-ῷ	καλ-οῖς

The Article

The article ("the") in Greek does not so much make another term definite as it specifies or points out a given entity. It may refer to a noun, pronoun, adjective, a verbal (i.e., an infinitive or participle), or even an entire clause or sentence. When the article occurs, it calls attention to that to which it points. The article may not translate smoothly into English (as is the case with the phrase "the poor in spirit," which has the article with both nouns), but its function as a highlighting device should be noted by the exegete.

When a word occurs without the article, it may or may not be definite in Greek. If it has a distinctive character, that must be determined by other factors in the context. Without the article a word may be translated and preceded by the English "a" or "an." These two words have no Greek equivalents.

The masculine article is formed by prefixing τ to the isolated endings of the masculine noun except in the nominative singular and plural. There, ὁ and οἱ are used. (Note the rough breathing marks.) The neuter article in the nominative and accusative singular adopts the corresponding neuter noun's ending, but without the ν: it is simply τό. Elsewhere the neuter article has precisely the endings of the noun, all prefixed with a τ (even the nominative). The article must agree with the term to which it is attached in gender, number, and case; e.g., ὁ ἄνθρωπος, but never οἱ ἀνθρώπους.

The nominative singular and plural of the article in the masculine and feminine genders are proclitics, i.e., words that have no accent of their own. Instead, they are so closely related euphonically to the following word as to be pronounced with that word.

ὁ and τό: the

	Singular		*Plural*	
	M.	N.	M.	N.
N.	ὁ	τό	οἱ	τά
G.	τοῦ	τοῦ	τῶν	τῶν
D.	τῷ	τῷ	τοῖς	τοῖς
A.	τόν	τό	τούς	τά

Function of Adjectives

Agreement

Because adjectives modify nominal forms, they must agree with the modified form in gender, number, and case. In the first example on page 16—ὁ ἄγγελός ἐστιν καλός—καλός is masculine, nominative singular because it is a predicate adjective, an adjective following the verb "to be" (see page 23 for more regarding εἰμί). Contrast this with βλέπω τὸν καλὸν ἄγγελον. καλὸν must shift to masculine, accusative singular because it modifies such a noun. A neuter noun would require the adjective to change to the neuter case, e.g., ἅγιον ἱερόν.

Position

A Greek adjective will be located—relative to the noun it modifies—in either (1) the attributive position or (2) the predicate position. The attributive position consists of the article followed immediately by the adjective. In the predicate position, by contrast, the adjective occurs without the article. In the attributive position the nominal form may follow or precede the article plus adjective: either ὁ καλὸς ἄγγελος or ὁ ἄγγελος ὁ καλός is "the beautiful angel." In the predicate position the adjective (N.B., without the article) may precede or follow the nominal form with its article: either ὁ ἄγγελος καλός or καλὸς ὁ ἄγγελος is "The angel [is] beautiful." A device which may help distinguish these two constructions is two abbreviations (using the first letters of the critical words) which express the relationships: A A A: *A*rticle, *A*djective = *A*ttributive position; A n P: *A*rticle, *n*oun = *P*redicate position. In sum, one finds the following:

ὁ καλὸς ἄγγελος
                                    = The beautiful angel (A A A)
ὁ ἄγγελος ὁ καλός

ὁ ἄγγελος καλός
                                    = The angel [is] beautiful. (A n P)
καλὸς ὁ ἄγγελος

When the adjective occurs with the article, i.e., in the attributive position, then the adjective is expressly qualifying or limiting the noun to which it is related to that category which is characterized by the attribute of the adjective. No complete sentence is thereby formed. In the first example not just any angel, but precisely the angel which is characterized by beautiful, is meant.

When the adjective occurs without the article, i.e., in the predicate position, then the adjective is not circumscribing the meaning of the noun to which it is related, but it is expressing or asserting something about that noun and is forming a complete sentence in which "is/are" should be supplied. The second example declares in sentence form that the angel has the quality of beauty. The verb "is" or "are" is supplied for the English idiom depending, of course, upon the number of the noun. Sometimes the verb will be present in the Greek; e.g., ὁ θεὸς ἀγάπη ἐστίν = "The God is love" (1 Jn. 4:8b).

Substantive

A further noteworthy function of the Greek adjective is its use as a noun substitute, i.e., a substantive. οἱ πονηροί is literally translated "the evil ones"; yet because it is masculine it means the same as οἱ πονηροὶ ἄνθρωποι, namely "the evil men." Alternatively, in the case of a Greek substantive, the article may not occur although English idiom would supply such. The familiar verse "He [God] causes his sun to rise upon [the] evil and [the] good and sends rain upon [the] righteous and [the] unrighteous" (Mt. 5:45) illustrates this phenomenon.

The Verb "To Be"

Conjugation and Accentuation

As in English, "to be" expresses a state of being, rather than action. Hence, it has neither active nor passive voices. The conjugation of the present tense indicative mood follows.

PRESENT INDICATIVE εἰμί

Singular		Plural	
1. εἰμί	I am	ἐσμέν	we are
2. εἶ	you are	ἐστέ	you are
3. ἐστί(ν)	he, she, it is	εἰσί(ν)	they are

Accents. Note carefully the irregular accent: ultima everywhere. Note also the movable ν's in the third person singular and plural, but never with first or second person singular.

The word εἰμί in all forms except εἶ is an enclitic; i.e., a term that will lose its own accent and be pronounced as if it were a part of the previous word. This running together, as it were, produces violations of the rule that only the last three syllables may be accented. Hence, Greek may modify the accentuation of the enclitic and/or the preceding word. The following patterns emerge.

1. The preceding word that is accented on the ultima will retain its accent and will not revert to a grave. The enclitic will lose its accent; thus υἱός ἐστιν.

2. When the preceding word has the acute on the antepenult or the circumflex on the penult add an acute to the ultima of that word; e.g., κύριός ἐστιν; δοῦλοί εἰσιν.

3. When the preceding word has an acute on the penult no additional accent is added for a monosyllabic enclitic; so λόγος μου (an enclitic personal pronoun yet-to-be-introduced; see page 36). If, however, the enclitic has two syllables, then it will have an acute on the ultima (which reverts to a grave if another word follows); thus λόγος ἐστίν or λόγος ἐστὶν καλός.

4. The enclitic, in addition to the previous instance, will retain its accent for emphasis or when it is the beginning of a clause or sentence.

Function of εἰμί

Grammarians label εἰμί a copulative verb because it links two parts of the sentence, the subject and the predicate. For example, in the sentence "The son is the Lord," *son* is the one of whom something is said; consequently, it is the subject and in the nominative case. *Lord*, the predicate noun,[6] is

---

[6]The predicate noun may be called the complement; it completes the thought being expressed by "the son is." An adjective may frequently occur in this same function.

describing *son* and must, therefore, be in the nominative case. *Is* links the two. In Greek one says ὁ υἱός ἐστιν ὁ κύριος.

A further explanatory comment regarding the article, nouns, adjectives and εἰμί is needed. The attributive adjective does not absolutely require the presence of the article (cf. Phil. 1:6 ἔργον ἀγαθὸν = "good work"). The article's presence, which is usual, makes the meaning unequivocal, whereas in its absence context must decide (cf. Mk. 10:17 διδάσκαλε ἀγαθέ = "good teacher"; 2 Thess. 2:17 λόγῳ ἀγαθῷ = "good word"). When there is no article used with the adjective/noun combination it is called an anarthrous construction; with the article, it is an articular construction.

One then appropriately concludes that the typical predicate construction is anarthrous, e.g., Jn. 1:1b θεὸς ἦν [a past tense form of "to be"] ὁ λόγος = "The Word was God"; 1 Jn. 1:5 ὁ θεὸς φῶς [a third declension nominative singular] ἐστιν = "The God is light"; Rom. 7:7 ὁ νόμος ἁμαρτία; [a first declension nominative singular] = "Is the law sin?" Whenever the article is expressed with one of these nominatives in a predicate construction, that one is undeniably the subject; it is definite and is having something asserted about it in the predicate. Note well that in such a construction the subject and predicate are not the same, equal, identical, or anything of the sort. One can always (according to 1 Jn.) say of God He is characterized by light; one cannot always say of light that it is God.

Conversely, if a predicate construction occurs in which both subject and predicate are articular (or if the subject is a pronoun or proper name) then, as Robertson says "Both are definite, treated as identical, one and the same, and interchangeable."[7] Consider Mt. 13:38 ὁ δὲ ἀγρός ἐστιν ὁ κόσμος = "And the field is the world"; 16:16 Σὺ εἶ ὁ Χριστὸς = "You are the Messiah."

Exercises

A. Translate the following sentences.

1. ὁ νόμος σῴζει. ὁ κύριος ἄξει τὸν υἱόν. οἱ θεοὶ σώσουσιν τὸν κόσμον.
2. οἱ ἅγιοι ἄνθρωποι εἰσὶν οἱ ἀδελφοὶ τῶν ἀγγέλων.
3. τὰ νεκρὰ βλέψουσιν τὸν θεόν.
4. λέγετε τοὺς λόγους τοῖς υἱοῖς τῶν ἀνθρώπων.
5. τῷ ἀγαθῷ ὁ οὐρανὸς πέμψει τὸν καλὸν ἄγγελον τῷ κόσμῳ τοῦ θεοῦ.
6. ὁ λόγος ὁ ἄλλος διδάξει τὰ ἀγαθά.
7. τὸ εὐαγγέλιον ἅγιον. ὁ κόσμος νεκρός.
8. τῷ προσώπῳ τοῦ τέκνου κηρύξω τὸν νόμον τὸν καλόν.

---

[7] *Robertson*, p. 768.

9. ὁ ἄνθρωπος ὁ ἀγαθὸς εὑρήσει τὰ ἅγια ἱερὰ τοῦ ἄλλου κόσμου.
10. τὰ ἔργα τοῦ κυρίου ἅγια, ἀγαθά, καλά.
11. ὁ ἀγαθὸς θεός ἐστιν πιστός.
12. ὁ κύριός ἐστιν ὁ υἱὸς τοῦ ἀνθρώπου.
13. οἱ ἄλλοι ἀδελφοὶ εὑρήσουσι τοὺς νόμους τῶν θεῶν τοῦ κοσμοῦ.
14. τὰ τέκνα ὁ θεὸς ἄγει τῷ οὐρανῷ; τὸ εὐαγγέλιον σώσει τοὺς νεκρούς;
15. τοῖς πιστοῖς ἀγγέλοις ὁ ἅγιος ἀνοίξει τὸ ἱερὸν τὸ καλόν.

B. Provide the requested information.

1. The structure of the attributive position is _____ or _____.

2. The structure of the predicate position is _____ or _____.

3. A substantive is _____.
4. The function of the Greek article is _____.
5. A proclitic is _____.
6. An adjective must agree with the word it modifies in _____, _____, and _____.
7. A copulative verb is _____. In the indicative mood its complement is in the _____ case.
8. Define declension; list the cases and the function of each.
9. An articular construction means that _____.
10. An anarthrous construction means that _____.
11. A predicate anarthrous structure signifies _____.
12. A predicate articular structure signifies _____.
13. An enclitic is _____.

CHAPTER 4

NOUN SYSTEM. II: FIRST DECLENSION.
CONDITIONAL SENTENCES

Vocabulary

Feminine Nouns: καρδία Type

ἀλήθεια, -ας, ἡ	truth
ἁμαρτία, -ας, ἡ	sin (cf. hamartiology)
βασιλεία, -ας, ἡ	kingdom, realm, reign (cf. basilica)
ἡμέρα, -ας, ἡ	day (cf. hemerocallis = a day lily)
καρδία, -ας, ἡ	heart (cf. cardiology)
χαρά, -ᾶς, ἡ	joy

Feminine Nouns: δόξα Type

γλῶσσα, -ης, ἡ	tongue, language (cf. glossolalia)
δόξα, -ης, ἡ	glory (cf. doxology)
θάλασσα, -ης, ἡ	sea (cf. thallasic = pertaining to the sea)

Feminine Nouns: φωνή Type

ἀγάπη, -ης, ἡ	love
γῆ, -ῆς, ἡ	earth (cf. geology)
ζωή, -ῆς, ἡ	life (cf. zoology)
φωνή, -ῆς, ἡ	voice (cf. phonograph)
ψυχή, -ῆς, ἡ	soul, life, a living creature (cf. psychology)

Adjectives of the καρδία Type Feminine

δίκαιος, -α, -ον	righteous, just
ἕτερος, -α, -ον	other (cf. heterosexual)
ἴδιος, -α, -ον	one's own (cf. idiom)
μακάριος, -α, -ον	blessed
πρεσβύτερος, -α, -ον	elder (cf. presbyter)

Adjectives of the φωνή Type Feminine

ἔσχατος, -η, -ον	last (cf. eschatology)
λοιπός, -ή, -όν	remaining, other
ὅλος, -η, -ον	whole, all* (cf. holocaust)
ὅσος, -η, -ον	as great as, as much as, all who*
πρῶτος, -η, -ον	first, earlier, earliest (cf. prototype)

Feminine Forms of Adjectives Already Presented

ἀγαθή, ἀγία, ἄλλη, καλή, νεκρά, πιστή

First Declension Masculine Nouns

Ἰωάν(ν)ης, -ου, ὁ	John
μαθητής, -οῦ, ὁ	disciple
προφήτης, -ου, ὁ	prophet

Second Declension Feminine Nouns

ἔρημος, -ου, ἡ	wilderness, desert; as adj.: desolate, empty (cf. eremite = a hermit)
ὁδός, -οῦ, ἡ	way, road, way of life (cf. electrode)
παρθένος, -ου, ἡ	virgin

Article

ἡ	the (fem., all types)

Conjunctions

καί	and, even, also
καὶ . . . καὶ	both . . . and
ἀλλά	but, yet, rather (final α often elides before a vowel: ἀλλ᾽)
εἰ	if, whether

Formation of First Declension
Nouns and Adjectives

Carefully review the sections in Chapter 3 on the characteristics and functions of the inflectional forms.

Nouns of the first declension presented in this text are all feminine except three which will be considered shortly. Feminine nouns and adjectives in their feminine form may be conveniently grouped into three classes:

*Term occurs in predicate position, but translates as if it were in the attributive position.

καρδία type, δόξα type, and φωνή type. This classification has no grammatical or lexical significance; it is structural. In all these classes the stem is found by deleting either the final α or η of the nominative singular (from which vowels the declension derives its name: the alpha declension). For an overview the endings of these three types are presented in the following chart. Then they are discussed separately.

Stem ends in:	ε, ι, ρ	double consonant (e.g., λλ, σσ), consonantal blend (ψ, ξ, ζ), σ or αιν-	anything else
Singular	κ α ρ δ ί α	δ ό ξ α	φ ω ν η
N.	ᾱ	α	η
G.	ᾱς	ης	ης
D.	ᾳ	ῃ	ῃ
A.	ᾱν	αν	ην
V.	ᾱ	α	η

Plural (regardless of stem ending)

- N./V.   αι
-   G.   ων
-   D.   αις
-   A.   ᾱς

καρδία *Type*

This group's stem ends in either ε, ι, or ρ. All the inflectional endings always will have a long α or diphthong except in two places: (1) the genitive plural, which is -ων throughout the first declension (that ω always receives—if a noun—a circumflex accent; the adjective does not), and (2) final -αι, which is short.

χαρά, -ᾶς, ἡ: joy

	Singular	*Plural*
N./V.	χαρ-ά	χαρ-αί
G.	χαρ-ᾶς	χαρ-ῶν
D.	χαρ-ᾷ	χαρ-αῖς
A.	χαρ-άν	χαρ-άς

Remember the earlier observation that when an ultima has the acute in the nominative singular (whether first or second declension) the genitives and datives will have a circumflex on the ultima, elsewhere an acute on the ultima. Know also that the final α of the nominative singular may be either long, as καρδία, or short, as ἀλήθεια. This conclusion is deduced from checking a lexicon to see where the accent is initially placed on the nominatives. Once that position is determined I can conclude the penult of καρδία will continue to be accented with an acute (in this word the penult has a short vowel) except for the genitive plural, where a circumflex always falls on the ultima.

The genitive feminine singular of the first declension is always long, either ᾱ or η. Thus I know, concerning ἀλήθεια, that the long genitive singular (-ας) and the datives (-ᾳ, -αις) (note the diphthongs) will attract the accent to the penult. Additionally, the accusative plural is always long and will accent the penult.

ἑτέρα: other

	Singular	Plural
N./V.	ἑτέρ-α	ἕτερ-αι
G.	ἑτέρ-ας	ἑτέρ-ων
D.	ἑτέρ-ᾳ	ἑτέρ-αις
A.	ἑτέρ-αν	ἑτέρ-ας

Note this accent. The α is long throughout the declension except in nominative plural; hence, that accent must shift to the antepenult.

δόξα Type

This group's stem ends in a consonantal blend (ψ, ξ, or ζ), a double consonant (e.g., λλ, σσ), a σ, or the letters αιν-. Short α is the final letter in the nominative and vocative singular; -αν (short) in the accusative singular. Only genitive and dative singular will change endings from the previous paradigm: α lengthens to an η.

θάλασσα, -ης, ἡ: sea

	Singular	Plural
N./V.	θάλασσ-α	θάλασσ-αι
G.	θαλάσσ-ης	θαλασσ-ῶν
D.	θαλάσσ-ῃ	θαλάσσ-αις
A.	θάλασσ-αν	θαλάσσ-ας

φωνή Type

This category encompasses all feminines whose nominative singular form ends with η. The η is retained throughout the singular; the plural remains unchanged.

φωνή, -ῆς, ἡ: voice

	Singular	Plural
N./V.	φων-ή	φων-αί
G.	φων-ῆς	φων-ῶν
D.	φων-ῇ	φων-αῖς
A.	φων-ήν	φων-άς

πιστή: faithful

	Singular	Plural
N./V.	πιστ-ή	πιστ-αί
G.	πιστ-ῆς	πιστ-ῶν
D.	πιστ-ῇ	πιστ-αῖς
A.	πιστ-ήν	πιστ-άς

Masculine Nouns of the First Declension

A few masculine nouns will be encountered in this declension. As masculines, they use the masculine form of the article and are modified by masculine adjectives. Illustrative of this type are ὁ μαθητής and ὁ προφήτης. Notice that in the following paradigm the only variation from the φωνή type occurs in the nominative and genitive singular and the vocative singular. Accents are normal. The ultima of the vocative is short.

μαθητής, -οῦ, ὁ: disciple

	Singular		Plural	
N.	ὁ	μαθητ-ής	οἱ	μαθητ-αί
G.	τοῦ	μαθητ-οῦ	τῶν	μαθητ-ῶν
D.	τῷ	μαθητ-ῇ	τοῖς	μαθητ-αῖς
A.	τὸν	μαθητ-ήν	τοὺς	μαθητ-άς
V.		μαθητ-ά		μαθητ-αί

Always remember the masculine article as a clue to use a masculine modifier with these terms—even when the article may have been omitted in context.

Formation of the First Declension Article

The article in this declension utilizes the singular and plural endings of the φωνή type—always. To these endings is prefixed a τ, except in the nominative singular and plural.

		Singular			*Plural*	
N.	ἡ	(χαρά;	δόξα)	αἱ	(χαραί;	δόξαι)
G.	τῆς	(χαρᾶς;	δόξης)	τῶν	(χαρῶν;	δοξῶν)
D.	τῇ	(χαρᾷ;	δόξῃ)	ταῖς	(χαραῖς;	δόξαις)
A.	τὴν	(χαράν;	δόξαν)	τὰς	(χαράς;	δόξας)

So, one encounters ἡ θάλασσα, τῆς καρδίας, τῇ ὥρᾳ.

Second Declension Feminines

Three nouns are encountered that have -ος endings of the second declension, but rather than being masculine, they are feminine. They have feminine articles and when modified by adjectives, pronouns, or participles will require the feminine case for their modifiers. The declension of ὁδός, -οῦ, ἡ: "road," together with an adjective modifier (for illustration) is representative.

		Singular			*Plural*	
N.	ἡ	ἀγία	ὁδός	αἱ	ἅγιαι	ὁδοί
G.	τῆς	ἀγίας	ὁδοῦ	τῶν	ἀγίων	ὁδῶν
D.	τῇ	ἀγίᾳ	ὁδῷ	ταῖς	ἀγίαις	ὁδοῖς
A.	τὴν	ἀγίαν	ὁδόν	τὰς	ἀγίας	ὁδούς
V.		ἀγία	ὁδέ		ἅγιαι	ὁδοί

Nouns in the Attributive Position

Nouns and certain constructions yet-to-be introduced (e.g., prepositional phrases, participles, infinitives, and adverbs) may occur in the attributive position just the same as an adjective. When this occurs, the noun or other form has an attributive adjectival force. The Greek word order of the first phrase in 1 Pet. 3:4 illustrates this: ἀλλ᾽ ὁ κρυπτὸς τῆς καρδίας ἄνθρωπος = "But the hidden man of the heart." κρυπτὸς ("hidden"), an articular attributive adjective, limits "man" to "the hidden one." Then follows an articular attributive genitive noun that further delimits "man," describing (the genitive's function) "man" as "heart." When the analysis is completed, no man at all is the subject, but "the inner person." Moreover, the context reveals that the inner person of woman is the subject.

Conditional Sentences

One element of richness in the Greek language is the variety of structures whereby one may express a conditional thought. In the Greek New

Testament there are four.[1] The first is the condition of reality, sometimes labeled a first class condition or a condition assumed to be real. Like all conditional sentences, it typically has two segments: the "if" or conditional clause, called the protasis; and the principal or conclusion clause, called the apodosis. The protasis will regularly use the particle εἰ ("if") with the present, imperfect, or future tense of the indicative mood. The apodosis will use any tense of the indicative (other moods may also be used, especially the imperative).

Earlier, it was observed that the indicative mood is the mood of declaration or statment of fact. Consequently, when this mood is used with εἰ, its significance is not to raise doubt. It is a way of expressing "a simple conditional assumption with emphasis on the reality of the assumption (not of what is being assumed): the condition is considered 'a real case.'"[2] Illustrative of this is Mt. 4:6: Εἰ υἱὸς εἶ τοῦ θεοῦ, κ.τ.λ. [καὶ τὰ λοιπά = and the remaining] ("If you are the Son of God, [cast yourself down]"). Matthew is not depicting the devil as one who believes Jesus to be the Son of God, but—by using the first class construction—is clearly communicating the devil's assumption for this encounter that Jesus is such. The actual reality or nonreality of the protasis must be ascertained by data provided elsewhere—either in the context or from other sources. The condition is assumed by the speaker to be real, although it may, in fact, not be real. Actual fact is irrelevant to the assumption.

Exercises

A. Translate the following sentences.

1. ἡ καλὴ ἡμέρα ἐστὶν τὸ ἔργον τοῦ κυρίου καί ἐστιν ἀγαθὴ τῷ τοῦ ἀνθρώπου προσώπῳ.
2. ὁ υἱὸς τοῦ θεοῦ κηρύσσει τὸ δίκαιον εὐαγγέλιον τῇ βασιλείᾳ τῇ νεκρᾷ καὶ πιστεύει.
3. ἡ καρδία ἡ ἁγία εὑρήσει καλὴν ζωήν.
4. ἡ γῆ καὶ ἡ θάλασσα καὶ ὁ οὐρανὸς λέγουσι τὴν δόξαν τοῦ θεοῦ.
5. εὑρίσκει τὸν ἀδελφὸν τὸν ἴδιον καὶ λέγει, Εὑρίσκομεν τὸν κύριον.

---

[1]Ernest DeWitt Burton, *Syntax of the Moods and Tenses in New Testament Greek* (3d ed.; Edinburgh: T. & T. Clark, 1898), pp. 100–112, provides a thorough analysis of the Greek conditional sentences from a perspective which is informed by the language structures in the classical period. The analysis is thorough and illuminating, but surpasses the beginner's level. *BDF* §§ 371, 372, and 360, survey the material in a less involved fashion. For the present needs of the beginner, the materials presented in this text will suffice for translation and analysis of the materials selected from the *GNT* and will provide an appropriate foundation for subsequent refinement.

[2]*BDF*, § 371 (1).

6. Κύριε τοῦ οὐρανοῦ καὶ τῆς γῆς, σώσεις τοὺς δικαίους καὶ ἀνοίξεις ταῖς ἀγαθαῖς τὴν βασιλείαν τοῦ θεοῦ.
7. ἡ καρδία ἁμαρτία, ἀλλ᾽ ὁ νόμος ἅγιος καὶ δίκαιος καὶ ἀγαθός.
8. εἰ τὴν τοῦ θεοῦ ἀγάπην ἄνθρωπος ἔχει, εὑρίσκει τὴν ζωήν.
9. μακάριοι οἱ πιστοί εἰ διδάσκουσι τὴν δικαίαν γλῶσσαν.
10. οἱ λοιποὶ πρεσβύτεροι κηρύξουσιν ὅλον τὸ εὐαγγέλιον καὶ ὅσοι πιστεύουσιν τοὺς λόγους τοὺς τοῦ κυρίου τὸν θεὸν βλέψουσιν.
11. ἡ καλὴ παρθένος ἕξει τέκνον τοῦ θεοῦ.
12. ἡ ὁδὸς ἡ ἑτέρα ἄξει τὰς ψυχὰς τῆς ἐρήμου εἰς [into] τὴν ζωὴν τῆς δικαίας.

B. Supply the requested information.

1. List three types of first declension feminine nouns.
2. Identify the distinct stem letters of each type.
3. Provide the singular case endings of these feminines.
4. Feminine plural nouns/adjectives, first declension have the following endings: _____ .
5. Decline ὁ ἀγαθὸς προφήτης; ἡ λοιπὴ ἔρημος.
6. "A noun is used with an attributive adjectival sense" means _____
   _____ .
7. What does a first class conditional sentence signify? What is its Greek structure?

CHAPTER 5

NOUN SYSTEM. III:
PERSONAL AND RELATIVE PRONOUNS

Vocabulary

Pronouns

αὐτός, -ή, -ό	he, she, it (in oblique cases only); in attributive position: same; in predicate position: himself, herself, itself (cf. autonomous)
ἐγώ	I (cf. egotism)
ὅς, ἥ, ὅ	who, which, what
σύ	you

Nouns

δαιμόνιον, -ου, τό	demon
δικαιοσύνη, -ης, ἡ	righteousness
δοῦλος, -ου, ὁ	slave, servant
δῶρον, -ου, τό	gift (cf. Dorothea, a gift of God)
εἰρήνη, -ης, ἡ	peace (cf. irenic)
ἐκκλησία, -ας, ἡ	church, assembly (cf. ecclesiology)
ἐξουσία, -ας, ἡ	power, authority
λαός, -οῦ, ὁ	people (cf. laity)
ὄχλος, -ου, ὁ	crowd (cf. ochlophobia)
σημεῖον, -ου, τό	sign (cf. semeiology)
ὥρα, -ας, ἡ	hour (cf. horoscope)

Conjunctions

The following are *postpositives*; i.e., they are never the first word in the sentence; rather, they are usually second.

γάρ	for (This is not the preposition "for," but a conjunction that functions with an explanatory force equivalent to "because.")
δέ	but, and (Sometimes it suggests contrast; at other times, it is simply a connective.)

οὖν   therefore (an inferential, transitional conjunc-
                                    tion)

Affirmative and Negative Particles

ναί   yes, certainly
οὐ   no, not (before a vowel with smooth breath-
                                    ing mark: οὐκ; before a vowel with rough
                                    breathing mark: οὐχ)
οὐδέ   and not, nor, neither, not even;
  οὐδὲ . . . οὐδέ . . .   neither . . . nor

Personal Pronouns

The first declension φωνή type endings and the second declension masculine and neuter forms will frequently be employed in this and the next
chapters. They should be carefully reviewed before going further.

A pronoun is a word that takes the place of a noun. In the sentence
"Jesus came to Martha to teach her, but Martha objected, saying 'I need to
serve you,'" "her," "I," and "you" are personal pronouns. Just as Greek
nouns and adjectives are declined, so too, Greek pronouns must be
declined. The gender and number of a personal pronoun must agree with
the antecedent (the word for which the pronoun substitutes) of the pronoun.
The case of the personal pronoun is determined by its use in its own clause.
In the above example, according to Greek grammar "her" is feminine
singular, corresponding to its antecedent "Martha." Its case is accusative
because it is the object of "to teach." "I" is feminine singular, corresponding
to its antecedent "Martha," and nominative because it is subject of the clause
"I need to serve." "You" is masculine singular, corresponding to its
antecedent "Jesus," and accusative since it is the object of "to serve."

Formation of Personal Pronouns

"I" and "you."   The first and second person personal pronouns, "I" and
"you," reflect little similarity to first and second declension words except in
the genitive forms. However, the endings for ἐγώ ("I") in all cases except
the nominative singular correspond with those for σύ ("you").

ἐγώ: I

	Singular			Plural	
N.	ἐγώ	I		ἡμεῖς	we
G.	ἐμοῦ, μου	of me (my)		ἡμῶν	of us (our)
D.	ἐμοί, μοι	to/for me		ἡμῖν	to/for us
A.	ἐμέ, με	me		ἡμᾶς	us

The forms ἐμοῦ, ἐμοί, ἐμέ are used for emphasis. The alternate forms μου, μοι, με are not emphatic. They are enclitics.[1]

σύ: you

	Singular			Plural	
N.	σύ	you		ὑμεῖς	you
G.	σοῦ	of you (your)		ὑμῶν	of you (your)
D.	σοί	to/for you		ὑμῖν	to/for you
A.	σέ	you		ὑμᾶς	you

"He," "she," "it." The third person personal pronoun in the masculine and feminine is declined precisely as the second declension masculine noun (e.g., λόγος) and the φωνή type of the feminine noun. The neuter declension varies from δῶρον only in that the nominative and accusative singular forms delete the final ν (just like ἄλλο).

αὐτός, αὐτή, αὐτό: he, she, it

	Singular			Plural		
	M.	F.	N.	M.	F.	N
N.	αὐτός	αὐτή	αὐτό	αὐτοί	αὐταί	αὐτά
G.	αὐτοῦ	αὐτῆς	αὐτοῦ	αὐτῶν	αὐτῶν	αὐτῶν
D.	αὐτῷ	αὐτῇ	αὐτῷ	αὐτοῖς	αὐταῖς	αὐτοῖς
A.	αὐτόν	αὐτήν	αὐτό	αὐτούς	αὐτάς	αὐτά

Function of Personal Pronouns

Emphasis or contrast. The first and second person personal pronouns (ἐγώ, σύ) may be used in the nominative case to express emphasis or contrast. For example, the question put to Jesus at his trial reads: Σὺ εἶ ὁ βασιλεὺς [king] τῶν Ἰουδαίων [Jew]; ("Are you the king of the Jews?"; Mt. 27:11). Σύ, strictly speaking, is unnecessary since a subject, "you," is an integral part of the verb εἶ. Its addition, however, underscores what Pilate felt to be the question's absurdity. To express the emphasis of the Greek construction in English is difficult. One may underscore the pronoun in a written text or change pitch in oral reading. Expositional commentary is the best solution.

Possession. The short form of the genitive, μου, is very common as a means of expressing possession; e.g., τῇ ἀγάπῃ μου ("for the love of me" [lit.] or "for my love").

[1]Review p. 23.

Objects. The oblique cases (i.e., genitive, dative, accusative) of ἐγώ/σύ are used in lieu of nouns just as one might employ nouns. For example, the dative μοι/σοι may occur as indirect object (see Mt. 18:26b: "And I shall repay to you [σοι]"); the accusative με/σε as the direct object (see Mt. 8:2b: "Lord, if you will, you are able to heal me [με]"); the genitive μου/σου as the object of certain verbs (see Mk. 7:14b: "You all hear me [μου]"[2]).

αὐτός, -ή, -ó. The use of the third person personal pronoun calls for special attention. When the term is used with the article in the attributive position the word is translated "same" and is, thus, an adjective. Consider a substantival use of αὐτός in Heb. 1:12: σὺ δὲ ὁ αὐτὸς εἶ ("But you are the same"). αὐτός may be used in oblique cases—in the attributive position—and mean "same." Note Mk. 14:39: "And again, after he had gone away, he prayed the same [τὸν αὐτὸν] prayer"; Lk. 23:40: "You are in the same [τῷ αὐτῷ] judgment."

By contrast αὐτός in the predicate position nominative case intensifies and is translated "himself," etc.; then, it is an adjectival pronoun. Second Thessalonians 2:16a is illustrative: Αὐτὸς δὲ ὁ κύριος ἡμῶν Ἰησοῦς Χριστὸς ("Now [may] our Lord Jesus Christ himself").

In addition to occurring with a noun, αὐτός may also occur with a verb, whether or not the verb has an expressed noun subject or an emphatic personal pronoun. Not having the article with αὐτός, it is said to be in the predicate position. Consequently, it will be intensive; translate it as "myself, yourself, herself," etc. Thus, in 2 Cor. 10:1 Paul writes Αὐτὸς δὲ ἐγὼ Παῦλος παρακαλῶ ὑμᾶς ("But I myself, Paul, exhort you"). Ἐγὼ emphasizes; αὐτὸς intensifies; Παῦλος identifies; the man was mustering all the expressiveness the language afforded.

In review, the uses of αὐτός are as follows:

ATTRIBUTIVE POSITION (Regardless of Case): "same"

ὁ αὐτὸς ἄγγελος λέγει = the same angel says
ὁ αὐτὸς   λέγει = the same one/man says

(Cf. Lk. 6:33; Rom. 10:12; 1 Cor. 1:10)

---

[2]This clause illustrates a phenomenon in Greek that is unlike English: ἀκούω may have a genitive as its object. *BDF* states the rule as follows: "Genitive with verbs of perception. . . . The person whose words are heard stands in the genitive, the thing (or person . . .) about which (or whom) one hears in the accusative." (§173[1]) This rule, however, does not always hold; cf. Jn. 15:20a.

PREDICATE POSITION

A. *Nominative Case:* "____self"

αὐτὸς,	λέγω	I myself say		λέγομεν	we ourselves say
αὐτή,	λέγεις	your yourself say	αὐτοί,	λέγετε	you yourselves say
αὐτό	λέγει	he, she, it, him-, her-, itself says	αὐταὶ, αὐτὰ	λέγουσι	they themselves say

(Cf. Rom. 7;25; Jn. 6:6b; Acts 20:34)

B. *Oblique Cases:* "his," "her," "them," etc.

Gen.   γράφω τὸν λόγον <u>αὐτοῦ</u> (αὐτῶν) = I write his (their) word. (Cf. 1 Cor. 15:10)

Dat.   ἄξω τοὺς λαοὺς αὐτῷ (αὐτοῖς) = I shall lead the people to him (them). (Cf. Jn. 4:7b, 17a)

Acc.   βλέπω τὸν κύριον (τοὺς κυρίους) καὶ βαπτίσω αὐτόν (αὐτούς) = I see the lord (the lords) and I shall baptize him (them). (Cf. Jn. 5:14)

The Relative Pronoun

The Formation of the Relative Pronoun

The relative pronoun is declined precisely as the article except the τ is everywhere deleted. All forms have a rough breathing mark. All nominatives and accusatives have acute accents (as long as contextual rules of accentuation will allow); all genitives and datives the circumflex.

ὅς, ἥ, ὅ: who, what, which

Singular

	M.			F.			N.	
N.	ὅς	who	ἥ	who		ὅ	what	
G.	οὗ	of whom	ἧς	of whom		οὗ	of what	
D.	ᾧ	to/for whom	ᾗ	to/for whom		ᾧ	to/for what	
A.	ὅν	whom	ἥν	whom		ὅ	what	

Plural

	M.			F.			N.	
N.	οἵ	who		αἵ	who		ἅ	what
G.	ὧν	of whom		ὧν	of whom		ὧν	of what
D.	οἷς	to/for whom		αἷς	to/for whom		οἷς	to/for what
A.	οὕς	whom		ἅς	whom		ἅ	what

Function of the Relative Pronoun

The relative, like the personal pronoun, agrees with its antecedent in number and gender. Like the personal pronoun, its case is normally determined by the function of the relative in its own clause. Consider 1 Cor 10:13: πιστὸς ὁ θεός, ὃς οὐκ ἐάσει [will permit] ὑμᾶς ("God is faithful, who will not permit you"). In this sentence ὅς, which is substituting for θεός, is accordingly masculine singular. It is nominative, not because θεός is, but because it is the subject of ἐάσει. ὃς οὐκ ἐάσει ὑμᾶς etc. is one ponderous, involved adjective. Properly speaking, it is a clause because it has both a subject and a predicate (ὃς and ἐάσει). Hence, one would call this entire concoction an adjectival relative clause. Its function is simply to describe ὁ θεός.

Occasionally, the relative will adopt the case of its antecedent regardless of what strict rules would have dictated. Such a situation is called the attraction of the relative to the case of its antecedent. This is especially true when the antecedent is in the genitive or dative cases. John 15:20a shows this: μνημονεύετε [remember] τοῦ λόγου οὗ ἐγὼ εἶπον [I said] ὑμῖν ("Remember the word which I spoke to you"). τοῦ λόγου, the object of μνημονεύετε, demonstrates the earlier observation[3] that some verbs take the genitive case for their direct objects. οὗ is the direct object of εἶπον and should be—strictly speaking—in the accusative case. It has adopted the case of λόγου, however, which adds "more internal unity" to the sentence structure.[4]

Exercises

A. Translate the following sentences.

1. ἡμεῖς οὐχ εὑρήσομεν αὐτόν; ναί, εἰ ἀκούομεν τοὺς λόγους αὐτοῦ καὶ πιστεύομεν αὐτούς.

2. Κύριε, σὺ εἶ ὁ υἱὸς τοῦ θεοῦ· σὺ ὁ δίκαιος εἶ τοῦ Ἰσραήλ.

3. λέγει αὐτῷ ὁ κύριος Σὺ εἶ ὁ δοῦλός μου. διδάξεις τοῖς λαοῖς μου τοὺς αὐτοὺς νόμους οὓς αὐτὸς διδάσκω σοι.

---

[3]See above, p. 38, note 2.

[4]*Robertson*, p. 715.

4. Ἀδελφέ, ὅς ἐστιν ἡ τῆς ζωῆς ὁδός, αὐτὸς βαπτίζει τοὺς ὄχλους οἳ εὑρίσκουσιν αὐτόν.
5. αὐτὸς δὲ ὁ θεὸς οὐ πέμπει τὸν ἄγγελον αὐτοῦ, ἀλλὰ τὸν υἱὸν αὐτοῦ ὃς κηρύσσει τὴν τοῦ θεοῦ ἀγάπην.
6. ὁ κόσμος οὐκ ἀνοίξει τὰ ἱερὰ αὐτοῦ, οἱ δὲ λαοὶ τοῦ θεοῦ ἀνοίξουσιν τὰς καρδίας αὐτῶν.
7. οὐ γάρ ἐστιν ἡ βασιλεία τοῦ θεοῦ ἁμαρτία, ἀλλὰ δικαιοσύνη καὶ εἰρήνη καὶ ἐξουσία τοῦ θεοῦ.
8. οὐκ ἀλήθειαν λέγομεν; οὐ δαιμόνιον ἔχεις ὃ ἄγει σε;
9. ἐγὼ δὲ νόμον ἔχω ὃν ὑμεῖς αὐτοὶ οὐ γινώσκετε.
10. βλέπω τὸν ἄνθρωπον ὃς λέγει μοι αἷς πιστεύω.[5]

B. Provide the requested information.

1. A postpositive is _____.
2. A pronoun agrees with its antecedent in _____ and _____.
3. The case of a personal pronoun is determined by _____
_____.
4. An enclitic is _____.
5. Personal pronouns are used to express _____, _____,
and _____.
6. In the predicate position αὐτός means _____ or _____.
7. In the attributive position αὐτός means _____.
8. The case of the relative pronoun is normally determined by _____
_____.
9. Explain "attraction to the case of the antecedent." _____
_____.

---

[5]πιστεύω frequently takes the dative case for its object. This is not an indirect object but a direct object. Since one thinks of the accusative case when a direct object is mentioned, one may call this construction a complementary object.

CHAPTER 6

NOUN SYSTEM III (CONT.):
DEMONSTRATIVE AND REFLEXIVE PRONOUNS

Vocabulary

Demonstrative Pronouns

ἐκεῖνος, -η, -ο	that; pl. those
οὗτος, αὕτη, τοῦτο	this; pl. these

Reflexive Pronouns

ἑαυτοῦ, ἑαυτῆς, ἑαυτοῦ	of himself, of herself, of itself; pl. of themselves
ἐμαυτοῦ (masc.) ἐμαυτῆς (fem.) [no neut.]	of myself; pl. of ourselves
σεαυτοῦ (masc.) σεαυτῆς (fem.) [no neut.]	of yourself; pl. of yourselves

Adjectives

ἀγαπητός, -ή, όν	beloved, dear
ἕκαστος, -η, -ον	each, every
Ἰουδαῖος, -α, -ον	Jewish; as a noun: Jew
πονηρός, -ά, -όν	evil

Nouns

Ἰησοῦς, -οῦ, ὁ	Jesus
οἶκος, -ου, ὁ	house
Χριστός, -οῦ, ὁ	the Anointed One, Messiah, Christ

Verbs

δοξάζω, δοξάσω	I glorify (cf. doxology)
εὐαγγελίζω, εὐαγγελίσω	I evangelize, proclaim the gospel
κράζω, κράξω	I cry out

Demonstrative Pronouns

Formation of Demonstrative Pronouns

οὗτος, αὕτη, τοῦτο. Confusion concerning formation of these stems can be avoided by observing a few simple patterns. (1) The stem οὑτ- has a prefix τ in the same forms as the article. Thus, masculine and feminine nominative singular and plural have no prefixed τ (but, N.B. the rough breathing mark); elsewhere the τ is a prefix. (2) The stem changes to (τ)αυτ- when the case ending has an α or η (N.B. neuter plural nominative and accusative). (3) Declension endings are first and second, following the pattern of αὐτός, αὐτή, αὐτό.

οὗτος, αὕτη, τοῦτο: this

	Singular Τhis			*Plural* Τhese		
	M.	**F.**	**N.**	**M.**	**F.**	**N.**
N.	οὗτος	αὕτη	τοῦτο	οὗτοι	αὗται	ταῦτα
G.	τούτου	ταύτης	τούτου	τούτων	τούτων	τούτων
D.	τούτῳ	ταύτῃ	τούτῳ	τούτοις	ταύταις	τούτοις
A.	τοῦτον	ταύτην	τοῦτο	τούτους	ταύτας	ταῦτα

that — ἐκεῖνος, -η, -ο. The stem is consistently ἐκειν-. The declension endings *those* are the same as οὗτος, etc. The accents will have the same changes for the same reasons: long penults followed by long ultimas demand an acute on the penult—if it is to be accented. This now makes five terms whose neuter nominative and accusative singular delete the ν: αὐτό, τοῦτο, ἐκεῖνο, the relative pronoun ὅ, and the article τό.

Functions of οὗτος *and* ἐκεῖνος.

οὗτος and ἐκεῖνος regularly occur without the article immediately preceding them in their relation to a noun or substantive. In other words, they stand in the predicate position. The demonstrative followed by the article and a noun is not translated as if it were an adjective in the predicate position. For example, ἀγαθὸς ὁ ἄνθρωπος is "the man is good," but οὗτος ὁ ἄνθρωπος is "this man."

To say "this one is . . ." one uses οὗτός ἐστιν, a simple substantival construction. The article is not used with οὗτος and ἐκεῖνος in the substantival construction because "this" and "that" specify without the use of the article. Thus, one reads οὗτός ἐστιν ὁ υἱός μου ("This one is my Son"—Mt. 17:5); μακάριος ὁ δοῦλος ἐκεῖνος ("Blessed is that servant"— Lk. 12:43); ἐκεῖνος ὑμᾶς διδάξει ("That one will teach you"—Jn. 14:26).

οὗτος usually refers to one present or in immediate proximity (either literally or mentally). So, when Mt. 17:5 reports that God said, "This is my

Son," one understands that God means one who is physically near the hearers. Likewise, in the interpretation of the parable of the sower (Mt. 13:19–23), "this" is used repeatedly, referring to something that is mentally near: The one of which I spoke, this one. By contrast, ἐκεῖνος frequently denotes a previous referent which is now absent. Consider Jn. 14:20, where "'that' day" is one in the yet-to-be-realized future. Like οὗτος, ἐκεῖνος may also be used in narratives simply to refer to a preceding thought. So, in Jn. 14:21, Jesus says, "He who has my commandments and keeps them, that one [ἐκεῖνος] is the one who is loving me."

Reflexive Pronouns

Formation and Function of Reflexive Pronouns

A reflexive pronoun is a combination of a personal pronoun plus ——self, e.g., "himself." In Greek the same is true. Reflexive pronouns are formed by combining the personal pronouns with αὐτός. "Of myself" (ἐμαυτοῦ) is αὐτοῦ with a prefixed ἐμ- from ἐμέ ("me"). "Of yourself" (σεαυτοῦ) is αὐτοῦ σ with σέ ("you") prefixed. "Of himself, herself, itself" (ἑαυτοῦ, ἑαυτῆς, ἑαυτοῦ) is αὐτοῦ with a prefixed ἑ (from an ancient form not found in the *GNT* but used by writers of the classical period and others of the Koine period). First and second declension forms of the αὐτός, -ή, -ό type are used for reflexive endings.

Two things are peculiar about reflexives. One is their lack of a nominative form; they occur only in the oblique cases. This is so because these pronouns are used to refer the expressed action back to their subject, an impossibility with the nominative. Thus, one reads "I see myself" (βλέπω ἐμαυτόν); "you see yourself" (βλέπεις σεαυτήν); "he is baptizing himself" (βαπτίζει ἑαυτόν). The thought "I myself speak to you" is not reflexive; the action is directed to "you," not "I." "Myself," in this instance, is intensive (so ἐγὼ αὐτὸς λέγω σοι).

The second unusual thing is that the masculine plural of all three terms, ἐμαυτοῦ, σεαυτοῦ, ἑαυτοῦ, is identical: ἑαυτῶν ("of our-, your-, them-selves"). Likewise, the feminine plural of all three terms is identical in formation: ἑαυτῶν. The neuter of ἑαυτοῦ, being formed with αὐτό, gives no surprises as regards formation.

The multiple occurrence of the same terms for the plurals means the context must determine which of the personal pronouns is being signified in any given instance. Translate them as first, second, or third person in keeping with the person and number of the verb whose action they reflect. Observe, moreover, that the gender of the reflexive pronoun provides the identification of the subject's gender. For example, κηρύσσομεν ἑαυτούς = "we (men [derived from the masculine ending of the reflexive]) preach ourselves"; κηρύσσετε ἑαυτούς = "you (men [same derivation]) preach yourselves"; κηρύσσουσι ἑαυτάς = "they (women [derived from the feminine ending of the reflexive]) preach themselves."

ἐμαυτοῦ, ἐμαυτῆς: of myself

	Singular			*Plural*		
	M.	F.	N.	M.	F.	N.
G.	ἐμαυτοῦ	ἐμαυτῆς	_____	ἑαυτῶν	ἑαυτῶν	_____
D.	ἐμαυτῷ	ἐμαυτῇ		ἑαυτοῖς	ἑαυταῖς	
A.	ἐμαυτόν	ἐμαυτήν		ἑαυτούς	ἑαυτάς	

σεαυτοῦ, σεαυτῆς: of yourself

G.	σεαυτοῦ	σεαυτῆς	_____	All forms are the same as the
D.	σεαυτῷ	σεαυτῇ		above
A.	σεαυτόν	σεαυτήν		

ἑαυτοῦ, ἑαυτῆς, ἑαυτοῦ: of him-, her-, itself

G.	ἑαυτοῦ	ἑαυτῆς	ἑαυτοῦ	All forms are the	ἑαυτῶν
D.	ἑαυτῷ	ἑαυτῇ	ἑαυτῷ	same as the	ἑαυτοῖς
A.	ἑαυτόν	ἑαυτήν	ἑαυτό	above	ἑαυτά

Ἰησοῦς: Jesus

The name "Jesus" occurs only in the singular. Its declension is as follows:

N.	Ἰησοῦς
G./D./V.	Ἰησοῦ
A.	Ἰησοῦν

Exercises

A. Translate the following sentences.

1. σὺ ἀκούεις τοῦ προφητοῦ ἐκείνου; οὐκ. ἀκούω τούτου τοῦ μαθητοῦ τοῦ κυρίου.
2. καὶ ὁ θεὸς πέμπει με, ἀλλ᾽ ὑμεῖς οὐκ ἀκούετε ἐκείνου οὐδὲ ἀκούετε φωνὴν αὐτοῦ.
3. ὁ ἄλλος μαθητὴς οὐ πιστεύει Ἰησοῦ, ἀλλ᾽ αὐτὸς πιστεύει ἑαυτῷ.
4. λέγει οὖν ὁ προφήτης ἐκεῖνος ὃν διδάσκει Ἰησοῦς Πιστεύω.
5. εἰ κηρύσσομεν Ἰησοῦν, αἱ Ἰουδαῖαι ἐκεῖναι εὑρήσουσι τὴν βασιλείαν τοῦ θεοῦ.
6. εὐαγγελίζετε ἑαυτοῖς καὶ βαπτίσουσιν ἑαυτοῖς καὶ πιστεύσομεν ἑαυταῖς.
7. οὗτός ἐστιν ὁ υἱός μου ὁ ἀγαπητὸς καὶ εἰ δοξάζετε αὐτὸν σώσει ὑμᾶς.

8. ὁ Ἰησοῦς ἀνοίξει ἑκαστῷ ὑμῶν τὴν ἁγίαν βασιλείαν εἰ ἀκούετε αὐτοῦ.
9. οὗτος ὁ ἄνθρωπος οὐ βλέπει καὶ κράζει Ἰησοῦ, Ἰησοῦ, σὺ δοξάσεις σεαυτόν;
10. ἐκεῖνος εὐαγγελίσει τούτους τοὺς λαούς.

B. Provide the requested information.

1. Contrast a reflexive and a demonstrative pronoun.
2. Where does α occur in the stem of οὗτος?
3. Demonstratives stand in the ＿＿＿＿＿＿ position. How does one say "That one is the man"?
4. Discriminate between the plural forms of the reflexive.

CHAPTER 7

PREPOSITIONS, COMPOUND VERBS, ὅτι

Vocabulary

Prepositions with One Case

ἀπό (Gen.)[1]	from (cf. apostate)
ἄχρι (Gen.) (or ἄχρις)	as far as, until; as a conjunction: until
εἰς (Acc.)	into, against, in order to (cf. eisegesis)
ἐκ (Gen.) (ἐξ before an initial vowel)	out of (cf. exegesis)
ἐν (Dat.)	in (cf. encephalograph)
ἐνώπιον (Gen.)	before
ἔξω (Gen.)	outside (cf. exotic)
ἕως (Gen.)	as far as, until
πρό (Gen.)	before (cf. propaedeutic)
πρός (Acc.)	to, toward, with (cf. prosthesis)
σύν (Dat.)	with (cf. synthesis)

Nouns

ἄρτος, -ου, ὁ	bread
γραφή, -ῆς, ἡ	writing, scripture (cf. graphic)
ἐντολή, -ῆς, ἡ	commandment, order
θάνατος, -ου, ὁ	death (cf. thanatology)
κεφαλή, -ῆς, ἡ	head (cf. encephalic)
ὀφθαλμός, -οῦ, ὁ	eye (cf. ophthalmology)

Compound Verbs

ἀπολύω, ἀπολύσω	I release, let go
ἐκβάλλω [fut. irregular]	I throw out, send out (cf. ballistics)
συνάγω, συνάξω	I gather, bring, lead together (cf. synagogue)

---

[1]The parentheses indicate the particular case in which the object of the preposition will occur.

Particle

ἀμήν so let it be, amen, truly

Conjunction

ὅτι that, because

Definitions and Purpose of Prepositions

A preposition is a word that usually occurs before a noun or substantive in order to link that word to a preceding term as a modifier, e.g., "He spoke *for* us"; "the book *of* John"; "the call *from* Tim." In English a preposition is said to have an object, a word that completes the thought of the preposition. Thus, in the above examples "us," "John," and "Tim" are objects and in the objective case (though no distinctive ending is employed to express such).

In Greek the object of the preposition may be in the genitive, dative, or accusative case, depending upon the thought being expressed by the author. Some prepositions will occur with their objects consistently occurring in one case. Others will occur with objects in two, or even three, possible cases. In this chapter only those that use one case are considered.

The choice of case has been fixed by time and practice. The case with which a preposition occurs must be learned as the English equivalent is memorized. The student will learn, for example, "ἐν with the dative expresses 'in'—location." The actual situation is that the dative case (or locative, in an eight-case system), which can express—by itself, without a preposition—location, is made quite explicit by the addition of ἐν with the dative. It should be clearly recognized that nouns with their case endings can and often do express precisely what prepositional phrases may. Prepositions add force, specificity, and clarity.

Compound Verbs

Prepositions do not always occur as separate words in Greek. Just as in English, they may be prefixed to verbs. When this occurs, some letter changes may result, which will be noted as they are encountered. The meaning of a compound verb, as these formations are called, may sometimes be determined from the component parts. Hence, συνάγω is "I lead together," a combination of σύν ("with") and ἄγω ("I lead"); ἐκβάλλω is "I cast out," from ἐκ ("out of") and βάλλω ("I throw"). This procedure, however, will not always work. One should always consult the lexicon when a new compound word is initially encountered.

Prepositions in Attributive Position
and as Substantives

Prepositional phrases may be used to describe nouns in the same fashion as adjectives or other nouns are used. Recall "the good man" is expressed by either ὁ ἀγαθὸς ἄνθρωπος or ὁ ἄνθρωπος ὁ ἀγαθός. One may say "The bread of heaven" by placing "of heaven" in the attributive position, thus, ὁ τοῦ οὐρανοῦ ἄρτος or ὁ ἄρτος ὁ τοῦ οὐρανοῦ.

The *GNT* uses prepositions in a similar way. One may observe either ὁ ἐκ τοῦ οὐρανοῦ ἄρτος or ὁ ἄρτος ὁ ἐκ τοῦ οὐρανοῦ = "the out-of-heaven-bread" or "the bread, the one out of heaven." In either instance an appropriate English equivalent would be "the bread that is out of heaven." ἐκ τοῦ οὐρανοῦ is a prepositional phrase functioning as an attributive adjective (cf. Jn. 6:50, 58).

Just as ὁ πονηρός is "the evil one" or "the evil man," so οἱ ἐκ τοῦ πονηροῦ is "the ones out of the evil one" or "the men out of the evil man." Here the prepositional phrase, taking the place of an adjective, functions with the article as a substantival phrase in the attributive position. Consider Mt. 5:16b: "that they may see your good works and glorify the Father ὑμῶν ~~of your~~ τὸν ἐν τοῖς οὐρανοῖς = "of you, the [Father] in the heavens." ἐν τοῖς οὐρανοῖς, the entire prepositional phrase, stands in the attributive position to the article τὸν (cf. Eph. 1:15b).

ὅτι

ὅτι is a conjunction, a particle that connects two clauses. The following are among its primary functions and meanings.

Causal Clauses

A clause introduced by ὅτι often provides the cause or basis for a preceding statement; e.g., ὑμῶν δὲ μακάριοι οἱ ὀφθαλμοὶ ὅτι βλέπουσιν, καὶ τὰ ὦτα ["ears"] ὑμῶν ὅτι ἀκούουσιν ("But blessed are your eyes because they see and your ears because they hear"—Mt. 13:16). Consider Mt. 5:3–10 where ὅτι is repeatedly used to explain the basis for declaring certain groups to be blessed.

Object Clauses

Whereas the object of a verb may often be simply a word (e.g., "John received a revelation"), the NT writers frequently use ὅτι to introduce a clause that serves as the object. Two common structures are these: (1) as an appositional, explanatory clause; (2) as object clause after verbs of sense or mental perception (i.e., taste, see, hear, think, perceive, read, etc.).

First John 4:10 illustrates the appositional use of ὅτι: ἐν τούτῳ ἐστὶν ἡ ἀγάπη, οὐχ ὅτι ἡμεῖς ἠγαπήκαμεν [pft. of ἀγαπάω: "we have loved"] τὸν θεόν, ἀλλ᾽ ὅτι αὐτὸς ἠγάπησεν [aor. of ἀγαπάω: "he loved"] ἡμᾶς ("In this is love, not that we have loved God, but that he himself loved us"). "Not that . . ., but that . . ." are in apposition to ἐν τούτῳ and explain wherein is love from the negative and positive perspectives.

First John 4:13 exemplifies, first, ὅτι with a verb of sense perception, and then, ὅτι introducing an explanatory causal clause. Ἐν τούτῳ γινώσκομεν ὅτι ἐν αὐτῷ μένομεν ["to abide"] καὶ αὐτὸς ἐν ἡμῖν, ὅτι ἐκ τοῦ πνεύματος ["Spirit"; a third declension genitive singular neuter noun] αὐτοῦ δέδωκεν [pft. of δίδωμι: "he has given"] ἡμῖν ("In this we know that we are abiding in him and he himself is abiding in us, because he has given to us out of his Spirit").

Direct Discourse

In Chapter 1 it was observed that direct discourse might be indicated by the use of a capital letter in the first word of the statement. Such a device is an editorial addition that was not a part of the original text and some editors choose not to employ it today. An indicator of direct discourse that was included in the original is the use of ὅτι. Both of these devices (plus a causal ὅτι) are illustrated in Jn. 10:36b: ὑμεῖς λέγετε ὅτι Βλασφημεῖς [pres. of βλασφημέω: "to blaspheme"], ὅτι εἶπον [aor. of λέγω: "I said"], Υἱὸς τοῦ θεοῦ εἰμι: ("Are you saying, 'You blaspheme,' because I said, 'I am the Son of God'?").

Exercises

Translate the following sentences.

1. οὐ πιστεύεις ὅτι ἐγὼ ἐν τῷ θεῷ καὶ ὁ θεὸς ἐν ἐμοί ἐστιν; τοὺς λόγους οὓς ἐγὼ λέγω ὑμῖν ἀπ᾽ ἐμαυτοῦ οὐ λέγω.
2. οἱ γὰρ προφῆται καὶ ὁ νόμος ἕως Ἰωάννου εὐαγγελίσουσιν.
3. Σὺ δέ, ἄνθρωπε θεοῦ, ταῦτα συνάξεις καὶ πέμψεις αὐτὰ τοῖς τέκνοις.
4. ἀμὴν γὰρ λέγω ὑμῖν ὅτι ἅγιοι προφῆται καὶ δίκαιοι κηρύσσουσιν ἃ βλέπετε καὶ πιστεύουσίν μοι ὅτι ἐγώ εἰμι ἀπὸ θεοῦ.
5. ἄνθρωποι λέγουσί μοι ἐν ταύτῃ τῇ ἡμέρᾳ, Κύριε, Κύριε, οὐκ ἐν ἐξουσίᾳ σου ἐκβάλλομεν δαιμόνια;
6. ἀπολύσω τὸν δοῦλόν μου, ἀλλ᾽ οὐκ ἄξω αὐτὸν ἔξω τῆς ἐκκλησίας πρὸς σέ.
7. καὶ λέγει αὐτοῖς ὁ Ἰησοῦς, Εἰ ἐκβάλλω ἐκείνους τοὺς πονηρούς, συνάξουσιν εἰς ταύτην τὴν βασιλείαν;
8. ὁ δὲ μαθητὴς ὁ ἀγαπητὸς καὶ ἐκεῖναι σὺν αὐτῷ διδάσκουσι τὴν ἀλήθειαν ἐνώπιον τοῦ θεοῦ καὶ τῶν βασιλειῶν τοῦ κόσμου.

9. πέμψω τὸν ἄγγελόν μου πρὸ προσώπου σου· ἐκεῖνος οὐ διδάξει ἀφ'² ἑαυτοῦ, ἀλλ' ἀνοίξει τοὺς ὀφθαλμοὺς τῶν υἱῶν τῶν ἀνθρώπων.

10. εὑρίσκει Φίλιππος³ τὸν Ναθαναὴλ καὶ λέγει αὐτῷ, Ὃν ἔγραψεν [aor. = "he wrote"] Μωϋσῆς ἐν τῷ νόμῳ εὑρίσκομεν, Ἰησοῦν υἱὸν τοῦ Ἰωσὴφ τὸν ἀπὸ Ναζαρέτ.

11. Ἰησοῦς διδάσκει τὰς ἀπὸ τῶν ἀγγέλων ἐντολὰς ἐνώπιον τῶν μαθητῶν αὐτοῦ ὧν κηρύξουσιν αὐτὰς πρὸ τῶν ὄχλων πρὸ τοῦ θανάτου αὐτῶν.

---

²ο of ἀπό deleted and π softened to φ.

³Pronouncing aloud this and the following place and person names (the capitalized terms) should provide adequate clues to their English counterparts.

CHAPTER 8

VERB SYSTEM. II: SECONDARY ACTIVE ENDINGS AND TENSES: IMPERFECT TENSE. IMPERFECT OF εἰμί. CONDITIONAL SENTENCES. ADVERBS

Vocabulary

Adverbs

ἔτι	still, yet
καθώς	just as (with οὕτως following: just as . . . so; with καί following: just as . . . so/also)
νῦν	now
ὅτε	when, while, as long as
οὕτως	thus
πάλιν	again, back
πῶς	how? in what way?
τότε	then, at that time
ὡς	as, about

Nouns

ἀπόστολος, -ου, ὁ	apostle
διδάσκαλος, -ου, ὁ	teacher (cf. didactic)
θρόνος, -ου, ὁ	throne
καρπός, -οῦ, ὁ	fruit
λίθος, -ου, ὁ	stone (cf. lithograph)
χρόνος, -ου, ὁ	time (cf. chronometer)

Particle

ἄν	an untranslated postpositive bit whose presence in a clause introduces an element of contingency.

Prepositions with Two Cases

διά	(Gen.)	through (cf. diameter)
	(Acc.)	on account of (cf. diacritical)
κατά	(Gen.)	down from, against (cf. catapult)
	(Acc.)	according to, throughout, during (cf. catalogue)
μετά	(Gen.)	with (cf. metabolic)
	(Acc.)	after (cf. metamorphosis)
περί	(Gen.)	concerning, about
	(Acc.)	around (cf. perimeter)
ὑπέρ	(Gen.)	in behalf of
	(Acc.)	above (cf. hypertension)
ὑπό	(Gen.)	by
	(Acc.)	under (cf. hypothermia)

Verbs

| ὑπάρχω | I am, I exist (This term regularly functions as a linking verb and will have the nominative case for its complement.) |
| ὑπάγω | I depart, I go |

Secondary Active Endings and Tenses

The secondary tenses are those that express past time: the imperfect, aorist, and pluperfect. To call the endings used with these tenses "secondary active" is somewhat misleading because one may infer that only active voice tenses will be formed. Such is not entirely the case. These endings are used in the following situations: (1) imperfect tense active voice, (2) first and second aorist tenses active voice, (3) first and second aorist tenses passive voice, (4) perfect tense active voice, and (5) pluperfect tense active voice. In this chapter only the imperfect tense will be considered.

Secondary Active Endings

Only two endings in this set are similar to ones previously encountered: the first and second person plural. The first person singular and the third person plural will exhibit some variation from tense to tense. Nevertheless, sufficient consistency in the pattern is observable to make this organization highly useful. First person singular and third person plural are alike. Context is the only distinguishing key.

	Singular		Plural
1.	-ν		-μεν
2.	-ς		-τε
3.	-	(no ending, but ν movable may occur)	-ν (or -σαν)

Imperfect Tense Active Voice[1]

Definition

The imperfect tense expresses an action that is viewed as in progress (kind of action) in a past time (time of action).

Formation

The imperfect tense uses the first principal part—the present stem—to form its parts. This is so because the present stem expresses a continuous or progressive kind of action. There are three steps to forming the imperfect tense active voice.

Isolate the verb stem. Delete the -ω from the first vocabulary form of a verb; thus βλεπ-, from βλέπω ("I see").

Attach a preformative to the verb stem. The preformative, in this instance called an augment, is an indicator of past time (cf. page 10). Prefix an ε if the stem begins with a consonant (ε + βλεπ-). If the stem begins with a vowel, lengthen the vowel according to the following patterns:

$$\begin{cases} \alpha \text{ or } \varepsilon = \eta; \text{ (e.g., } \H{\alpha}\gamma\omega = \H{\eta}\gamma\text{-)} \\ o = \omega; \text{ (e.g., } \dot{o}\mu\nu\acute{u}\omega \text{ ["I swear"]} = \dot{\omega}\mu\nu\upsilon\text{-)} \\ \iota \text{ or } \upsilon = \text{no change} \end{cases}$$

These patterns are reflected in diphthongs:

αυ or ευ = ηυ, (e.g., εὑρίσκω = ηὑρισκ-)

αι or ει = ῃ, (αἴρω ["I lift up"] = ᾖρ-)

οι = ῳ, (οἰκέω ["I dwell"] = ᾠκε-)

(N.B. the iota shifts to subscript.)

---

[1]The definitions of tense that are given here and with regard to other past tenses concerning past time are relevant *ONLY IN THE INDICATIVE MOOD.* In other moods time of action is relative and not an inherent aspect of the tenses.

The augment must be placed upon the stem; it does not occur upon a prefixed preposition. One must identify any such prepositions and carefully not augment them. ἐκβάλλω will become ἐξεβαλλ- (remember, the κ of ἐκ changes to ξ before a subsequent vowel), not ἠκβαλλ-. The final vowel of a preposition in a compound verb (except περί and πρό) will delete before an augment; thus, ἀπολύω, but ἀπέλυον; περιπατέω, περιεπάτουν.[2]

③ *Attach the secondary active endings to the augmented stem.* These endings couple to the stem by using as connectors the variable vowels ο or ε in this fashion: before an ending beginning with μ or ν, use ο; elsewhere, use ε. Applying this one finds the following.

	Singular			*Plural*	
1.	ἔβλεπον	I was seeing		ἐβλέπομεν	we were seeing
2.	ἔβλεπες	you were seeing		ἐβλέπετε	you were seeing
3.	ἔβλεπε	he, she, it was seeing		ἔβλεπον	they were seeing

Functions

Progressive past action. This is the most common use of the imperfect tense. Acts 18:25 is illustrative: "This one [Apollos] had been taught the way of the Lord and, being zealous in spirit, *he was speaking* [ἐλάλει = a contract verb's third person singular imperfect that differs from the above paradigm] and *he was teaching* [ἐδίδασκεν] accurately the things concerning Jesus." Not one sermon or witness, but an on-going lifestyle of speaking and teaching was in mind. Reflect upon the continuative qualities of ἔβαλλον ("were throwing") in Mk. 12:41 and ἐφίλει in Jn. 11:36 (the same form as ἐλάλει above; English fails to capture the verbal force succinctly; try "he was accustomed to love").

Attempted past action. Grammarians label this the conative imperfect. Mt. 3:14 is a well-known example: "But John *tried to prevent* him [διεκώλυεν]." Note the verb is a compound form exhibiting the internal augment.

Repeated past action. This type is called the iterative imperfect. Consider Lk. 21:37: "Day by day he was teaching [a yet-to-be introduced construction that also expresses durative past action] in the temple, but when the evenings came, *he customarily spent the night* ηὐλίζετο [from αὐλίζομαι[3]] on the mount which is called Olivet." Observe the augment of

---

[2]This verb, and the above example οἰκέω, are "contract verbs." For these see Chapter 15.

[3]This is a "deponent" verb. Its conjugation will be introduced in Chapter 11.

this example. Whether the unaugmented form begins with α or ε can be determined only by checking each possibility in a lexicon.

Beginning a past action. This is the inceptive imperfect. Of the man who has been crippled 38 years (Jn. 5:5), John writes, "He took up his pallet and *began walking about"* (περιεπάτει [5:9]; note the prefixed preposition περί and the internal augment. This verb, too, is a contract type; thus, the different ending.) Cf. Jn. 5:16a: ἐδίωκον = "[the Jews] *began persecuting."*

One has, in summary, four ways in which the imperfect may be used and translated:

1. Progressive (I was seeing)

2. Conative (I tried to see)

3. Iterative (I kept on seeing)

4. Inceptive (I began seeing)

Which aspect is present in a given example depends upon the context and the lexical meaning of the term. For example, "I die" could hardly be iterative.

Imperfect of εἰμί

The imperfect tense of εἰμί is irregular, but its endings have common elements with the secondary active endings, except in the third person singular.

IMPERFECT: εἰμί

	Singular			*Plural*	
1.	ἤμην	I was		ἦμεν	we were
2.	ἦς	you were		ἦτε	you were
3.	ἦν	he, she, it was		ἦσαν	they were

Conditional Sentences

Previously the condition assumed to be real (Type I) was introduced. Conditions of unreality (Type II)—frequently called "supposition contrary to fact"—use the past tenses, either the imperfect, aorist, or pluperfect, in both the protasis and the apodosis. The protasis will be regularly introduced by εἰ. The condition of unreality indicates something is not or was not actualized. By using the imperfect tense in these conditions the Greek indicates on-going kind of action. The time of that action, when the imperfect is used, is regularly the present. (Conditions referring to past time use the aorist or pluperfect.) Thus, in Gal. 1:10 Paul wrote εἰ ἔτι ἀνθρώποις ἤρεσκον [impft. of ἀρέσκω = "to strive to please"], Χριστοῦ δοῦλος οὐκ ἂν ἤμην, "If I were still striving to please men, I would not be a slave of Christ." The imperfects in both clauses, plus the ἂν in the apodosis, tell the reader this is a "contrary-to-fact" condition. However, the ἂν may not occur if the context makes clear the type of condition (cf. Jn. 15:22).

The translation "if I were . . . , I would . . ." in Gal. 1:10 is used in conformity to the demand of English grammar that present suppositional statements use the simple past tense of the subjunctive mood. Recall the conjugation of an English past tense active voice subjunctive mood:

	Singular	*Plural*
1.	I were speaking	we were speaking
2.	you were speaking	you were speaking
3.	he, she, it were speaking	they were speaking

So, correct English dictates: "If they [the parts of the body] were all one member, where would the body be?" (1 Cor. 12:19)—another illustration of the condition of unreality, this time couched as a question.

To balance these English past tense subjunctive mood terms in the "if clause" (protasis), one uses "would" in all persons and numbers of the conclusion clause (apodosis). Consider Lk. 7:39: Οὗτος εἰ ἦν ὁ προφήτης, ἐγίνωσκεν ἂν "If this one were the prophet, he would be in the process of knowing" (Type II); Jn. 5:46a: εἰ γὰρ ἐπιστεύετε Μωϋσεῖ [dat. sing. = "Moses"], ἐπιστεύετε ἂν ἐμοί "For if you were in the process of believing Moses, you would be in the process of believing in me" (Type II). Both of these examples, although using Greek imperfect tenses, have present time of action.

Another essential element of the Type II condition is that the condition does not necessarily express reality. Whatever is expressed as "contrary-to-fact" is such from the perspective of the speaker (Cf. the Type I condition). Thus, in Lk. 7:39, cited above, the speaker's statement is in actual fact erroneous. The contrary to fact assertion is assumed to be so by the speaker, but he is wrong. So, be very careful to note whether or not *past tenses* are used in the conditions. If they are, one usually is dealing with Type II conditions. Then, examine the context carefully to ascertain whether or not the condition is contrary to fact and if the assertion is indeed valid.

Adverbs

Definition and Function

Adverbs are modifiers of verbs, infinitives, participles, adjectives, or other adverbs. Adverbs may even be used substantively. They indicate manner, time, place, reason, degree to which something is or happens, and the like. The following are examples of English adverbs: "haughtily," "quickly," "here," "last." Greek adverbs may be single words, as these. Alternatively, prepositional phrases may function adverbially to give such information (e.g., "She came *on the morning plane*"). One also encounters the adverb per se used as the object of a preposition. An article may be present. If it is, its case will be determined by the preposition and it will be neuter singular. ἀπὸ τοῦ νῦν, for example, means "from the present"; ἀπὸ τότε is "from that time on."

Formation

Adverbs are sometimes formed by a modification of the second declension genitive plural of a given adjective. For example, ὅμοιος is the adjective; ὁμοίων is its genitive plural. Delete the final ν and replace it with ς to derive the adverb ὁμοίως. Other adverbs reflect various case endings, e.g., ποῦ = a genitive singular; ἰδίᾳ = dative singular; σήμερον and πάλιν = accusative singular. These examples illustrate that one is well advised simply to learn adverbs by rote and ignore any kind of attempt to categorize them by structure.

Exercises

Translate the following sentences.

1. εἰ ὁ θεὸς κύριος ὑμῶν ἦν, ἐπιστεύετε ἂν ἐμοί.
2. εἰ δὲ ὑμεῖς Χριστοῦ, τοῦ Ἀβραὰμ τέκνα ἐστέ.
3. ὁ δὲ υἱὸς τοῦ διδασκάλου ὑπάξει καθὼς λέγω περὶ αὐτοῦ.
4. Κύριε, καθὼς καὶ Ἰωάννης ἐδίδασκεν τοὺς μαθητὰς αὐτοῦ, οὕτως διδάξεις ἡμᾶς;
5. ἀλλὰ καὶ νῦν ἡ ὥρα ἐστίν, ὅτε οἱ διδάσκαλοι οἱ πιστοὶ κηρύξουσιν ὅτι ὑπάγω τῷ θρόνῳ τοῦ θεοῦ.
6. πάλιν δὲ λέγω ὑμῖν ὅτι ὡς ἦσαν ἐν ταῖς ἡμέραις ἐκείναις, οὕτως εὑρήσετε ὅτε ὁ θρόνος ὁ πονηρός ἐστι σὺν τοῖς λαοῖς.
7. ὑπῆρχε γὰρ ὁ Χριστὸς ἐν τῇ δόξῃ τοῦ θεοῦ αὐτοῦ μετὰ τῶν ἀγγέλων αὐτοῦ, καὶ τότε ὁ θεὸς ἔπεμπε αὐτὸν δι᾽ οὐρανοῦ διὰ τὸν κόσμον.
8. πῶς οὖν ἀνοίξεις τοὺς ὀφθαλμούς σου, οὐκ εἰ ὑπ᾽ ἐξουσίαν τῶν δαιμονίων;
9. αὕτη ἔστιν ἡ ἡμέρα δι᾽ ἣν βαπτίσομεν τὸν διδάσκαλον τῆς δικαιοσύνης.
10. ὡς γὰρ δι᾽ ἀνθρώπου θάνατος, καὶ δι᾽ ἀνθρώπου ζωὴ ἐκ τῶν νεκρῶν.
11. οὐχ ὑπάρχει ὑπὲρ τῶν ἀποστόλων; ναί. ὃς ἦν πρὸς τὸν θεὸν ὑπάρχει μεθ᾽ ἡμῶν καὶ αὐτὸς συνάξει τοὺς καρποὺς αὐτοῦ ἀπὸ τοῦ κόσμου εἰς τὴν βασιλείαν αὐτοῦ.

CHAPTER 9

VERB SYSTEM. II (CONT.):
SECONDARY ACTIVE ENDINGS. AORIST TENSES

Vocabulary

PRESENT A.	FUTURE A.	AORIST A.	PERFECT A.[1]	PERFECT M/P.[2]	AORIST P.
ἀγοράζω I buy	———[3]	ἠγόρασα	———	———	ἠγοράσθην
ἄγω I lead συνάγω:[4] I gather together ὑπάγω: I go away, I depart, I go	ἄξω	ἤγαγον	———	ἦγμαι	ἤχθην
ἀκούω I hear	ἀκούσω	ἤκουσα	ἀκήκοα	———	ἠκούσθην
ἁμαρτάνω I do wrong, I sin	ἁμαρτήσω	ἥμαρτον ἡμάρτησα	ἡμάρτηκα		
ἀνοίγω I open	ἀνοίξω	ἀνέῳξα ἤνοιξα ἠνέῳξα	ἀνέῳγα	ἀνέῳγμαι ἤνοιγμαι ἠνέῳγμαι	ἀνεῴχθην ἠνοίχθην ἠνεῴχθην
ἀποθνῄσκω I die	ἀποθανοῦμαι*	ἀπέθανον			
ἅπτω I light, kindle	———	ἧψα			

---

[1]See Chapter 10 for discussion of this principal part and tenses.

[2]See Chapter 11 for discussion of the perfect middle/passive and all present and future tense formations ending in -μαι.

[3]A line signifies this part does not occur in the *GNT*. No entry in a column, such as the fourth column of ἀποθνῄσκω, means no such part exists.

[4]Compound verbs presented in this indented format use the principal parts of the verb under which they are placed; e.g., συνάγω, συνάξω, συνήγαγον, etc.

*See Chapter 15 for these forms.

PRESENT A.	FUTURE A.	AORIST A.	PERFECT A.	PERFECT M/P.	AORIST P.
βαπτίζω I baptize	βαπτίσω	ἐβάπτισα	———	βεβάπτισμαι	ἐβαπτίσθην
βλέπω I see	βλέψω	ἔβλεψα			
γινώσκω I know ἀναγινώσκω: I read ἐπιγινώσκω: I come to know, recognize	γνώσομαι	ἔγνων	ἔγνωκα	ἔγνωσμαι	ἐγνώσθην
γράφω I write	γράψω	ἔγραψα	γέγραφα	γέγραμμαι	ἐγράφην
διδάσκω I teach	διδάξω	ἐδίδαξα	———	———	ἐδιδάχθην
διώκω I pursue, persecute	διώξω	ἐδίωξα	———	δεδίωγμαι	ἐδιώχθην
δοξάζω I glorify	δοξάσω	ἐδόξασα	———	δεδόξασμαι	ἐδοξάσθην
ἐγγίζω I come near, approach	ἐγγιῶ*	ἤγγισα	ἤγγικα		
εἰμί I am, I exist	ἔσομαι				
ἐκβάλλω I throw out, expel; send out	ἐκβαλῶ*	ἐξέβαλον	ἐκβέβληκα	ἐκβέβλημαι	ἐκβλήθην
ἐλπίζω I hope	ἐλπιῶ*	ἤλπισα	ἤλπικα		
ἐσθίω I eat	φάγομαι	ἔφαγον			
ἑτοιμάζω I prepare	ἑτοιμάσω	ἡτοίμασα	ἡτοίμακα	ἡτοίμασμαι	ἡτοιμάσθην
εὐαγγελίζω I evangelize, bring good news	———	εὐηγγέλισα	———	εὐηγγέλισμαι	εὐηγγελίσθην
εὑρίσκω I find	εὑρήσω	εὗρον	εὕρηκα	———	εὑρέθην
ἔχω I have	ἕξω	ἔσχον	ἔσχηκα		

———

*See Chapter 15 for these forms.

PRESENT A.	FUTURE A.	AORIST A.	PERFECT A.	PERFECT M/P.	AORIST P.
θαυμάζω I marvel, wonder at	θαυμάσομαι	ἐθαύμασα	——	——	ἐθαυμάσθην
θεραπεύω I heal, care for, serve	θεραπεύσω	ἐθεράπευσα	——	τεθεράπευμαι	ἐθεραπεύθην
καθαρίζω I cleanse	καθαριῶ*	ἐκαθάρισα	——	κεκαθάρισμαι	ἐκαθαρίσθην
καθίζω I seat, sit	καθίσω καθιῶ*	ἐκάθισα	κεκάθικα		
κηρύσσω I preach, proclaim	κηρύξω	ἐκήρυξα	——	——	ἐκηρύχθην
κλαίω I weep, cry out	κλαύσω	ἔκλαυσα			
κράζω I cry out	κράξω	ἔκραξα	κέκραγα		
λαμβάνω I take, receive	λήμψομαι	ἔλαβον	εἴληφα	εἴλημμαι	ἐλήμφθην

παραλαμβάνω: I receive, take along or with

λέγω I say, utter	ἐρῶ*	εἶπον	εἴρηκα	εἴρημαι	ἐρρέθην ἐρρήθην
λείπω I leave	λείψω	ἔλιπον	——	λέλειμμαι	ἐλείφθην
λύω I loose, set free, untie, abolish	λύσω	ἔλυσα	λέλυκα	λέλυμαι	ἐλύθην

ἀπολύω: I set free, release, dismiss,send away

πάσχω I suffer, endure	——	ἔπαθον	πέπονθα		
πείθω I persuade	πείσω	ἔπεισα	πέποιθα	πέπεισμαι	ἐπείσθην
πειράζω I try, attempt, put to the test, tempt	πειράσω	ἐπείρασα	——	πεπείρασμαι	ἐπειράσθην
πέμπω I send	πέμψω	ἔπεμψα	——	——	ἐπέμφθην
περισσεύω I abound, am rich	περισσεύσω	ἐπερίσσευσα	——	——	ἐπερισσεύθην

*See Chapter 15 for these forms.

PRESENT A.	FUTURE A.	AORIST A.	PERFECT A.	PERFECT M/P.	AORIST P.
πίνω I drink	πίομαι	ἔπιον	πέπωκα	——	ἐπόθην
πίπτω I fall	πεσοῦμαι	ἔπεσον ἔπεσα	πέπτωκα		
πιστεύω I believe	πιστεύσω	ἐπίστευσα	πεπίστευκα	πεπίστευμαι	ἐπιστεύθην
πράσσω I do, accomplish	πράξω	ἔπραξα	πέπραχα	πέπραγμαι	ἐπράχθην
σκανδαλίζω I cause to sin, cause to fail; give offense to	——	ἐσκανδάλισα	——	ἐσκανδάλισμαι	ἐσκανδαλίσθην
στρέφω I turn [future occurs only in compounds] ἐπιστρέφω: I return, turn around, turn back ὑποστρέφω: I return, turn back	-στρέψω	ἔστρεψα	——	——	ἐστράφην
σῴζω I save	σώσω	ἔσωσα	σέσωκα	σέσω(σ)μαι	ἐσώθην
ὑπάρχω I am, exist	ὑπάρξω	ὑπῆρξα			
ὑποτάσσω active: I subject, subordinate; passive: subject oneself, be subjected	——	ὑπέταξα	——	ὑποτέταγμαι	ὑπετάγην
φεύγω I flee, escape	φεύξομαι	ἔφυγον			
φυλάσσω I watch, guard, keep	φυλάξω	ἐφύλαξα	πεφύλαχα	——	ἐφυλάχθην

This completes the list of all -ω conjugation verbs that occur more than 30 times in the *GNT*. Divide them into four parts and complete your memorization task before beginning Chapter 12. The exercises are constructed with this in mind.

Aorist Tense Active Voice

Definition

Aorist indicative is the tense used in Greek to express simple past time. It views action as an event; it neither declares the action to have been progressive (as the imperfect) nor does it indicate abiding results (as the perfect). Thus, the aorist tense is often described as having a snapshot kind of action. Robertson wrote of this tense that it "just *treats* the act as a single whole entirely irrespective of the parts or time involved."[5] He emphasized *"treats"* precisely because the action may not have been a simple unitary experience. One can say "she drank," and denote thereby one gulp. The action involved in drinking is such that one may spend half an hour drinking, but still describe the experience by saying, "She drank a glass of tea." The use of the aorist tense in such a context would view the act as a single experience, regardless of the component aspects. The verb-idea, by contrast, would suggest a nonpoint kind of activity. Hence, when analyzing a text, one must consider both the significance of the tense and the verb-idea per se.

Two structural types exist: the first and the second aorist. No difference in grammatical significance is intended any more than in a common English pattern. "I walked" and "I broke" are merely two different ways of forming past tense. As in English, one may not interchange the patterns ("breaked" is never acceptable). With rare exceptions, a verb will always be either first or second aorist. Consequently, one must learn the tense stems of a given verb as one learns the lexical significance of the term. Then one has the basic building blocks to form the conjugation.

To ascertain whether a verb is first or second aorist observe the third form in the vocabulary list. If the term ends in -σα (the σ may be in a consonantal blend), it is first aorist. If it ends in -ov, it is second aorist.

Formation of the First Aorist Tense Active Voice

The following three steps illustrate how the third principal part—the aorist tense—is derived. Memorization of the principal parts obviates going through these three steps.

Isolate the verb stem. Do this by deleting the -ω of the first principal part. So, one has, for example, πειθ- from πείθω.

Attach a prefixed augment. The rules of augment for the imperfect tense (see pages 57f.) apply in the aorist also. So, with the above example, one forms ἐπειθ-.

Add the suffix -σα to the stem. Review the consonantal blends which occur when σ is attached to palatal, dental, and labial consonants (see page 12). These same rules apply in the first aorist. So, ἐπειθ + σα = delete the θ and attach -σα = ἐπεισα-. This -σα is called the first aorist tense suffix. When one sees -σα (or a consonantal blend that contains -σα), one should think "first aorist."

---

[5] *Robertson*, p. 832; his italics.

Attach secondary active endings. These are placed on the augmented verb stem with its tense suffix. One modification of the secondary endings must be made. First person singular does not use ν or any other consonant. Third person singular modifies the tense suffix -σα to -σε (use no ending), thereby differentiating first and third persons.

	Singular			Plural	
1.	ἔ πει σα	I persuaded	ἐ πεί σα μεν	we persuaded
2.	ἔ πει σα ς	you persuaded	ἐ πεί σα τε	you persuaded
3.	ἔ πει σε	he, she, it persuaded	ἔ πει σα ν	they persuaded

Formation of the Second Aorist Tense Active Voice

The second aorist tense stem is best learned by rote memory from a vocabulary list. These verbs undergo internal vowel and, sometimes, consonant changes in the stem. Hence, systematic deduction from the present stem is difficult, if not impossible.

After identifying the stem, the conjugation is simple. The second aorist tense endings are a replica of the imperfect—even to the use of the variable vowels ο/ε, but they are placed on the second aorist stem, i.e., the third principal part.

The verb λείπω ("I leave") has a second aorist form; its aorist stem is λιπ- ("I left"). The conjugation of ἔλιπον follows.

	Singular			Plural	
1.	ἔ λιπ ο ν	I left	ἐ λίπ ο μεν	we left
2.	ἔ λιπ ε ς	you left	ἐ λίπ ε τε	you left
3.	ἔ λιπ ε	he, she, it left	ἔ λιπ ο ν	they left

Again, note the use of the same augment, variable vowels, and secondary active endings as the imperfect. The stem alone is altered, from λειπ- (present) to λιπ- (aorist). Remember, the imperfect is ἔλειπον.

First Aorist Endings on Second Aorist Stems

A peculiarity of Greek is the attaching of first aorist endings (minus the sigma) to the second aorist stem. This is irregular and not a commonplace, but it will occur. In such cases the verbs are second aorists. Consider in 1 Thess. 4:6 προείπαμεν.

Functions of the Aorist Tense

Constative aorist. The aorist tense is used to express the simple event as a point of action. The earlier description is usually labeled the constative aorist; it emphasizes neither beginning nor completion, but the totality of action as a unit. The verb of Jn. 2:20a is such: "This temple was built [aorist passive] in forty-six years." A simple event did not occur, but the perspective is one which views all the work as one whole. Observe from Jn. 6:58: "not just as your fathers ate [ἔφαγον] and died [ἀπέθανον]." There were many times of eating and dying, but from the perspective of the speaker they are viewed as a totality.

Sometimes the aorist tense needs to be translated by an English perfect form, but it does not take on a perfective force. Consider *RSV*'s translation of Jn. 10:18b: "This charge I have received [ἔλαβον] from my Father"; in Mk. 5:35 and 39, ἀπέθανεν is translated as "is dead."

Inceptive aorist. A second function of the aorist tense is to express an action with a view to its inception or beginning (this function is sometimes called ingressive). The point or unitary aspect, common to all the functions of the aorist, is maintained, but the spotlight focuses upon the commencement of the action—usually a state or condition of existence.

Consider Rom. 14:9: εἰς τοῦτο γὰρ Χριστὸς ἀπέθανεν καὶ ἔζησεν, "For this very reason, Christ died and returned to life." (*NIV*) The aorist ἔζησεν decidedly looks to the commencement of the act. However, does not ἀπέθανεν have the same quality? In this context surely it does. Burton observes: "The Aorist of a verb whose Present denotes a state or condition, commonly denotes the beginning of that state." He also emphasizes that "the Aorist of such verbs is not, however, necessarily inceptive. The same form may be in one sentence inceptive and in another historical."[6]

The student is here confronted with another of the difficulties of Greek: Though the aorist tense expresses unitary kind of action, the aspect is sometimes not immediately apparent. The *intrinsic meaning* of the tense, the *lexical signification* of the verb stem and the *context* must all three always be kept in mind as one seeks to discriminate precisely what was in the mind of the author of the text when he chose the term/tense in question.

Culminative aorist. In contrast to the preceding functions one may view an action from the vantage of its conclusion—the culminative aorist (sometimes called resultative[7] or effective[8]). Nothing is implied or affirmed by the tense regarding the continued effects of the concluded activity (a province of the perfect tense), although such information may be gleaned from either the lexical meaning of the word itself or the context. With the

---

[6]Burton, *Moods*, §41. "Historical" is his label for "constative."

[7]Ibid., 35.

[8]*Robertson*, p. 834.

culminative aorist, although the verb simply related the act, the focus of attention is upon the results or consequences of that act. English translations will often use the perfect tense for this function.

Revelation chapter 18 offers several excellent illustrations of the culminative aorist. Since the vocabulary and a number of the forms have not yet been introduced, only the references and the key words are provided. The translations are those of *NIV*. Verse 2: "Fallen! Fallen" (Ἔπεσεν, ἔπεσεν); "she has become" (ἐγένετο); v. 3: "grew rich" (ἐπλούτησαν); v. 5: "are piled up" (ἐκολλήθησαν); "has remembered" (ἐμνημόνευσεν); v. 10: "has come" (ἦλθεν); v. 14: "is gone" (ἀπῆλθεν), etc. Hebrews 2:14a uses the perfect tense followed by the aorist in a culminative sense: "Since therefore the children have shared [κεκοινώνηκεν] flesh and blood, he himself also likewise shared [μετέσχεν] the same things." The children's experience continues to be one of sharing flesh and blood, but not so with Jesus. What he became for the purpose of his atoning work (cf. 2:14b, 17) he did not remain.

Aorist Tense Passive Voice

Meaning of Passive Voice

The passive voice is common to both the English and Greek languages. It expresses in Greek, as in English, that the subject receives the action of the verb. One reads, not "Jesus raised himself," but "Jesus has been raised"— passive (cf. 1 Cor. 15:13f.). "Jesus," the subject, is the recipient, not the doer, of the action in the verb. Paul, writing the Romans concerning their new life in Christ, used a number of passives: "we were baptized," "we were buried," "he was raised" (Rom. 6:3f.).

The personal agent who actually does the action expressed by the passive constructions is often identified by using the preposition ὑπό with the genitive. (This is one of the contextual indicators of the passive voice.) An illustration of this is Mk. 1:9: "He was baptized in the Jordan by John [ὑπὸ Ἰωάννου]." However, in Rom. 6:3f. the direct agent of baptizing and raising is not indicated. The intermediate agent of Christ's raising is stated: "through the glory of the Father [διὰ τῆς δόξης τοῦ πατρός]." The student must discriminate between the direct agent (ὑπό and the genitive) and the intermediate agent (or means) (διά and the genitive) in a given text. Often it will be necessary to examine a much wider context to ascertain the direct agent.

Formation of the Aorist Tense Passive Voice

The functions of the aorist tense, as previously presented, continue to be relevant. One need be concerned here only with the structures of the passive voice. Greek has both the first and second aorist forms in the passive voice. These are formed on the sixth principal part, the aorist passive stem.

First aorist passive. With a regular verb the first aorist passive stem is formed by the following steps:

1. Prefix to the verb stem, e.g., λυ-, the usual augment (see page 57); so ἐλυ-.

2. The sign of the first aorist passive -θη is attached to the stem as a suffix; thus, ἐλυθη-.

3. The secondary active endings, almost without change, are attached to conjugate a verb. The third person plural shifts from -ν to -σαν; otherwise, they are quite familiar.

	Singular			*Plural*	
1.	ἐ λύ θη ν	I was loosed	ἐ λύ θη μεν	we were loosed
2.	ἐ λύ θη ς	you were loosed	ἐ λύ θη τε	you were loosed
3.	ἐ λύ θη	he, she, it was loosed	ἐ λύ θη σαν	they were loosed

This formation is modified when a regular verb stem (e.g., ἀγ-, εὐαγγελιζ-, λειπ-) ends with a palatal, dental, or labial consonant. Observe the following changes:

palatals: κ, γ, χ + θη = χθη

dentals: τ, δ, θ (or ζ) + θη = σθη

labials: π, β, φ + θη = φθη

Consequently, ἄγω becomes ἤχθην; εὐαγγελίζω becomes εὐηγγελίσθην, λείπω becomes ἐλείφθην. Although these observations are valid, there are so many other possible internal changes which may modify the verb stem that the student should simply consult a verb chart for the stem's formation. Attempts to deduce this form according to the rules all too frequently simply result in frustration. In seeking to translate the form, one should bear in mind the above guides. Then, observe the constant sign of the first aorist passive: θη-; note the augment; consider which secondary active ending is used; identify the stem and, in turn, translate accurately.

Second aorist passive. The second aorist passive verb formation differs from the first only in that the θ of the aorist passive stem is missing. So, ὑποτάσσω in the aorist passive is second aorist: ὑπετάγην. Otherwise, no change occurs. Note that ὑποτάσσω in the aorist active is first aorist. When such a change may occur is unpredictable and must be learned by observation.

Singular		Plural	
1. ὑπ ε τάγ η ν	I was subjected	ὑπ ε τάγ η μεν	we were subjected
2. ὑπ ε τάγ η ς	you were subjected	ὑπ ε τάγ η τε	you were subjected
3. ὑπ ε τάγ η	he, she, it was subjected	ὑπ ε τάγ η σαν	they were subjected

Exercises

Translate the following sentences

1. ὁ Ἰησοῦς ὁ διδάσκαλος ὑπήγαγε εἰς τὴν Ἰουδαίαν ἔρημον· τότε ἐδίδαξε μετ᾽ ἀνθρώπων αὐτοῦ.
2. ἐπιγινώσκομεν γὰρ ὅτι καλὴν καρδίαν ἔχομεν ὅτι ὁ κύριος τῆς ζωῆς εὗρε ἡμᾶς.
3. τότε ἐκεῖναι αἱ παρθένοι ἤκουσαν τὴν φωνὴν αὐτοῦ καὶ συνήγαγον εἰς τὴν ὁδόν, ἀλλὰ ὁ ἄνθρωπος οὐκ ἔγνω αὐτάς.
4. αὐτὸς γὰρ ὁ θεὸς σώσει ὑμᾶς, ὅτι ὑμεῖς ἐπιστεύσατε ὅτι ἐγὼ παρὰ ["from"] τοῦ θεοῦ εἰμί.
5. εἰ ἐκ κόσμου ἦτε, ὁ κόσμος ἂν ὑμᾶς ἐπεγίνωσκε· ὅτι δὲ συνήχθητε ἐκ τοῦ κόσμου, οὐ ἐπιγινώσκει ὑμᾶς.
6. ὑμεῖς οὐκ ἀκούετε ὅτι ἐκ τοῦ θεοῦ οὐκ ἐστέ.
7. γινώσκομεν δὲ ὅτι ἃ ὁ νόμος λέγει τοῖς ὑπὸ τὸν νόμον λέγει.
8. ταῦτα ἔγραψα ὑμῖν ὅτι ζωὴν ἔχετε καλήν.
9. εἰς Χριστὸν ἁμαρτάνετε εἰ εἰς τὸν ἀδελφὸν ἁμαρτάνετε.
10. οὗτός ἐστιν ὁ Ἰωάνης καὶ βαπτίσει λαοὺς ὅτι πιστεύουσιν τοῖς λογοῖς αὐτοῦ.
11. ὁ θεὸς κύριος ἠνέῳξε τὸν θρόνον αὐτοῦ ὅτε ἔπεμψε τὸν υἱὸν ἑαυτὸν Ἰησοῦν.
12. οὗτοι ἠγοράσθησαν ἀπὸ τῶν ἀνθρώπων καρποὶ τῷ θεῷ καὶ ἐν τούτοις οὐχ εὑρέθη ψεῦδος ["lie"].

CHAPTER 10

VERB SYSTEM. II (CONT.): SECONDARY ACTIVE ENDINGS. PERFECT ACTIVE; PLUPERFECT ACTIVE. CONDITIONAL SENTENCES

Vocabulary

Nouns

ἀρχή, -ῆς, ἡ	beginning, ruler (cf. archeology)
ἐπαγγελία, -ας, ἡ	promise
οἰκία, -ας, ἡ	house
παραβολή, -ῆς, ἡ	parable
σοφία, -ας, ἡ	wisdom (cf. sophistry)
συναγωγή, -ῆς, ἡ	synagogue
πλοῖον, -ου, τό	boat
παιδίον, -ου, τό	child
τόπος, -ου, ὁ	place (cf. topography)

Adjectives

αἰώνιος, -ον	eternal (masc. and fem. are the same form)
δεξιός, -ά, -όν	right
ἐμός, -ή, -όν	my
μέσος, -η, -ον	middle, in the midst of (cf. Mesozoic)
μόνος, -η, -ον	only (cf. monopoly)
τοιοῦτος, τοιαύτη, τοιοῦτον (or τοιοῦτο)	such

Prepositions

ἐπί	(Gen.)	on, over (cf. epidermis)
	(Dat.)	on the basis of, at
	(Acc.)	on, at, to
παρά	(Gen.)	from alongside (cf. parameter)
	(Dat.)	beside, in the presence of
	(Acc.)	alongside of

Verb

οἶδα	I know

Perfect Tense Active Voice

Definition

The perfect tense indicates that a past event that is now completed or accomplished has a continuing effect or consequence in the present. The action itself does not continue; the results do. Consider 1 Cor. 15:14: "But if Christ has not been raised [perfect passive], then our preaching is without basis, and your faith is without basis." "Has been raised," by being perfect tense, highlights the present, existing result of a past act. Paul's message is not that Jesus is continuing to be raised, but, rather, the event has happened and not been nullified—or else his preaching and the reader's faith are baseless.

The notion of an event in the past that has continuing results is graphically expressed by (. _____). The dot signifies an act occurred at some past time. When this was is not specified by the tense. The line signifies that a consequence of that act continues into the present.

Formation

Identify the stem.   The perfect tense active voice is formed on the fourth principal part, the perfect active stem. By dropping the -ω of any regular verb's first principal part—the present active, one has identified the unit with which to work. So, one has πιστευ-.

Attach the letters of reduplication.   Stems that begin with a consonant will have the same consonant plus ε attached as a prefix. This is called reduplication. Thus, one forms πε-πιστευ-.

The consonants φ, χ, and θ reduplicate in a modified form. Note carefully the following patterns:

     φ = πε, e.g., φιλέω = πεφιλ-

     χ = κε, e.g., χαρίζομαι = κεχαρισ-

     θ = τε, e.g., θύω = τεθυ-

A verb with an initial vowel may lengthen the vowel according to the usual vowel patterns; i.e.,

     α or ε lengthens to η;

     o   lengthens to ω;

     ι or υ do not change form.

So, ἐλπίζω = ἠλπι-. However, the initial vowel α, ε, or o is often not changed.

Other changes for reduplication may be observed from the vocabulary list of Chapter 9. Many of these can be explained, but the beginner is well advised simply to memorize the forms there set forth, consider the terms as irregular, and delay until advanced study a consideration of the intricacies of these verb formations.[1]

Add the suffix κ to the reduplicated stem. Perfects are subdivided into two groups: first perfects, which add κ to the reduplicated stem; second perfects, which lack the κ. As with first and second aorists, this distinction is simply one of formation, not grammatical significance. One finds πεπίστευκα and πέποιθα (an obviously irregular stem for the word πείθω); both are perfect tense (N.B. the reduplication), but they are first and second perfects, respectively.

Attach the secondary active endings. The first person singular (like the first aorist) does not use the ν; it has only the coupler letter. Second person singular and successive forms are -ς, —, -μεν, -τε, -σι. These endings are joined to the reduplicated stem (either first or second perfect) by the coupler α, except in the third singular, where ε alone appears. The change thereby distinguishes first and third persons singular.

FIRST PERFECT: πεπίστευκα

Singular		Plural	
1. πε πίστευκ α	I have believed and the effect continues	πε πιστεύκ α μεν	we have believed and the effect continues
2. πε πίστευκ α ς	you have believed, etc.	πε πιστεύκ α τε	you have believed, etc.
3. πε πίστευκ ε(ν)	he, she, it has believed, etc.	πε πιστεύκ α σι	they have believed, etc.

SECOND PERFECT: πέποιθα

Singular		Plural	
1. πέ ποιθ α	I have persuaded and the effect continues	πε ποίθ α μεν	we have per- suaded, etc.
2. πέ ποιθ α ς	you have per- suaded, etc.	πε ποίθ α τε	you have per- suaded, etc.
3. πέ ποιθ ε(ν)	he, she, it has persuaded, etc.	πε ποίθ α σι	they have per- suaded, etc.

---

[1]For particulars, cf. R. W. Funk, *A Beginning-Intermediate Grammar of Hellenistic Greek*, I (2d. ed.; Missoula: Scholars Press, 1973), pp. 239–245.

Do not consider the θ of πέποιθα as a "sign of the perfect." It is part of the second perfect stem for the word πείθω; cf. κέκραγα (reduplicated stem of κράζω) and εἴληφα (reduplicated stem of λαμβάνω) where the γ and φ are parts of the stems, not tense indicators per se.

Function

To express an existing state. The perfect tense regularly indicates a past action has some consequence to the present. One of the most common of these is to declare an existing state (called "present perfect" by *Robertson* and *BDF*[2]). This significance is seen with πέποιθα (Phil. 2:24 = "I trust") and other verbs where the emphasis is not at all on the past activity, but on the resultant state. The English translations may at times sound more like a present tense than the above paradigm's clear perfect tense. The exegete should carefully elucidate the distinct force of the Greek tense underlying the English.

To express a completed action. To assert that an action is completed and that consequences or results of this action still exist use the perfect tense. The action itself does not continue; the effects of the now past action continue. Consider Mt. 19:27: Peter says, "Behold, we have left [ἀφήκαμεν = pft. act. of ἀφίημι] everything and we followed [ἠκολουθήσαμεν = aor. act. of ἀκολουθέω] you." Matthew's intent is to express a break with the past which has not been resumed; the departure is an accomplished act that has present consequences. Cf. 1 Jn. 1:1; 2:12–14.

Pluperfect Tense Active Voice

Function

The pluperfect tense makes the perfect tense past. It expresses action that had occurred in a past setting and the resultant effect continued up to a time that is now in the past. Both action and effect are past experiences.

The pluperfect, like the perfect, may denote either a state that had existed up to a time in the past (cf. Jn. 18:16, 18) or a completed action (cf. Jn. 11:19).

Formation

The pluperfect is formed on the stem of the fourth principal part. As a past tense one might expect it to have an augment. It should, but in the Koine period the augment usually is missing. So, one simply uses the perfect active principal part; e.g., πεπιστευκ-; ἐληλυθ-.

---

[2] *Robertson*, pp. 894ff. and *BDF* §341.

To this stem attach the secondary active endings -ν, -ς, ——, -μεν, -τε, -σαν, using -ει- as the coupler letters.

FIRST PLUPERFECT: πεπιστεύκειν

Singular		*Plural*	
1. πε πιστεύκ ει ν	I had believed and the effect had continued	πε πιστεύκ ει μεν	we had believed, etc.
2. πε πιστεύκ ει ς	you had believed, etc.	πε πιστεύκ ει τε	you had believed, etc.
3. πε πιστεύκ ει	he, she, it had believed, etc.	πε πιστεύκ ει σαν	they had believed, etc.

SECOND PLUPERFECT: ἐληλύθειν

Singular		*Plural*	
1. ἐ ληλύθ ει ν	I had come and the effect had continued	ἐ ληλύθ ει μεν	we had come, etc.
2. ἐ ληλύθ ει ς	you had come, etc.	ἐ ληλύθ ει τε	you had come, etc.
3. ἐ ληλύθ ει	he, she, it had come, etc.	ἐ ληλύθ ει σαν	they had come, etc.

οἶδα and ᾔδειν

These terms function as the present and imperfect of a very common Greek word that is not clearly distinguished in meaning from γινώσκω. οἶδα, whose stem is said to be ἰδ-, is a second perfect in its form and its endings. It has no explainable reduplication,[3] nor does it have the sense of a perfect tense in terms of stressing a past event whose effect continues in the present. It has, rather, a continuative present sense.[4] Likewise the pluperfect form ᾔδειν (N.B. the iota subscript) has no sense of a past effect continuing.[5] It is an imperfect in sense. The conjugation of these follows.

SECOND PERFECT: οἶδα

Singular		*Plural*	
1. οἶδ α	I know	οἶδ α μεν	we know
2. οἶδ α ς	you know	οἶδ α τε	you know
3. οἶδ ε (ν)	he, she, it knows	οἶδ α σι	they know

---

[3] *Robertson*, p. 357 (g).

[4] Ibid., p. 881 (c).

[5] Ibid., p. 904 (γ).

SECOND PLUPERFECT: ᾔδειν

Singular		Plural	
1. ᾔδ ει ν	I was knowing	ᾔδ ει μεν	we were knowing
2. ᾔδ ει ς	you were knowing	ᾔδ ει τε	you were knowing
3. ᾔδ ει	he, she, it was knowing	ᾔδ ει σαν	they were knowing

Aorist Tense in Contrary-to-fact Conditional Sentences

The second class conditional sentence using the imperfect tense was introduced in Chapter 8. There the continuous kind of action that is fundamental to the present and imperfect tense was noted as appertaining to the contrary-to-fact conditional sentence (see pages 59f.).

When a Type II condition uses the aorist tense, the kind of action is that of a simple event. The time of action, past, is expressed in English by the use of the past perfect tense. 1 Corinthians 2:7–8 illustrate the *Aktionsart* and time of action involved: "But we are speaking the wisdom of God . . . which no one of the rulers of this age has known [ἔγνωκεν = pft. act.], for if they had known [ἔγνωσαν: lit. = "they knew"—aorist], they would not have crucified [ἐσταύρωσαν: lit. = "they crucified"—aorist] the Lord of glory." ἔγνωσαν and ἐσταύρωσαν, as aorist tenses, express the constative perspective: "had the rulers known," an overview of all their actions; "they would not have crucified," a single event. The time of the action is prior to that of the perfect tense main verb ἔγνωκεν. To express this, English uses the past perfect subjunctive.

Exercises

Translate the following sentences.

1. ἔγνωκε τοῦτον τὸν ἄνθρωπον ἀπ᾽ ἀρχῆς κόσμου ἕως τοῦ νῦν.
2. εἶπον οὖν αὐτῷ οἱ Ἰουδαῖοι, Νῦν ἐγνώκαμεν ὅτι δαιμόνιον ἔχεις.
3. εἰ τὸ παιδίον πιστεύει τῇ ἐπαγγελίᾳ, ἕξει ζωὴν αἰώνιον τὴν ἀπὸ θεοῦ.
4. εἶπεν οὖν ἡ ἀρχὴ πρὸς τὸν Ἰησοῦν, Κύριε, εἰ ἦς ἐν τῇ οἰκίᾳ τῇ ἐμῇ οὐκ ἂν ἀπέθανεν ὁ ἀδελφός μου.
5. ὁ ἄγγελος πέπτωκε· οἱ λαοὶ ἐσκανδαλίσθησαν· αἱ ψυχαὶ πεπόνθασι· ἡ ἐκκλησία ἐσώθη.
6. ἐγώ σε ἐδόξασα ἐπὶ τοῦ κόσμου καὶ νῦν δοξάσεις με σύ, θεέ, παρὰ σεαυτῷ τῇ δόξῃ ᾗ εἶχον[6] πρὸ τοῦ κόσμου.
7. εὑρήκαμεν ὅτι τὸ πλοῖον ἦν ἐπὶ τὴν θάλασσαν ὅτι Ἰησοῦς μόνος ἀπέλυε τοὺς μαθητάς· αὐτὸν ἐβλέψαν αὐτοὶ παρὰ αὐτοὺς καὶ ὑπέστρεφον.

---

[6]The imperfect of the verb ἔχω is εἶχον, εἶχες, etc.

8. εἰ τὴν τοιαύτην παραβολὴν εἶπεν, ἡ συναγωγὴ ἐμοῦ ἄν ἐπίστευσε εἰς αὐτόν.

9. εἰ δὲ ὁ ὀφθαλμός σου ὁ δεξιὸς πράσσει πονηρόν, ἀπολύσει αὐτὸν παρὰ σεαυτοῦ.

10. οὕτως ὁ Παῦλος ἐπέστρεφε πρὸς αὐτοὺς καὶ χαρὰ ἐλήμφθη ὑπὸ τῶν τῆς οἰκίας τῆς ἀρχῆς διὰ τὴν ἐπαγγελίαν.

11. οὗτος ἔφυγε πρὸς αὐτὸν ἡμέρας⁷ καὶ εἶπεν αὐτῷ, ῾Ραββί,⁸ οἴδαμεν ὅτι ἀπὸ θεοῦ ὑπάρχεις διδάσκαλος.

12. ἤδεισαν γὰρ οἱ λαοὶ ἐν τῷ τόπῳ ἐκείνῳ ὅτι οὗτοι οἱ ἄνθρωποι δοῦλοι τοῦ θεοῦ τοῦ ἁγίου ὑπῆρχον.

---

⁷The genitive case may express kind of time. The descriptive aspect of the case is to the fore, so that one understands neither point of time (dative) nor extent of time (accusative), but type of time. See page 199.

⁸"Rabbi," from a Hebrew word meaning "Lord," "teacher."

CHAPTER 11

VERB SYSTEM. III: PRIMARY MIDDLE ENDINGS AND TENSES, INDICATIVE MOOD. DEPONENT VERBS. FUTURE OF εἰμί. RECIPROCAL PRONOUN

The primary tenses, it will be recalled, are the present, future, and perfect. In this chapter attention will focus upon those tenses that use Set III of the verb endings, the primary middle. With this set one constructs the present tense middle and passive voices (one formation serves for both), the future tense middle voice, the future tense passive voice, and the perfect tense middle and passive voices (one formation serves for both).

Vocabulary

Nouns

ἱμάτιον, -ου, τό	garment
καιρός, -οῦ, ὁ	time
σάββατον, -ου, τό	Sabbath

Reciprocal Pronoun

ἀλλήλων	of one another (no nominative forms)

Conjunction

οὔτε	and not
οὔτε . . . οὔτε	neither . . . nor

Deponent Verbs

PRESENT A.	FUTURE A.	AORIST A.[1]	PERFECT A.	PERFECT M/P.	AORIST P.[2]
ἀποκρίνομαι I answer, reply	———	ἀπεκρινάμην	———	———	ἀπεκρίθην

---

[1]The conjugation of aorist deponent forms uses the secondary middle endings which will be introduced on pp. 91f. Note ἔρχομαι is not deponent in the aorist or perfect tenses.

[2]The aorist passive is sometimes deponent, carrying an active sense. Sometimes it is a genuine passive. Only context and basic lexical meaning will enable one to discriminate. For example, a passive notion simply will not fit ἐγενήθην.

PRESENT A.	FUTURE A.	AORIST A.	PERFECT A.	PERFECT M/P.	AORIST P.

ἅπτομαι　　　　ἅψομαι　　　ἡψάμην
　I touch, take hold of [takes the genitive as its complement]

ἀσπάζομαι　　　　——　　　ἠσπασάμην
　I greet, welcome

βούλομαι　　　——　　　　——　　　——　　　——　　　ἐβουλήθην
　I wish, am willing

γίνομαι　　　γενήσομαι　　ἐγενόμην　　γέγονα　　γεγένημαι　　ἐγενήθην
　I come to be, become, happen (often a substitute for εἰμί)
　　παραγίνομαι: I come, arrive

δέχομαι　　　——　　　ἐδεξάμην　　　——　　　δέδεγμαι　　ἐδέχθην
　I receive, take

ἐργάζομαι　　　——　　　ἠργασάμην　　　——　　　εἴργασμαι
　I work, do, accomplish

ἔρχομαι　　　ἐλεύσομαι　　ἦλθον　　ἐλήλυθα
　I come, go
　　ἀπέρχομαι: I go away, depart (with various prepositions following)
　　διέρχομαι: I go, pass through (with accusative or various prepositions)
　　εἰσέρχομαι: I enter, come into, go into (with various prepositions)
　　ἐξέρχομαι: I come out, go out (with various prepositions)
　　παρέρχομαι: I pass away, pass by (with various prepositions)
　　προσέρχομαι: I come to, go to (with the dative)
　　συνέρχομαι: I come together (with the dative or various prepositions)

κάθημαι　　　καθήσομαι
　I sit; stay, reside

λογίζομαι　　　——　　　ἐλογισάμην　　　——　　　——　　　ἐλογίσθην
　I reckon, consider, count

πορεύομαι　　πορεύσομαι　　　——　　　——　　　πεπόρευμαι　　ἐπορεύθην
　I go, proceed, travel
　　ἐκπορεύομαι: I go out

προσεύχομαι　　προσεύξομαι　　προσηυξάμην
　I pray

Significance of Middle and Passive Voices

Middle Voice

In the active voice the subject of the verb performs an action, e.g., "he finds" (εὑρίσκει). In the middle voice the subject of the verb is involved in the action, but the specific manner must be detected from the context. In some way the action is in the interest of the subject.

　The subject may perform an act directly upon itself. This is known as the direct middle. It is essentially reflexive in force, but the reflexive pronoun used in English translation does not occur in the Greek. Matthew 27:5b, "he *hanged himself*"; 1 Cor. 6:11, "you *washed yourselves*"; 2 Cor. 11:14, "Satan himself *disguises himself* as an angel," are illustrative. This form will not be encountered frequently. The *GNT* will more often use the reflexive pronoun and the active voice to express a reflexive thought.

More often, the middle voice will occur when the subject is acting so as to cause an effect in the subject's own interest. This is called the indirect middle. In this instance the actor (subject) is emphasized as taking part in the action expressed by the verb. It is illustrated by Heb. 10:36: "You have need of endurance in order that when you have done the will of God, *you may receive* [aorist subjunctive middle] the promise" (Heb. 11:13, 39 have two more uses of the same aorist middle verb). Consider Heb. 9:12: "And not through the blood of goats and calves, but through his own blood, he [Christ] entered once and for all into the sanctuary, *having obtained* [εὑράμενος = second aorist middle participle from εὑρίσκω] an eternal redemption." He obtained, not "for himself," but "in his interest"—that he might fulfill his priestly ministry.

Passive Voice

Review the significance of the passive voice on page 82. Whether one has a middle or a passive voice is not clear in the present and perfect tenses because the forms used are the same. To distinguish between the two voices one must rely upon the context and the verb-idea itself.

Formation and Translation of Primary Middle Tenses

PRIMARY MIDDLE ENDINGS

Singular	*Plural*
1. -μαι	-μεθα
2. -σαι	-σθε
3. -ται	-νται

These endings will be attached to the stem of any regular verb to form the above-listed tenses. One must, however, use certain sufformatives and preformatives as indicated below.

Present Tense Middle and Passive Voice

These tenses are identical in form. The present active stem is isolated and to it is attached the variable vowel ο or ε in the same fashion as previously observed: before an ending that begins with μ or ν, use ο; elsewhere, use ε. Then, attach the above endings.

PRESENT TENSE MIDDLE/PASSIVE VOICE: ἄγομαι

	Singular	*Plural*
1.	ἄγ ο μαι	ἀγ ό μεθα
2.	ἄγ ῃ	ἄγ ε σθε
3.	ἄγ ε ται	ἄγ ο νται

The second person singular form has undergone a deletion of the σ from the ending and the remaining ε + α contracts to form η with final ι placed as iota subscript.

Since this conjugation may be translated as either middle or passive, context will regularly be the guide as to which voice is being employed. Here are translations of the previous paradigm, listing first the middle and then the passive.

Singular	*Plural*
1. I lead/am leading in my own interest	we lead/are leading in our own interest
2. you lead/are leading in your own interest	you lead/are leading in your own interest
3. he, she, it leads/is leading in his/her/its own interest	they lead/are leading in their own interest

1. I am led/being led	we are led/being led
2. you are led/being led	you are led/being led
3. he, she, it is led/being led	they are led/being led

Future Tense Middle Voice

The future tense forms the middle and passive voices separately. Observe, in the future middle, the sign of the future—σ (or σ in a consonantal blend)—and the primary middle endings. The ο/ε variable vowel continues as the coupler between the future stem and the primary middle endings.

	Singular			*Plural*	
1.	ἄξ ο μαι	I shall lead in my own interest	ἀξ ό μεθα	we shall lead in our own interest
2.	ἄξ ῃ	you will lead in your own interest	ἄξ ε σθε	you will lead in your own interest
3.	ἄξ ε ται	he, she, it will lead, etc.	ἄξ ο νται	they will lead in their own interest

Future Tense Passive Voice

Delete the augment and the secondary endings. The sixth principal part, the aorist passive form, is used. Because the future tense is a primary tense, the augment must be removed from the stem. Thus, ἤχθην reverts back to ἀχθην; ἐδέχθην becomes δεχθην, etc. These unaugmented stems will further delete the secondary active endings ν, ς etc.

Attach the future couplers σο/σε. To the unaugmented stem without the secondary active endings is attached the sign of the future—σ— with the variable vowels ο/ε. The same pattern as the future middle prevails: ο before μ or ν; ε elsewhere. Thus, ἀχθησο/σε; δεχθησο/σε.

Attach the primary middle endings. The same endings as in the present middle/passive and the future middle are used with no modifications. The variations in the stem and the tense coupler are the clues to the voice.

FUTURE PASSIVE: ἀχθήσομαι: I shall be led

Singular	*Plural*
1. ἀχ θή σο μαι	ἀχ θη σό μεθα
2. ἀχ θή σ ῃ	ἀχ θή σε σθε
3. ἀχ θή σε ται	ἀχ θή σο νται

Perfect Tense Middle and Passive Voices

The perfect tenses middle and passive voices occur as the same forms. Like the present middle and passive, the voice is distinguished by context. The primary middle endings are added directly to what is called the fifth principal part which is given in the verb charts (e.g., ἤγμαι; δέδεγμαι). Note there is no variable vowel to link the stem and the ending. This is one of the distinctives of the perfect middle and passive tenses. As there is no variable vowel, the second person singular form does not contract; it remains -σαι.

The second distinction of these tenses is the reduplication of the stem. This follows the same patterns as the perfect active (see page 74). Rather than trying to predict the final formations, the student should carefully memorize them from the vocabulary lists.

Even though the fifth principal part may be memorized, there will still be some difficulty when the endings -μαι, -σαι, -ται, etc. are joined to stems ending with palatals, labials, and dentals. Consonants in these categories will undergo changes, but the beginner need not be concerned to memorize all of them. By noting the stem's reduplication and the primary middle endings, together with the absence of the variable vowel, one should be able to parse and translate any given form. The following paradigms are included for illustrative and reference purposes only.

PERFECT MIDDLE/PASSIVE
(Stem ending in a vowel): λέλυμαι

Singular	Plural
1. λέ λυ μαι	λε λύ μεθα
2. λέ λυ σαι	λέ λυ σθε
3. λέ λυ ται	λέ λυ νται

A translation of the perfect middle:

Singular	Plural
1. I have loosed in my own interest and the effect continues	we have loosed in our own interest, etc.
2. you have loosed in your own interest etc.	you have loosed in your own interest etc.
3. he, she, it has loosed in his, her, its own interest etc.	they have loosed in their own interest etc.

A translation of the perfect passive:

Singular	Plural
1. I have been loosed and the effect continues	we have been loosed etc.
2. you have been loosed etc.	you have been loosed etc.
3. he, she, it has been loosed etc.	they have been loosed etc.

PERFECT MIDDLE/PASSIVE
(Stem ending in a palatal [κ, γ, χ]): ἦγμαι:
I have led in my own interest/I have been led

Singular	Plural
1. ἦγμαι	ἦγμεθα
2. ἦξαι	ἦχθε
3. ἦκται	ἦγμένοι εἰσί*

PERFECT MIDDLE/PASSIVE
(Stem ending in a labial [π, β, φ]): πέπεμμαι:
I have sent in my own interest/I have been sent

Singular	Plural
1. πέπεμμαι	πεπέμμεθα
2. πέπεμψαι	πέπεμφθε
3. πέπεμπται	πεπεμμένοι εἰσί*

---

*A perfect middle/passive participle plus the verb εἰμί in a form that has not yet been introduced.

PERFECT MIDDLE/PASSIVE
(Stem ending in a dental [τ, δ, θ]): πέπεισμαι:
I have persuaded in my own interest/I have been persuaded

Singular	Plural
1. πέπεισμαι	πεπείσμεθα
2. πέπεισαι	πέπεισθε
3. πέπεισται	πεπεισμένοι εἰσί*

PERFECT MIDDLE/PASSIVE
(Stem ending in a σ):
ἔγνωσμαι: I have known in my own interest/I have been known

Singular	Plural
1. ἔγνωσμαι	ἐγνώσμεθα
2. ἔγνωσαι	ἔγνωσθε
3. ἔγνωσται	ἐγνωσμένοι εἰσί*

PERFECT MIDDLE/PASSIVE
(Stem ending in a liquid [λ, μ, ν, or ρ]): ἦρμαι:
I have taken up in my own interest/I have been taken up

Singular	Plural
1. ἦρμαι	ἦρμεθα
2. ἦρσαι	ἦρσθε
3. ἦρται	ἦρμένοι εἰσί*

Instrumental Dative of Impersonal Means

Often the dative's idea of personal interest recedes and it instead expresses the impersonal instrument by which or in relation to which/whom something happens (e.g., Jn. 13:5: "and to dry them with a towel [τῷ λεντίῳ]"). This is in contrast to ὑπό with its object in the genitive case to indicate the personal means by which something occurs (e.g., Mt. 1:22: "the word which was spoken by the Lord [ὑπὸ κυρίου]"). Note the passive voice verb. The instrumental dative of impersonal means needs no preposition in order to convey its significance. Nevertheless, Greek frequently employs ἐν with the dative to denote the same thought. Compare 1 Cor. 14:2 with Rom. 5:9: "For he who speaks with a tongue [γλώσσῃ = impersonal means] speaks, not to men [ἀνθρώποις = indirect object]"; "having been justified by his blood [ἐν τῷ αἵματι (a yet-to-be introduced third declension dative singular) αὐτοῦ = impersonal means]."

---

*A perfect middle/passive participle plus the verb εἰμί in a form that has not yet been introduced.

Deponent Verbs

Some verbs occur with middle/passive voice endings, but are active in meaning. These are called deponents. ἔρχομαι is such a verb. It has no present tense active voice form ἔρχω. It and other deponents are regularly conjugated as middle/passives, but *translated* into English as though they were in the *active voice*. Such is the way the Greeks understood deponents. Thus, Jn. 21:13, ἔρχεται Ἰησοῦς καὶ λαμβάνει τὸν ἄρτον, is "Jesus comes and takes the bread."

Deponents may occur in any tense. A good example of tenses and uses of deponents is provided by 1 Cor. 3:1–2 where the deponent δύναμαι ("I am able") is used three times. Paul first uses the aorist passive form—ἠδυνήθην—with reference to his entire manner of relating to the Corinthians: "I was unable [to speak to you]." Note carefully, this is not an English passive verb; it is simple past tense state of being. In v. 2 ἐδύνασθε, the imperfect deponent, expresses the on-going past inability of the readers: "You were not yet able [to eat solid food]." δύνασθε, the present deponent, expresses the on-going present inability of the readers: "And yet you still are not now able."

Although a verb may be deponent in the present tense (e.g., ἔρχομαι), it may not be in the future or some other tense (e.g., ἦλθον). Consult a lexicon to ascertain which principal parts appear as deponents. Even then, one may still experience uncertainty because a verb that occurs as deponent in a given tense, e.g., γνώσομαι (future deponent of γινώσκω meaning "I shall know") may yet occur with a genuine passive sense in that very tense. Note Luke 12:2: "But there is nothing that has been concealed which shall not be revealed, or hidden which shall not be made known [γνωσθήσεται]." Again, let it be emphasized: Test the form in view of the context.

εἰμί: Future Tense

After having learned the primary middle endings, the future endings of εἰμί present no difficulties. The stem must be learned by rote memory.

	Singular			*Plural*	
1.	ἔσομαι	I shall be		ἐσόμεθα	we shall be
2.	ἔσῃ	you will be		ἔσεσθε	you will be
3.	ἔσται	he, she, it will be		ἔσονται	they will be

Reciprocal Pronoun

The middle voice expresses action performed by the subject in his/her own interest. The passive voice expresses action that is done to the subject. To express action that reciprocates between two or more persons, use the active voice and the reciprocal pronoun. Only the following masculine plural forms are found in the *GNT*:

G. ἀλλήλων
D. ἀλλήλοις
A. ἀλλήλους

Exercises

Translate the following.

1. γεγένησαι. πεπορεύμεθα. δέδεχθε. ἀνέῳκται. ἀσπάζεσθε.
2. ἐγνώσμεθα πρὸ τούτων τῶν καιρῶν, ἀλλ' οὗτος οὐ βεβαπτίσται εἰς τὸν Ἰησοῦν.
3. ὅσοι δὲ ὑπήγαγον εἰς τὴν ἔρημον καὶ ἔφαγον τὸ αὐτὸ καὶ ἔπιον τὸ αὐτό· ἤσθιον γὰρ καὶ ἔπινον ἐκ τοῦ Χριστοῦ.
4. ἐξελεύσεται ἐκ τοῦ τέκνου σου τὸ δαιμόνιον τῷ λόγῳ τοῦ προφήτου.
5. ὁ λόγος γενήσεται ὅτι ὁ πρεσβύτερος ὁ ἀγαπητὸς λέγει τὴν ἀλήθειαν ἐν τοῖς καιροῖς τούτοις.
6. τῇ ἀγάπῃ δὲ θεοῦ εἰμὶ ὅ εἰμι καὶ ὅτι θεὸς ἀγάπη ἐστίν ἐσόμεθα λαοὶ ἀγάπης.
7. ὁ ἄρτος ὃν φάγεσθέ ἐστιν ἡ ζωὴ τοῦ κυρίου ἡμῶν.
8. ἅγιοι ἔσεσθε ὅτι ἐγὼ ἅγιος.
9. ἡ δικαιοσύνη ὑμῶν ἡ πρὸ τοῦ θεοῦ κηρυχθήσεται ἕως τῆς ἡμέρας τοῦ κυρίου.
10. γέγραπται γὰρ ὅτι Τὸ σάββατον πρῶτον ἔσται ἐν ταῖς καρδίαις ἀνθρώπων.
11. ἀλλὰ βεβάπτισθε ἐν τῷ κυρίῳ Ἰησοῦ Χριστῷ.
12. ἅψομαι αὐτοῦ καὶ τότε προσελεύσομαι τῷ ἱερῷ καὶ προσεύξομαι τῷ θεῷ.
13. ἔλεγον οὖν οἱ μαθηταὶ πρὸς ἀλλήλους Νῦν καθησόμεθα ἐν σοφίᾳ καὶ χαρᾷ παρὰ τῷ κυρίῳ τῷ μακαρίῳ.
14. οὐκ ἐπέστρεψα εἰς Ἱεροσόλυμα πρὸς τοὺς πρὸ ἐμοῦ ἀποστόλους, ἀλλὰ ὑπήγαγον εἰς Ἀραβίαν, καὶ πάλιν ὑπέστρεψα εἰς Δαμασκόν.
15. ὁ Χριστὸς ἐκηρύχθη· ἐπείσθην· οὐκ ἐσκανδαλίσθημεν· ἐσώθησαν σὺν ἡμῖν.
16. ἐφάγομεν ἐνώπιόν σου καὶ ἐπίομεν, καὶ ἐν ταῖς οἰκίαις ἡμῶν ἐδίδαξας.
17. τότε ἀποκριθήσονται αὐτῷ οἱ δίκαιοι, Κύριε, ὅτε σε ἐβλέψαμεν ἐν τῷ ἱερῷ καὶ ἤλθομεν πρός σε;
18. Παιδία, ἐσχάτη ὥρα ἐστίν, καὶ καθὼς ἠκούσατε ὅτι ἀντίχριστος ὑπάρξει, καὶ νῦν ἀντίχριστοι γεγόνασιν· νῦν γινώσκομεν ὅτι ἐσχάτη ὥρα ἐστίν.

CHAPTER 12

VERB SYSTEM. IV: SECONDARY MIDDLE ENDINGS AND TENSES, INDICATIVE MOOD: IMPERFECT MIDDLE/PASSIVE TENSE; FIRST AND SECOND AORIST MIDDLE TENSES; PLUPERFECT MIDDLE/PASSIVE TENSE

We continue to examine the secondary tenses: the imperfect, the aorist (first and second), and the pluperfect. In this chapter the student will learn those tenses that complete the Indicative Mood: the middle and passive voice forms of the imperfect, the aorist tenses middle voice, and the pluperfect tense middle and passive forms. No new tenses or voices are introduced in this chapter. One should review the significances of the imperfect tense (pp. 58f.), the aorist tenses (pp. 66–70), the pluperfect tense (page 76), and the middle and passive voices (pp. 82f., 70).

Formation and Translation of Secondary Middle Tenses

The following are the endings of the secondary middle tenses:

	Singular	*Plural*
1.	-μην	-μεθα
2.	-σο	-σθε
3.	-το	-ντο

Having reviewed the active voice forms of the secondary tenses, one can readily form the secondary middle/passive tenses.

Imperfect Tense Middle and Passive Voice

Like the present tense middle and passive voices, one set of terms functions as either middle or passive. Delete the active voice endings of the imperfect tense, e.g., ἠγ- from ἦγον. Use the ο/ε variable vowel (see page 58), e.g., ἠγο-, ἠγε-. To these stems attach the above endings. In the second person singular the σ of -σο deletes and the remaining ε (variable vowel) plus ο combine to yield -ου. The imperfect tense middle or passive voice is thus:

		Singular			Plural
1.	ἠγ ό μην	I was leading in my interest; I was being led	ἠγ ό μεθα		we were leading in our interest; we were being led
2.	ἤγ ου	etc.	ἤγ ε σθε		etc.
3.	ἤγ ε το	etc.	ἤγ ο ντο		etc.

Aorist Tenses Middle Voice

First aorist tense. The first aorist stem, the third principal part (e.g., ἔλυσα), is utilized. (Remember, the first and second aorist passives are formed on the sixth principal part with secondary active endings.) Simply attach the above middle endings to the first person singular of the third principal part. The second person singular, theoretically -σασο, deletes the second -σ and the remaining -σαο consistently combines to form -σω. Thus, one has the following first aorist middle:

		Singular			Plural
1.	ἐ λυ σά μην	I loosed in my interest	ἐ λυ σά μεθα		we loosed in our interest
2.	ἐ λύ σω (ἐλύσασο)	etc.	ἐ λύ σα σθε		etc.
3.	ἐ λύ σα το	etc.	ἐ λύ σα ντο		etc.

Second aorist tense. To the second aorist stem or the third principal part, e.g., ἤγαγον, add the above middle endings after deleting the ν of the first person singular. Second person singular follows the contraction pattern of the imperfect. Remember, the only difference in appearance between the imperfect (e.g., ἠγόμην) and the second aorist (e.g., ἠγαγόμην) is the *stem.*

		Singular			Plural
1.	ἠ γαγ ό μην	I led in my interest	ἠ γαγ ό μεθα		we led in our interest
2.	ἠ γάγ ου	etc.	ἠ γάγ ε σθε		etc.
3.	ἠ γάγ ε το	etc.	ἠ γάγ ο ντο		etc.

Pluperfect Tense Middle and Passive Voices

The middle and passive voices of the pluperfect tense are identical. They are formed on the fifth principal part and, like the perfect middle or passive (see pp. 85–87), use no coupling variable vowel. Simply add the secondary middle endings to the fifth principal part minus the -μαι. Sometimes the stem will occur with an augment. In the Koine period this element was optional.

	Singular			*Plural*	
1.	(ἐ) λε λύ μην	I had loosed in my interest and the effect continued/had been loosed and the effect continued	(ἐ) λε λύ μεθα		we had loosed in our interest and the effect continued/had been loosed and the effect continued
2.	(ἐ) λέ λυ σο	etc.	(ἐ) λέ λυ σθε		etc.
3.	(ἐ) λέ λυ το	etc.	(ἐ) λέ λυ ντο		etc.

Like the perfect middle and passive, the pluperfect middle or passive tenses have consonantal changes when the verb tense stem, e.g., ἡγίασμαι (from the verb ἁγιάζω = "I sanctify"), has the secondary middle endings attached.[1] The following is representative.

	Singular			*Plural*	
1.	ἡγιάσ μην	I had sanctified in my interest etc.	ἡγιάσ μεθα		we had sanctified in our interest etc.
2.	ἡγία σο	etc.	ἡγία σθε		etc.
3.	ἡγίασ το	etc.	ἡγιασ μένοι ἦσαν		etc.

The consonantal deletions in the second person singular and plural are due to euphonic considerations. The third person plural is a combination of the perfect middle/passive participle and the imperfect tense of the verb "to be." This is a convenient pronounceable circumvention of an impossible ἡγιάσντο.

The Indicative Mood: A Review

The student has now been introduced to all tenses and voices of the indicative mood that are encountered in the *GNT*. The following charts bring them together in tabular form. First the tenses are organized under the headings of the four sets of verb endings; then follows a chart organized about the respective principal parts upon which the tenses are constructed. Both of these use the regular verb λύω. Then follows the verb ἄγω which illustrates (1) the changes of augment and reduplication when the initial letter is a vowel, (2) the second aorist active and middle tenses, and (3) the consonantal changes in the perfect and pluperfect middle/passive tenses when the stem ends with a consonant.

---

[1]Cf. the illustrations on pages 86f. N.B. the first and second persons plural of the perfect middle passive and pluperfect middle passive are identical. Thus, context must be one's guide in their translations.

New Testament Greek

λύω, A Regular Verb of the -ω Conjugation, Indicative Mood

PRIMARY ACTIVE ENDINGS		SECONDARY ACTIVE ENDINGS				
Present A.	*Future A.*	*Imperfect A.*	*Aorist A.*	*Aorist P.*	*Perfect A.*	*Pluperfect A.*
Singular						
1. λύω	λύσω	ἔλυον	ἔλυσα	ἐλύθην	λέλυκα	λελύκειν
2. λύεις	λύσεις	ἔλυες	ἔλυσας	ἐλύθης	λέλυκας	λελύκεις
3. λύει	λύσει	ἔλυε	ἔλυσε	ἐλύθη	λέλυκε	λελύκει
Plural						
1. λύομεν	λύσομεν	ἐλύομεν	ἐλύσαμεν	ἐλύθημεν	λελύκαμεν	λελύκειμεν
2. λύετε	λύσετε	ἐλύετε	ἐλύσατε	ἐλύθητε	λελύκατε	λελύκειτε
3. λύουσι(ν)	λύσουσι(ν)	ἔλυον	ἔλυσαν	ἐλύθησαν	λελύκασι	λελύκεισαν

PRIMARY MIDDLE ENDINGS				SECONDARY MIDDLE ENDINGS		
Present M./P.	*Future M.*	*Future P.*	*Perfect M./P.*	*Imperfect M./P.*	*First Aorist M.*	*Pluperfect M./P.*
Singular						
1. λύομαι	λύσομαι	λυθήσομαι	λέλυμαι	ἐλυόμην	ἐλυσάμην	(ἐ)λελύμην
2. λύῃ	λύσῃ	λυθήσῃ	λέλυσαι	ἐλύου	ἐλύσω	(ἐ)λέλυσο
3. λύεται	λύσεται	λυθήσεται	λέλυται	ἐλύετο	ἐλύσατο	(ἐ)λέλυτο
Plural						
1. λυόμεθα	λυσόμεθα	λυθησόμεθα	λελύμεθα	ἐλυόμεθα	ἐλυσάμεθα	(ἐ)λελύμεθα
2. λύεσθε	λύσεσθε	λυθήσεσθε	λέλυσθε	ἐλύεσθε	ἐλύσασθε	(ἐ)λέλυσθε
3. λύονται	λύσονται	λυθήσονται	λέλυνται	ἐλύοντο	ἐλύσαντο	(ἐ)λέλυντο

PRINCIPAL PARTS λύω				λύσω		ἔλυσα	
Present A.	*Present M./P.*	*Imperfect A.*	*Imperfect M./P.*	*Future A.*	*Future M.*	*Aorist A.*	*Aorist M.*
Singular							
1. λύω	λύομαι	ἔλυον	ἐλυόμην	λύσω	λύσομαι	ἔλυσα	ἐλυσάμην
2. λύεις	λύῃ	ἔλυες	ἐλύου	λύσεις	λύσῃ	ἔλυσας	ἐλύσω
3. λύει	λύεται	ἔλυε	ἐλύετο	λύσει	λύσεται	ἔλυσε	ἐλύσατο
Plural							
1. λύομεν	λυόμεθα	ἐλύομεν	ἐλυόμεθα	λύσομεν	λυσόμεθα	ἐλύσαμεν	ἐλυσάμεθα
2. λύετε	λύεσθε	ἐλύετε	ἐλύεσθε	λύσετε	λύσεσθε	ἐλύσατε	ἐλύσασθε
3. λύουσι	λύονται	ἔλυον	ἐλύοντο	λύσουσι	λύσονται	ἔλυσαν	ἐλύσαντο

PRINCIPAL PARTS λέλυκα		λέλυμαι		ἐλύθην	
Perfect A.	*Pluperfect A.*	*Perfect M./P.*	*Pluperfect M./P.*	*Aorist P.*	*Future P.*

Singular

1. λέλυκα	λελύκειν	λέλυμαι	(ἐ)λελύμην	ἐλύθην	λυθήσομαι
2. λέλυκας	λελύκεις	λέλυσαι	(ἐ)λέλυσο	ἐλύθης	λυθήσῃ
3. λέλυκε	λελύκει	λέλυται	(ἐ)λέλυτο	ἐλύθη	λυθήσεται

Plural

1. λελύκαμεν	λελύκειμεν	λελύμεθα	(ἐ)λελύμεθα	ἐλύθημεν	λυθησόμεθα
2. λελύκατε	λελύκειτε	λέλυσθε	(ἐ)λέλυσθε	ἐλύθητε	λυθήσεσθε
3. λελύκασι	λελύκεισαν	λέλυνται	(ἐ)λέλυντο	ἐλύθησαν	λυθήσονται

ἄγω, A Regular Verb of the Omega Conjugation, Indicative Mood.
Stem Beginning with a Vowel and Ending with a Consonant.
Second Aorist Active and Middle Tenses; Second Perfect
and Pluperfect Tenses

PRIMARY ACTIVE ENDINGS		SECONDARY ACTIVE ENDINGS					
			Second	*First*			
Present A.	*Future A.*	*Imperfect A.*	*Aorist A.*	*Aorist P.*	*Perfect A.*	*Pluperfect A.*

Singular

1. ἄγω	ἄξω	ἦγον	ἤγαγον	ἤχθην *	ἦχα	ἤχειν
2. ἄγεις	ἄξεις	ἦγες	ἤγαγες	ἤχθης	ἦχας	ἤχεις
3. ἄγει	ἄξει	ἦγε	ἤγαγε	ἤχθη	ἦχε	ἤχει

Plural

1. ἄγομεν	ἄξομεν	ἤγομεν	ἠγάγομεν	ἤχθημεν	ἤχαμεν	ἤχειμεν
2. ἄγετε	ἄξετε	ἤγετε	ἠγάγετε	ἤχθητε	ἤχατε	ἤχειτε
3. ἄγουσι	ἄξουσι	ἦγον	ἤγαγον	ἤχθησαν	ἤχασι	ἤχεισαν

PRIMARY MIDDLE ENDINGS				SECONDARY MIDDLE ENDINGS		
					Second	
Present M./P.	*Future M.*	*Future P.*	*Perfect M./P.*	*Imperfect M./P.*	*Aorist M.*	*Pluperfect M./P.*

Singular

1. ἄγομαι	ἄξομαι	ἀχθήσομαι	ἦγμαι	ἠγόμην	ἠγαγόμην	ἤγμην
2. ἄγῃ	ἄξῃ	ἀχθήσῃ	ἦξαι	ἤγου	ἠγάγου	ἦξο
3. ἄγεται	ἄξεται	ἀχθήσεται	ἦκται	ἤγετο	ἠγάγετο	ἦκτο

(*) indicates that the fourth principal part of this particular verb does not occur in the *GNT*. These forms are included, nevertheless, for illustration.

Present *M./P.* *Plural*	*Future* *M.*	*Future* *P.*	*Perfect* *M./P.*	*Imperfect* *M./P.*	*Aorist* *M.*	*Pluperfect* *M./P.*
1. ἀγόμεθα	ἀξόμεθα	ἀχθησόμεθα	ἤγμεθα	ἠγόμεθα	ἠγαγόμεθα	ἤγμεθα
2. ἄγεσθα	ἄξεσθε	ἀχθήσεσθε	ἦχθε	ἤγεσθε	ἠγάγεσθε	ἦχθε
3. ἄγονται	ἄξονται	ἀχθήσονται	ἠγμένοι εἰσίν	ἤγοντο	ἠγάγοντο	ἠγμένοι ἦσαν

Exercises

Translate the following sentences.

1. ὁ οὐρανὸς καὶ ἡ γῆ παρελεύσεται, οἱ δὲ λόγοι μου οὐ παρελεύσονται.

2. οἱ δὲ πρὸς αὐτὸν εἶπον· ἡμεῖς οὔτε λόγους περὶ σοῦ ἐδεξάμεθα ἀπὸ τῆς Ἰουδαίας, οὔτε οἱ ἀδελφοὶ εἰρήκασι περὶ σοῦ πονηρόν.

3. ὁ πονηρὸς οὐχ ἅψεται αὐτοῦ ὅτι γέγονε υἱὸς τοῦ θεοῦ καὶ ἔγνωκε τὴν ἀλήθειαν ἣν εἴρηται ὑπὸ τοῦ Ἰησοῦ.

4. καθὼς δὲ ἤγγιζεν ὁ χρόνος τῆς ἐπαγγελίας ἧς εἶπεν ὁ θεὸς τῷ Ἀβραάμ, ἡμάρτησαν οἱ λαοὶ καὶ ἀπήρχοντο εἰς τοὺς ἑτέρους θεούς.

5. πέπεισμαι γὰρ ὅτι οὔτε θάνατος οὔτε ζωὴ οὔτε ἄγγελοι λήμψεται ταύτας τὰς πιστὰς ἀπὸ τῆς ἀγάπης τοῦ θεοῦ τῆς ἐν Χριστῷ Ἰησοῦ τῷ κυρίῳ ἡμῶν.

6. διὰ τοῦτο ὡς δι᾿ ἀνθρώπου ἡ ἁμαρτία εἰς τὸν κόσμον εἰσῆλθεν καὶ διὰ ἁμαρτίας ὁ θάνατος, καὶ οὕτως εἰς ὅλους ἀνθρώπους ὁ θάνατος ἦλθεν.

7. λήμψεσθε Τιμόθεον ὅτι τὸ ἔργον κυρίου ἐργάζεται ὡς κἀγώ.[2]

8. καὶ ἐγένετο ὡς ἀπῆλθον ἀπ᾿ αὐτῶν εἰς τὸν οὐρανὸν οἱ ἄγγελοι, οἱ ἄνθρωποι ἔλεγον πρὸς ἀλλήλους· νῦν διελευσόμεθα ἕως Βηθλέεμ καὶ βλεψόμεθα τὸν λόγον τοῦτον ὃν ὁ κύριος ἐκήρυξε ἡμῖν.

9. ἐξῆλθε ἐκ τῆς ὁδοῦ ἐκείνης καὶ ἔπιπτεν ἐπὶ τῆς γῆς, καὶ προσηύχετο.

10. ὁ δὲ Ἰησοῦς εἶπεν αὐτοῖς· ἀμὴν λέγω ὑμῖν ὅτι ὑμεῖς καθήσεσθε καὶ αὐτοὶ ἐπὶ θρόνους. Πολλοὶ ["many"] δὲ ἔσονται πρῶτοι ἔσχατοι καὶ ἔσχατοι πρῶτοι.

11. αἱ γλῶσσαι προφητῶν ὑποτεταγμένοι εἰσὶν τῇ ἐκκλησίᾳ ὑπὸ τοῦ θεοῦ.

12. καὶ καθὼς ἐγένετο ἐν ταῖς ἡμέραις Νῶε, οὕτος ἔσται καὶ ἐν ταῖς ἡμέραις τοῦ υἱοῦ τοῦ ἀνθρώπου·

13. ἤσθιον, ἔπινον, ἄχρι ἧς ἡμέρας εἰσῆλθεν Νῶε εἰς τὴν κιβωτόν ["ark"], καὶ ἦλθεν ὁ κατακλυσμός ["flood"].

---

[2]A combination (called crasis) of καὶ and ἐγώ. Dative singular (κἀμοί) and accusative singular (κἀμέ) forms also occur. Translate as "and I," "but I," "I also."

CHAPTER 13

NOUN SYSTEM. III: THIRD DECLENSION MASCULINE AND FEMININE NOUNS

The third declension is comprised of all nouns that do not occur in either the first or the second declensions. Consequently, one finds terms in all three genders. This is a most important declension, both because some very significant theological vocabulary is of this declension, and more critically, because certain endings of the declension provide the fundamental pattern for a significant portion of the present, aorist, and perfect participles.

Third declension stems are not readily discernable, nor is their gender. One must memorize from the vocabulary list the nominative singular, the genitive singular, and the article (which will be the same as in first and second declension nouns) when one learns the English equivalent(s). It is totally inadequate simply to learn "ἄρχων = ruler." One must learn "ἄρχων ἄρχοντος, ὁ = ruler." Anything less will result in frustration and failure. The stem is not ἀρχ-, but ἀρχοντ-, a fact that is gleaned from the genitive singular. Nor is it sufficient to learn only the genitive singular, since the nominative singular cannot be readily deduced thereby. Learn nominative singular, genitive singular, article, English equivalent. Success will follow.

Vocabulary

Masculine Nouns: Consonant Stems

αἰών, αἰῶνος, ὁ	eternity, age; εἰς τοὺς αἰῶνας = forever
ἀνήρ, ἀνδρός, ὁ	man (in contrast to "woman" or "boy"; cf. androgynous) Dative pl. = ἀνδράσι
ἄρχων, ἄρχοντος, ὁ	ruler (cf. oligarchy)
μάρτυς, μάρτυρος, ὁ	witness, martyr
πατήρ, πατρός, ὁ	father (cf. patron)
πούς, ποδός, ὁ	foot (cf. podiatry)
Σίμων, Σίμωνος, ὁ	Simon (occurs only in the singular)

Feminine Nouns: Consonant Stems

γυνή, γυναικός, ἡ	woman (cf. androgynous)
ἐλπίς, ἐλπίδος, ἡ	hope
μήτηρ, μητρός, ἡ	mother (cf. matron) (decline like ὁ πατήρ)
νύξ, νυκτός, ἡ	night (cf. nocturnal)
σάρξ, σαρκός, ἡ	flesh (cf. sarcophagus)
χάρις, χάριτος, ἡ	grace, favor
χείρ, χειρός, ἡ	hand [the dative pl. stem deletes the ι = χερσί(ν)]

Feminine Nouns: Vowel Stems

ἀνάστασις, ἀναστάσεως, ἡ	resurrection
δύναμις, δυνάμεως, ἡ	power, might; ability (cf. dynamic)
θλῖψις, θλίψεως, ἡ	tribulation, affliction
κρίσις, κρίσεως, ἡ	judgment (cf. critic)
πίστις, πίστεως, ἡ	faith, trust
πόλις, πόλεως, ἡ	city (cf. metropolis)
συνείδησις, συνειδήσεως, ἡ	consciousness, conscience

Masculine Nouns: Vowel Stems

ἀρχιερεύς, ἀρχιερέως, ὁ	high priest
βασιλεύς, βασιλέως, ὁ	king
γραμματεύς, γραμματέως, ὁ	scribe, expert in the law
ἱερεύς, ἱερέως, ὁ	priest (cf. hierarchy)

Conjunction

τέ	and (enclitic)
τὲ ... τέ	as ... so; not only ... but also
τε καὶ	and

Formation of Third Declension Masculine and Feminine Nouns: Stems Ending with a Consonant

With regard to formation two groups are discernable: those whose stems end with a consonant (e.g., ἐλπιδ-) and those whose stems end with a vowel (e.g., πολε-).

Basic Endings

The most frequently encountered masculine and feminine endings of the third declension are presented in the box below.

	Singular	Plural
	M./F.	M./F.
N.	-ς, none	-ες
G.	-ος	-ων
D.	-ι	-σι
A.	-α or -ν	-ας
V.	Like the Nom. or learn by observation	-ες

Accents

In the third declension rules of accent are difficult, if not impossible, to articulate. In all the grammars consulted I have found very few explanations to the phenomena; they are simply observed. In this text relevant observations will be made and a few distinct patterns will be noted, but inexplicable variations abound. The sure approach is to use a lexicon or concordance to check the accent of the word in question.

One will observe that monosyllables in the nominative singular usually accent the ultima in the genitive and dative, but the penult in either accusative or the nominative plural.

Consonant Contractions

The astute student will immediately recognize where a problem will develop in joining the above endings to a consonantal ending: with the nominative singular and the dative plural. Moreover, the student will surmise that the problem consonants are the gutturals (κ, γ, χ), the dentals (τ, δ, θ), the labials (π, β, φ) and the liquids (λ or ρ).[1] Most all of these are handled precisely as with the future and aorist tense contractions (see page 12). Consequently, as the nominative singular or dative plural is introduced, look for the following formations (but, you may find exceptions).

gutturals (κ, γ, χ) + σ = ξ (e.g., σάρξ, σαρξί)

dentals (τ, δ, θ) + σ = σ (e.g., ἐλπίς, ἐλπίσι)

labials (π, β, φ) + σ = ψ (rare)

liquids (λ, ρ) + σ = observe the individual word

---

[1] This is a group of consonants not previously introduced. Verbs whose stems end in liquids will be considered in Chapter 15.

Masculine Nouns

Stems ending in dentals. A masculine pattern of infrequent occurrence, yet of paramount significance because its structure is analogous to the participle's masculine and neuter forms, is represented by ὁ ἄρχων, τοῦ ἄρχοντος = ruler. Remembering that the genitive singular reveals the stem, learn the following paradigm:

		Singular		*Plural*
N.	ὁ	ἄρχων	οἱ	ἄρχοντες
G.	τοῦ	ἄρχοντος	τῶν	ἀρχόντων
D.	τῷ	ἄρχοντι	τοῖς	ἄρχουσι(ν)
A.	τὸν	ἄρχοντα	τοὺς	ἄρχοντας
V.		ἄρχων		ἄρχοντες

Nominative singular has lengthened the o of the stem, deleted the τ of the stem, and not accepted the usual σ of the nominative singular. The accent is normal.

When the stem ends in a dental (as the above paradigm), not only will the dental delete before σ in the dative plural, but the then exposed ν, being treated as a dental, will also delete. With the deletion of two consonants "compensatory lengthening" of the remaining stem vowel usually occurs. The following patterns will be encountered.

αντ + σι = ασι (e.g., πᾶσι*)

εντ + σι = εισι (e.g., λυθεῖσι*)

οντ + σι = ουσι (e.g., ἄρχουσι)

Stems ending in liquids. Stems ending in ρ are those of concern. Three distinct patterns of stem structure are encountered, although the endings are typical. In the simplest structure the dative plural deletes the ρ.

ὁ μάρτυς, τοῦ μάρτυρος: witness

		Singular		*Plural*
N./V.	ὁ	μάρτυς	οἱ	μάρτυρες
G.	τοῦ	μάρτυρος	τῶν	μαρτύρων
D.	τῷ	μάρτυρι	τοῖς	μάρτυσι(ν)
A.	τὸν	μάρτυρα	τοὺς	μάρτυρας

---

*No forms that are familiar have occurred with this pattern. πᾶσι is the dative plural of the adjective πᾶς (see p. 109); λυθεῖσι is a masculine/neuter dative plural aorist passive participle (see p. 139).

The second structure is seen in ὁ ἀνήρ, τοῦ ἀνδρός ("man"). Note the vocative singular and dative plural.

	Singular			*Plural*
N.	ὁ	ἀνήρ	οἱ	ἄνδρες
G.	τοῦ	ἀνδρός	τῶν	ἀνδρῶν
D.	τῷ	ἀνδρί	τοῖς	ἀνδράσι(ν)
A.	τὸν	ἄνδρα	τοὺς	ἄνδρας
V.		ἄνερ		

A potential string of four consecutive consonants (dative plural) was avoided by the addition of a vowel between the stem and ending.

The final structure is that of ὁ πατήρ, τοῦ πατρός ("father"). The feminine noun ἡ μήτηρ, τῆς μητρός ("mother") also follows this pattern. Note how the stem fluctuates between πατρ- and πατερ-. Dative plural adds an α for euphony.

	Singular			*Plural*
N.	ὁ	πατήρ	οἱ	πατέρες
G.	τοῦ	πατρός	τῶν	πατέρων
D.	τῷ	πατρί	τοῖς	πατράσι(ν)
A.	τὸν	πατέρα	τοὺς	πατέρας
V.		πάτερ		

Feminine Stems Ending with Consonants

This group of words presents no problem so long as one bears in mind the principles of contraction reviewed above (p. 99). Add the regular endings to the stem.[2]

ἡ σάρξ, τῆς σαρκός: flesh

	Singular			*Plural*
N.	ἡ	σάρξ	αἱ	σάρκες
G.	τῆς	σαρκός	τῶν	σαρκῶν
D.	τῇ	σαρκί	ταῖς	σαρξί(ν)
A.	τὴν	σάρκα	τὰς	σάρκας
V.		σάρξ		σάρκες

---

[2]νύξ, νυκτός deletes the τ before nominative singular's ς and dative plural's σι as a proper dental should; then (having a guttural exposed) it blends the κ + σ to yield νύξ, νυξί.

ἡ ἐλπίς, τῆς ἐλπίδος: hope

	Singular			*Plural*
N.	ἡ	ἐλπίς	αἱ	ἐλπίδες
G.	τῆς	ἐλπίδος	τῶν	ἐλπίδων
D.	τῇ	ἐλπίδι	ταῖς	ἐλπίσι(ν)
A.	τὴν	ἐλπίδα	τὰς	ἐλπίδας
V.		ἐλπί		ἐλπίδες

The noun ἡ χάρις is a notable exception to the σάρξ pattern in the vocabulary list of terms occurring more than thirty times. It varies only in the accusative singular, where χάριν occurs.

ἡ χάρις, τῆς χάριτος: grace

	Singular			*Plural*
N./V.	ἡ	χάρις	αἱ	χάριτες
G.	τῆς	χάριτος	τῶν	χαρίτων
D.	τῇ	χάριτι	ταῖς	χάρισι(ν)
A.	τὴν	χάριν	τὰς	χάριτας

Formation of Third Declension Feminine and Masculine Nouns: Stems Ending with a Vowel

Stems Ending in ι/ε

The stems of this group of feminine nouns end in ε, although nominative and accusative singular has an ι in the final syllable. These nouns can easily be mastered if one observes the following features: (1) Genitive and dative singular and plural form as with previous third declension patterns, except genitive singular has become ως, rather than ος. (2) Accusative singular is ιν, not α. (3) Nominative and accusative plural have the same form: εις. A typical paradigm follows.

ἡ πόλις, τῆς πόλεως: city

	Singular			*Plural*
N.	ἡ	πόλις	αἱ	πόλεις
G.	τῆς	πόλεως	τῶν	πόλεων
D.	τῇ	πόλει	ταῖς	πόλεσι(ν)
A.	τὴν	πόλιν	τὰς	πόλεις
V.		πόλι		πόλεις

Observe the accent of the genitives is on the antepenult, the only instance where a long ultima does not draw the accent to the penult. This is due to the accentuation of an earlier Homeric form from which these are derived.[3]

Stems Ending in ε/ευ

A quite similar group likewise has a stem ending in ε, but the nominative singular is ευς. These are masculine in gender. The accusative singular has the familiar α; genitive singular has εως (cf. πόλις, πόλεως) and nominative and accusative plural are alike: εῖς. Dative plural reflects the vowels of the nominative singular: ευ, so εῦσι.

ὁ βασιλεύς, τοῦ βασιλέως: king

	Singular			Plural	
N.	ὁ	βασιλεύς	οἱ	τῶν	βασιλεῖς
G.	τοῦ	βασιλέως	τῶν		βασιλέων
D.	τῷ	βασιλεῖ	τοῖς		βασιλεῦσι(ν)
A.	τὸν	βασιλέα	τοὺς		βασιλεῖς
V.		βασιλεῦ			βασιλεῖς

Neuter Plural Subjects with Singular Verbs

To see neuter plural subjects with verbs in the singular is a commonplace in Greek. If the writer has the collective entity in view, then the neuter plural subject with the singular verb will likely be used. If the individuals or things that comprise the collective are more prominent, then a plural verb will be used. John 10:25 and 27 illustrate the matter. In v. 25 Jesus says, "τὰ ἔργα which I am doing in the name of my Father ταῦτα μαρτυρεῖ [third person singular of a contract verb = "testify"] concerning Me." Then, in v. 27, He says, "My sheep [plural] hear [ἀκούουσιν] my voice." "The works," as a group, bear witness; "the sheep," each one of them, is hearing the Shepherd.

Exercises

Translate the following sentences.

1. ἔλεγον οὖν αὐτῷ, Ποῦ*[4] ἐστιν ὁ πατήρ σου; ἀπεκρίθη Ἰησοῦς, Οὔτε ἐμὲ οἴδατε οὔτε τὸν πατέρα μου· εἰ ἐμὲ ᾔδειτε, καὶ τὸν πατέρα μου ἂν ᾔδειτε.

---

[3]So *G.G.* §254.

[4]When the asterisks (*) occur in this and subsequent exercises the vocabulary item has not been introduced in this text. The term may be readily identified by consulting a standard Greek lexicon. I begin at this point to do this in order to help the student develop proficiency with such a reference work.

2. οὐ γάρ ἐστιν ἀνὴρ ἐκ γυναικός, ἀλλὰ γυνὴ ἐξ ἀνδρός· καὶ γὰρ οὐκ ἐκτίσθη* ἀνὴρ διὰ τὴν γυναῖκα, ἀλλὰ γυνὴ διὰ τὸν ἄνδρα.

3. ἄλλοι ἔλεγον, Ἄγγελος αὐτῷ λελάληκεν.* ἀπεκρίθη καὶ εἶπεν Ἰησοῦς, Οὐ δι᾽ ἐμὲ ἡ φωνὴ αὕτη γέγονεν ἀλλὰ δι᾽ ὑμᾶς. νῦν κρίσις ἐστὶν τοῦ κόσμου τούτου, νῦν ὁ ἄρχων τοῦ κόσμου τούτου ἐκβληθήσεται ἔξω·

4. ὁ δὲ Σίμων καὶ αὐτὸς ἐπίστευεν ὅτε ἔβλεψε δυνάμεις σου.

5. ἐν ἐκείνῃ τῇ ἡμέρᾳ γνώσεσθε ὑμεῖς ὅτι ἐγὼ ἐν τῷ πατρί μου καὶ ὑμεῖς ἐν ἐμοὶ κἀγὼ ἐν ὑμῖν.

6. εἰ καὶ ἐγνώκαμεν κατὰ σάρκα Χριστόν, ἀλλὰ νῦν οὐκέτι* γινώσκομεν.

7. χάριτι δὲ θεοῦ εἰμι ὅ εἰμι, καὶ ἡ χάρις αὐτοῦ ἡ εἰς ἐμὲ οὐ κενὴ* ἐγενήθη.

8. ἀλλὰ λήμψεσθε δύναμιν καὶ ἔσεσθέ μου μάρτυρες.

9. καὶ ἔργα τῶν χειρῶν σού εἰσιν οἱ οὐρανοί.

10. Μετὰ δὲ ἐκείνας τὰς ἡμέρας ὁ Φῆλιξ* καὶ ἤκουσεν αὐτοῦ περὶ τῆς εἰς Χριστὸν Ἰησοῦν πίστεως.

11. ὀργὴ* γὰρ ἀνδρὸς δικαιοσύνην θεοῦ οὐκ ἐργάζεται.

12. Σὺ πίστιν ἔχεις κἀγὼ ἔργα ἔχω.

13. καὶ νῦν, ἀδελφοί, οἶδα ὅτι κατὰ ἄγνοιαν* ἐπράξατε, ὥσπερ* καὶ οἱ ἄρχοντες ὑμῶν.

14. ἡγίασται* γὰρ ὁ ἀνὴρ ὁ ἄπιστος* ἐν τῇ γυναικί, καὶ ἡγίασται ἡ γυνὴ ἡ ἄπιστος ἐν τῷ ἀδελφῷ· ἐπεὶ* ἄρα* τὰ τέκνα ὑμῶν ἀκάθαρτά* ἐστιν, νῦν δὲ ἅγιά ἐστιν.

15. Οὐκ εἰμὶ ἐλεύθερος;* οὐκ εἰμὶ ἀπόστολος; οὐχὶ* Ἰησοῦν τὸν κύριον ἡμῶν ἑώρακα;* οὐ τὸ ἔργον μου ὑμεῖς ἐστε ἐν κυρίῳ;

CHAPTER 14

NOUN SYSTEM. III (CONT.): THIRD DECLENSION NEUTER NOUNS; ADJECTIVES AND NUMERALS; INDEFINITE/INTERROGATIVE PRONOUNS

Vocabulary

-μα/-ματος Type Neuter Nouns

αἷμα, αἵματος, τό	blood (cf. hematology)
θέλημα, θελήματος, τό	will
ὄνομα, ὀνόματος, τό	name (cf. onomatopoeia)
πνεῦμα, πνεύματος, τό	spirit, breath, wind (cf. pneumatic)
ῥῆμα, ῥήματος, τό	word, saying
σπέρμα, σπέρματος, τό	seed, descendant(s) (cf. sperm)
στόμα, στόματος, τό	mouth (cf. stomach)
σῶμα, σώματος, τό	body (cf. somatic)

-ος/-ους Type Neuter Nouns

γένος, γένους, τό	race, descendants (cf. geneology)
ἔθνος, ἔθνους, τό	nation, Gentile (cf. ethnic)
ἔτος, ἔτους, τό	year
μέλος, μέλους, τό	member, part, limb (of the body, whether literal or figurative)
μέρος, μέρους, τό	part (often geographical or quantitative)
ὄρος, ὄρους, τό	mountain (cf. orography)
πλῆθος, πλήθους, τό	multitude, crowd (cf. plethora)
σκότος, σκότους, τό	darkness
τέλος, τέλους, τό	end (cf. teleology)

Stems Ending in a Liquid or τ (not -ματ)

οὖς, ὠτός, τό	ear (cf. otology)
πῦρ, πυρός, τό	fire (cf. pyre)
ὕδωρ, ὕδατος, τό	water (cf. hydroplane)
φῶς, φωτός, τό	light (cf. photograph)

Adjectives and Numerals

ἀληθής (M. and F.) -ές (N.)	true
δύο	two (cf. duet)
εἷς, μία, ἕν	one
οὐδείς, οὐδεμία, οὐδέν	no, no one, nobody, nothing
μηδείς, μηδεμία, μηδέν	no, no one, nobody, nothing
μέγας, μεγάλη, μέγα	great, large (cf. megalomania)
πᾶς, πᾶσα, πᾶν	all, every, whole
ἅπας, ἅπασα, ἅπαν	whole, all, everybody
πολύς, πολλή, πολύ	much, many (cf. polychrome)
τέσσαρες (M. and F.)	four (cf. tetragrammaton)
τέσσαρα (N.; may occur as τέσσερα)	
τρεῖς (M. and F.), τρία (N.)	three (cf. triangle)

Pronouns

τίς (M. and F.), τί (N.)	who? which? what?; τί, as an adverb: why?
τις (M. and F.), τι (N.)	someone, a certain one, something

Formation of Third Declension Neuter Nouns

Basic Endings

		Singular	Plural
N.		none	-α
G.		-ος	-ων
D.		-ι	-σι
A.		none	-α
V.		none	-α

-μα/-ματος Type

From the genitive singular one deduces that the stem ends in -ματ-; thus from σπέρματος one has σπερματ-. The nominative and accusative singular of these third declension neuter nouns alike show -α. This is simply the stem without its final τ because a Greek word, if ending in a consonant, can only end in ν, σ or ρ. The plural of these cases adds to the stem a familiar α as in neuters of the second declension. Genitive and dative singular and plural correspond to their respective forms in the ἄρχων type: -ος, -ι, -ων, -σι.

τὸ σπέρμα, τοῦ σπέρματος: seed

	Singular		Plural	
N.	τὸ	σπέρμα	τὰ	σπέρματα
G.	τοῦ	σπέρματος	τῶν	σπερμάτων
D.	τῷ	σπέρματι	τοῖς	σπέρμασι
A.	τὸ	σπέρμα	τὰ	σπέρματα
V.		σπέρμα		σπέρματα

-ος/-ους Type

A significant group of neuter nouns has the nominative singular ending in -ος, a modification of an underlying original stem that ended in -εσ. An analysis of the various forms following the rules for contraction of vowels (to which the student will be introduced later) would reveal the original forms and modifications. Although the student need simply learn the resultant formations, the uncontracted forms are included in parentheses so that one may see how the endings of the -μα type are, in fact, still being employed in all cases except the nominative, accusative, and vocative singular.

τό μέρος, τοῦ μέρους: part

	Singular		Plural	
N./V.	τὸ	μέρος	τὰ	μέρη (μερεσα)
G.	τοῦ	μέρους (μερεσος)	τῶν	μερῶν (μερεσων)
D.	τῷ	μέρει (μερεσι)	τοῖς	μέρεσι (μερεσσι)
A.	τὸ	μέρος	τὰ	μέρη (μερεσα)

A warning. These nouns are notorious for confusing the beginner due to obvious likenesses to the masculine and feminine nouns of the first and second declensions. Give careful attention to clues provided in contexts by the article and/or other modifiers.

Stems Ending in a Liquid or τ (not -ματ-)

These neuter nouns very closely follow the τὸ σπέρμα type, except they do not use -ματ in the oblique cases. Representative are τὸ πῦρ, τοῦ πυρός ("fire"); τὸ φῶς, τοῦ φωτός ("light"); τὸ ὕδωρ, τοῦ ὕδατος ("water").

	Singular					
N./V.	τὸ	πῦρ	τὸ	φῶς	τὸ	ὕδωρ
G.	τοῦ	πυρός	τοῦ	φωτός	τοῦ	ὕδατος
D.	τῷ	πυρί	τῷ	φωτί	τῷ	ὕδατι
A.	τὸ	πῦρ	τὸ	φῶς	τὸ	ὕδωρ

Plural

N./V.	τὰ (πυρά)*	τὰ (φῶτα)	τὰ ὕδατα
G.	τῶν (πυρῶν)	τῶν φώτων	τῶν ὑδάτων
D.	τοῖς (πυρσί)	τοῖς (φωσί)	τοῖς ὕδασι
A.	τὰ (πυρά)	τὰ φῶτα	τὰ ὕδατα

Third Declension Nouns Presented in This Text: A Summary[1]

CONSONANT STEMS				VOWEL STEMS		NEUTER NOUNS		
Masculines		Feminines		Feminine	Masculine	-μα Type	-ος Type	Liquid or τ

Singular

ἄρχων	νύξ	ἐλπίς	χάρις	πόλις	βασιλεύς	ὄνομα	γένος	ὕδωρ
ἄρχοντος	νυκτός	ἐλπίδος	χάριτος	πόλεως	βασιλέως	ὀνόματος	γένους	ὕδατος
ἄρχοντι	νυκτί	ἐλπίδι	χάριτι	πόλει	βασιλεῖ	ὀνόματι	γένει	ὕδατι
ἄρχοντα	νυκτά	ἐλπίδα	χάριν	πόλιν	βασιλέα	ὄνομα	γένος	ὕδωρ

Plural

ἄρχοντες	νύκτες	ἐλπίδες	χάριτες	πόλεις	βασιλεῖς	ὀνόματα	γένη	ὕδατα
ἀρχόντων	νυκτῶν	ἐλπίδων	χαρίτων	πόλεων	βασιλέων	ὀνομάτων	γενῶν	ὑδάτων
ἄρχουσι	νυξί	ἐλπίσι	χάρισι	πόλεσι	βασιλεῦσι	ὀνόμασι	γένεσι	ὕδασι
ἄρχοντας	νύκτας	ἐπίδας	χάριτας	πόλεις	βασιλεῖς	ὀνόματα	γένη	ὕδατα

Adjectives and Numerals

In Chapters 3 and 4 the student was introduced to first and second declension adjectives that had three distinct sets of forms for the masculine, feminine, and neuter genders (e.g., ἀγαθός, ἀγαθή, ἀγαθόν). There are adjectives that mix the third and first declensions to form their genders (e.g., πᾶς, πᾶσα, πᾶν). Some adjectives (and pronouns) will have common masculine and feminine forms, but distinct neuter patterns (e.g., τίς, τί). Some even display a mixture of all three declensions within the genders (e.g., πολύς, πολλή, πολύ). As in earlier sections some more obscure forms (less than 30 times frequency) are found in the *GNT*, but these are not addressed in this text.

---

*This and the following forms in parentheses do not occur in the *GNT* for these particular words. They are included for illustration.

[1]N.B. the underscored endings are uniform. There are other third declension terms of low frequency occurrence, but seldom will these so diverge from the patterns presented in this text as to stymie the student.

Third-First-Third Declension Type

πᾶς, πᾶσα, πᾶν. This adjective and its derivative ἅπας are the only words of this precise type occurring more than 30 times. It is significant in its own right, occurring some 1226 times in the *GNT*. It gains significance, however, in that it is analogous to the basic paradigm of the aorist participle.

The following observations should enable one easily to master the declension. The masculine uses the endings of ἄρχων, ἄρχοντος. The feminine gender πᾶσα is a first declension δόξα type. Neuter genitive and dative, singular and plural are the same as the respective masculine forms. Neuter nominative singular simply deletes the τ of the stem παντ-; plural uses that familiar ending α.

πᾶς, πᾶσα, πᾶν: all, every, whole

	Singular			*Plural*		
	M.	F.	N.	M.	F.	N.
N.	πᾶς	πᾶσα	πᾶν	πάντες	πᾶσαι	πάντα
G.	παντός	πάσης	παντός	πάντων	πασῶν	πάντων
D.	παντί	πάσῃ	παντί	πᾶσι(ν)	πάσαις	πᾶσι(ν)
A.	πάντα	πᾶσαν	πᾶν	πάντας	πάσας	πάντα
V.	πᾶς	πᾶσα	πᾶν	πάντες	πᾶσαι	πάντα

Note that the feminine is everywhere accented on the penult except the genitive plural, where the ultima receives the circumflex.

εἷς, μία, ἕν. The numeral "one" calls to mind the preposition εἰς ("into") and ἐν ("in"), but note well the numeral is accented and has a rough breathing mark. The declension occurs only in the singular.

	M.	F.	N.
N.	εἷς	μία	ἕν
G.	ἑνός	μιᾶς	ἑνός
D.	ἑνί	μιᾷ	ἑνί
A.	ἕνα	μίαν	ἕν

The masculine forms are using the third declension consonant stem masculine endings. The feminine gender is a familiar καρδία type. The neuter follows the scheme of the masculine, except for a typical nominative and accusative correspondence.

Like this pattern in declension is οὐδείς, οὐδεμία, οὐδέν and μηδείς, μηδεμία, μηδέν. οὐδείς, etc., is used with the indicative mood; μηδείς, etc., is used with the subjunctive and other moods yet-to-be introduced.

δύο. "Two" has only two forms (understood as plurals, of course): δύο functions for the nominative, genitive, or accusative; δυσί(ν) the dative.

πολύς, πολλή, πολύ; μέγας, μεγάλη, μέγα. Carefully study the following paradigms together with the subsequent comments. Except for the two noted peculiarities, the words present no problems.

πολύς, πολλή, πολύ: much, many

	Singular			Plural		
	M.	F.	N.	M.	F.	N.
N.	πολύς	πολλή	πολύ	πολλοί	πολλαί	πολλά
G.	πολλοῦ	πολλῆς	πολλοῦ	πολλῶν	πολλῶν	πολλῶν
D.	πολλῷ	πολλῇ	πολλῷ	πολλοῖς	πολλαῖς	πολλοῖς
A.	πολύν	πολλήν	πολύ	πολλούς	πολλάς	πολλά

μεγάς, μεγάλη, μέγα: great, large

	Singular			Plural		
	M.	F.	N.	M.	F.	N.
N.	μέγας	μεγάλη	μέγα	μεγάλοι	μεγάλαι	μεγάλα
G.	μεγάλου	μεγάλης	μεγάλου	μεγάλων	μεγάλων	μεγάλων
D.	μεγάλῳ	μεγάλη	μεγάλῳ	μεγάλοις	μεγάλαις	μεγάλοις
A.	μέγαν	μεγάλην	μέγα	μεγάλους	μεγάλας	μεγάλα
V.	μεγάλε	μεγάλη	μέγα			

Two things should be noted with these adjectives; then, everything is straightforward first declension φωνή type and second declension endings. (1) The singular stem shifts: concerning πολύς the nominative and accusative masculine and neuter stem is πολ-; elsewhere, it is πολλ-. These cases of μέγας have a stem μεγ-; elsewhere, the stem is μεγαλ-. (2) These four terms have third declension type endings. For πολύς, it is respectively -υς, -υν (cf. πόλις), -υ, -υ;[2] for μέγας: -ας, -αν (cf. πόλις), -α, -α (cf. ὄνομα).

Third (Masculine-Feminine Same), Third (Neuter) Declensions

τρεῖς, τρία. The numeral "three" (occurring only in the plural) follows the third declension pattern of πόλις. The masculine and feminine genders have common terms that even the neuter shares in genitive and dative (a repeated phenomenon with this class of words). Observe there are only four different forms.

---

[2] An infrequently found third declension neuter form.

Plural

	M./F.	M./F./N.	N.
N.	τρεῖς		τρία
G.		τριῶν	
D.		τρισί(ν)	
A.	τρεῖς		τρία

τέσσαρες; τέσσαρα. These plural forms for "four" use the typical third declensional endings. Note again the common genitive and dative.

Plural

	M./F.	M./F./N.	N.
N.	τέσσαρες		τέσσαρα
G.		τεσσάρων	
D.		τέσσαρσι(ν)	
A.	τέσσαρας		τέσσαρα

ἀληθής; ἀληθές. Adjectives such as "true" are numerous, but none occurs more than twenty-seven times in the *GNT*. Nevertheless, the student should be familiar with their pattern. ἀληθής is typical. Its stem is ἀληθεσ- (cf. τὸ γένος).

		Singular			*Plural*	
	M./F.	M./F./N.	N.	M./F.	M./F./N.	N.
N.	ἀληθής		ἀληθές	ἀληθεῖς		ἀληθῆ
G.		ἀληθοῦς			ἀληθῶν	
D.		ἀληθεῖ			ἀληθέσι(ν)	
A.	ἀληθῆ		ἀληθές	ἀληθεῖς		ἀληθῆ

The genitive and dative singular and plural forms were encountered with τὸ γένος, as were the neuter plural nominative and accusative forms. Nominative and accusative singular masculine and feminine have the ς and α that are often used with third declension nouns. In the nominative ε of the stem has lengthened to η; in the accusative this ε has combined with α to form η. Neuter singular simply exhibits the stem without any endings—true to neuter patterns.

Indefinite and Interrogative Pronouns

The personal pronouns ἐγώ, σύ, αὐτός, and the relative pronoun ὅς were introduced in Chapter 5. The demonstratives οὗτος and ἐκεῖνος and the reflexives ἐμαυτοῦ, ἑαυτοῦ, and σεαυτοῦ were presented in Chapter 6. In this section the interrogative pronoun τίς, τί and the indefinite pronoun τις, τι are presented.

These two pronouns are one of the instances where accent is critical for identification. Note carefully in the table below that the interrogative pronoun has the acute accent on the single syllable forms (and this never changes to a grave). The two syllable forms consistently have the accent on the penult. These two points of accent provide an unchanging identification mark.

By contrast, the indefinite relative τις, τι is an enclitic; it almost never has the accent on the single syllable forms. The two syllable forms will occur with an accented ultima if the word begins a clause, is used for emphasis, or is preceded by a word which is itself accented on the penult.

τίς, τί: who? which?

	Singular			Plural		
	M./F.	M./F./N.	N.	M./F.	M./F./N.	N.
N.	τίς		τί	τίνες		τίνα
G.		τίνος			τίνων	
D.		τίνι			τίσι(ν)	
A.	τίνα		τί	τίνας		τίνα

τις, τι: a certain one, someone

	Singular			Plural		
	M./F.	M./F./N.	N.	M./F.	M./F./N.	N.
N.	τις		τι	τινες		τινα
G.		τινος			τινων	
D.		τινι			τισι(ν)	
A.	τινα		τι	τινας		τινα

Exercises

Translate the following sentences.

1. ἀλλὰ κεκηρύκαμεν τὸ εὐαγγέλιον ὃ οὐδεὶς τῶν ἀρχόντων τοῦ αἰῶνος τούτου ἔγνωκεν, εἰ γὰρ ἔγνωσαν, οὐκ ἂν τὸν κύριον τῆς δόξης ἐσταύρωσαν.*
2. τίς γὰρ οἶδεν ἀνθρώπων τὰ τοῦ ἀνθρώπου εἰ μὴ ["except"] τὸ πνεῦμα τοῦ ἀνθρώπου τὸ ἐν αὐτῷ;
3. καὶ ἡμεῖς ἐσμεν μάρτυρες τῶν ῥημάτων τούτων, καὶ τὸ πνεῦμα τὸ ἅγιον.
4. ἀλλ᾽ εἰσὶν ἐξ ὑμῶν τινες οἳ οὐ πιστεύουσιν.

5. ὁ δὲ³ εἶπεν αὐτοῖς, Οἱ βασιλεῖς τῶν ἐθνῶν ἔλαβον τούτους τοὺς ἄνδρας ἐκ τοῦ ἔθνους τῶν Ἰουδαίων.
6. σὺ δὲ ὁ αὐτὸς εἶ καὶ τὰ ἔτη σου οὐκ ἐκλείψουσιν.*
7. ᾔδεισαν γὰρ ἅπαντες τὸν πατέρα αὐτοῦ ὅτι Ἕλλην* ὑπῆρχεν.
8. ὅσοι γὰρ εἰς Χριστὸν ἐβαπτίσθητε, Χριστὸν ἐνεδύσασθε.*
9. πάντες γὰρ ὑμεῖς εἷς ἐστε ἐν Χριστῷ Ἰησοῦ.
10. οὐκ οἴδατε ὅτι τὰ σώματα ὑμῶν μέλη Χριστοῦ ἐστιν;
11. ἡ γὰρ ἀγάπη τοῦ Χριστοῦ συνέχει* ἡμᾶς, ὅτι γινώσκομεν τοῦτο ὅτι εἷς ὑπὲρ πάντων ἀπέθανεν· ἄρα* οἱ πάντες ἀπέθανον.
12. ὥσπερ* γὰρ τὸ σῶμα χωρὶς πνεύματος νεκρόν ἐστιν, οὕτως καὶ ἡ πίστις χωρὶς ἔργων νεκρά ἐστιν.
13. οὐκ οἴδατε ὅτι τὸ σῶμα ὑμῶν ναὸς* τοῦ ἐν ὑμῖν ἁγίου πνεύματός ἐστιν, οὗ ἔχετε ἀπὸ θεοῦ, καὶ οὐκ ἐστὲ ἑαυτῶν;
14. ἠγοράσθητε γὰρ τιμῆς· δοξάσετε δὴ* τὸν θεὸν ἐν τῷ σώματι ὑμῶν.
15. ἡ γυνὴ τοῦ ἰδίου σώματος οὐκ ἐξουσιάζει* ἀλλὰ ὁ ἀνήρ· ὁμοίως* δὲ καὶ ὁ ἀνὴρ τοῦ ἰδίου σώματος οὐκ ἐξουσιάζει* ἀλλὰ ἡ γυνή.
16. τί γὰρ οἶδας, γύναι, εἰ τὸν ἄνδρα σώσεις; ἢ* τί οἶδας, ἄνερ, εἰ τὴν γυναῖκα σώσεις;

---

³This is the article used as a demonstrative pronoun. Translate as "But this one," or "But he."

CHAPTER 15

CONTRACT VERBS; LIQUID VERBS; NOMINATIVE TO NAME
SOMEONE; NOMINATIVE ABSOLUTE; COMPARATIVE AND
SUPERLATIVE OF ADVERBS AND ADJECTIVES

Vocabulary

-εω Contract Verbs

ζητέω	I seek, I look for
καλέω	I call
ἐπικαλέω	I call, name; middle: I invoke, appeal to
παρακαλέω	I beseech, exhort, console
λαλέω	I speak, give forth a sound
ποιέω	I do, make, practice
τηρέω	I keep, observe, fulfill

-αω Contract Verbs

ἀγαπάω	I love
γεννάω	I beget
ἐρωτάω	I ask, ask a question, request
ἐπερωτάω	I ask
ζάω	I live
ὁράω	I see [Irregular future: ὄψομαι; second aorist: εἶδον; perfect: ἑώ[ό]ρακα]

-οω Contract Verbs

δικαιόω	I justify, pronounce righteous
πληρόω	I fulfill, fill
σταυρόω	I crucify
φανερόω	I manifest, reveal

LIQUID VERB STEMS ENDING IN λλ OR λ

Present A.	Future A.	Aorist A.	Perfect A.	Perfect M./P.	Aorist P.
ἀπαγγέλλω	ἀπαγγελῶ	ἀπήγγειλα	— — —	— — —	ἀπηγγέλην

I report, announce, proclaim
παραγγέλλω: I give orders, command

ἀποστέλλω	ἀποστελῶ	ἀπέστειλα	ἀπέσταλκα	ἀπέσταλμαι	ἀπεστάλην

I send away, send out

βάλλω	βαλῶ	ἔβαλον	βέβληκα	βέβλημαι	ἐβλήθην

I throw, put, place

ὀφείλω.
I owe, am indebted, I ought, must, am obligated (with infinitive following).
Only the present and imperfect tenses occur.

LIQUID VERB STEMS ENDING IN ν

ἁμαρτάνω	ἁμαρτήσω	ἡμάρτησα	ἡμάρτηκα
		ἥμαρτον	

I do wrong, sin

ἀναβαίνω	ἀναβήσομαι	ἀνέβην	ἀναβέβηκα

I go up, ascend
καταβαίνω: I come down, go down

ἀποκτείνω	ἀποκτενῶ	ἀπέκτεινα	— — —	— — —	ἀπεκτάνθην

I kill

κρίνω	κρινῶ	ἔκρινα	κέκρικα	κέκριμαι	ἐκρίθην

I judge, consider, decide

μένω	μενῶ	ἔμεινα	μεμένηκα

I remain, stay, abide

φαίνω	— — —	ἔφανα	— — —	— — —	ἐφάνην

I shine, give light, become visible

The ω class of verbs has two subcategories that present special problems when adding the previously learned personal endings to the stems. They are those verbs whose stems end in α, ε, or ο (called contract verbs) and those verbs whose stems end in a liquid consonant, either λ, λλ, ν, or ρ. Both categories of verbs use the regular endings of the ω conjugation. The variations concern coupler vowels, stem changes, and changes in accentuation. No changes in the significance of the various tenses occur. The issues are strictly formational.

Formation of Contract Verbs

In the *GNT* one will not find the precise forms ποιέω, σταυρόω, or ὁράω; rather, the contracted forms will occur: ποιῶ, σταυρῶ, ὁρῶ. In the vocabulary lists the uncontracted forms will be given so that the student may be able to determine without question the basic stem. In the present system, i.e., present active, middle, and passive; imperfect active, middle, and passive, one must make the following modifications to the coupler vowels and to the initial vowel(s) of the personal endings. Remember, there are no new endings; there are modified couplers.

Accents

In observing the following paradigms it will become evident that few new rules of accentuation are needed. If, in the uncontracted form, either of the contracting vowels or diphthongs has the accent, then the resultant contraction receives the accent. Should the final vowel of the uncontracted stem be accented (e.g., σταυρόεις, ἐποιέοντο), the resultant contraction will have the circumflex (so σταυροῖς, ἐποιοῦντο). Should the variable vowel of the personal ending be accented (e.g., ἐποιεόμην, ἐποιεόμεθα), the resultant contraction will have the acute (so ἐποιούμην, ἐποιούμεθα). If none of the syllables involved in the contraction were accented prior to contraction, then usual rules are followed and none of the contracted vowels receives an accent (e.g., ἐποίεον = ἐποίουν).

-εω Contract Verbs

Stem ending	+	Initial vowel(s) of personal ending	=	Resultant contraction
ε	+	ω	=	ω
ε	+	o or ου	=	ου
ε	+	ε or ει	=	ει
ε	+	η	=	η

So, ε deletes before a long vowel or diphthong (η, ω, ει, ου); ε plus ε or o becomes a diphthong (ει or ου).

PRESENT ACTIVE INDICATIVE: ποιέω: I do

Singular	*Plural*
1. ποι ῶ (ἐ + ω)	ποι οῦ μεν (ἐ + ομεν)
2. ποι εῖς (ἐ + εις)	ποι εῖ τε (ἐ + ετε)
3. ποι εῖ (ἐ + ει)	ποι οῦ σι (ἐ + ουσι)

PRESENT MIDDLE/PASSIVE INDICATIVE

Singular	*Plural*
1. ποι οῦ μαι (ἐ + ομαι)	ποι ού μεθα (ε + όμεθα)
2. ποι ῇ (ἐ + η)	ποι εῖ σθε (ἐ + εσθε)
3. ποι εῖ ται (ἐ + εται)	ποι οῦ νται (ἐ + ονται)

IMPERFECT ACTIVE INDICATIVE

Singular	*Plural*
1. ἐποί ουν (ἐ + ον)	ἐποι οῦ μεν (ἐ + ομεν)
2. ἐποί ει ς (ἐ + ες)	ἐποι εῖ τε (ἐ + ετε)
3. ἐποί ει (ἐ + ε)	ἐποί ου ν (ε + ον)

IMPERFECT MIDDLE/PASSIVE INDICATIVE

Singular	*Plural*
1. ἐποι ού μην (ε + όμην)	ἐποι ού μεθα (ε + όμεθα)
2. ἐποι οῦ (ἐ + ου)	ἐποι εῖ σθε (ἐ + εσθε)
3. ἐποι εῖ το (ἐ + ετο)	ἐποι οῦ ντο (ἐ + οντο)

-αω Contract Verbs

Stem ending	+	Initial vowel(s) of personal ending	=	Resultant contraction
α	+	o sound (o, ου, or ω)	=	ω
α	+	e sound (ε or η)	=	α
α	+	e sound (ει or η)	=	ᾳ

Remember, α overcomes any ε/η sound; α succumbs to any o sound; iota subscript is tenacious.

PRESENT ACTIVE INDICATIVE: ὁράω: I see

Singular	*Plural*
1. ὁρ ῶ (ά + ω)	ὁρ ῶ μεν (ά + ομεν)
2. ὁρ ᾷς (ά + εις)	ὁρ ᾶ τε (ά + ετε)
3. ὁρ ᾷ (ά + ει)	ὁρ ῶ σι (ά + ουσι)

PRESENT MIDDLE/PASSIVE INDICATIVE

Singular	*Plural*
1. ὁρ ῶ μαι (ά + ομαι)	ὁρ ώ μεθα (α + όμεθα)
2. ὁρ ᾷ (ά + η)	ὁρ ᾶσθε (ά + εσθε)
3. ὁρ ᾶ ται (ά + εται)	ὁρ ῶ νται (ά + ονται)

IMPERFECT ACTIVE INDICATIVE

Singular	*Plural*
1. ἑώρ ω ν (α + ον)	ἑωρ ῶ μεν (ά + ομεν)
2. ἑώρ ας (α + ες)	ἑωρ ᾶ τε (ά + ετε)
3. ἑώρ α (α + ε)	ἑώρ ω ν (α + ον)

IMPERFECT MIDDLE/PASSIVE INDICATIVE

Singular	*Plural*
1. ἐωρ ώ μην (α + όμηω)	ἐωρ ώ μεθα (α + όμεθα)
2. ἐωρ ῶ (ά + ου)	ἐωρ ᾶ σθε (ά + εσθε)
3. ἐωρ ᾶ το (ά + ετο)	ἐωρ ῶ ντο (ά + οντο)

-οω Contract Verbs

Stem ending	+	Initial vowel(s) of personal ending	=	Resultant contraction
ο	+	ω or η	=	ω
ο	+	ο, ου, or ε	=	ου
ο	+	η or ει	=	οι or ῳ

Observe that ο is overcome by long vowels (η or ω), but only results in ω. An ε/η sound never survives. When encountering an ε sound diphthong, ο overcomes, resulting in οι or ῳ.

PRESENT ACTIVE INDICATIVE: σταυρόω: I crucify

Singular	*Plural*
1. σταυρ ῶ (ό + ω)	σταυρ οῦ μεν (ό + ομεν)
2. σταυρ οῖς (ό + εις)	σταυρ οῦ τε (ό + ετε)
3. σταυρ οῖ (ό + ει)	σταυρ οῦ σι (ό + ουσι)

PRESENT MIDDLE/PASSIVE INDICATIVE

Singular	*Plural*
1. σταυρ οῦ μαι (ό + ομαι)	σταυρ ού μεθα (ο + όμεθα)
2. σταυρ οῖ (ό + η)	σταυρ οῦ σθε (ό + εσθε)
2. σταυρ οῦ ται (ό + εται)	σταυρ οῦ νται (ό + ονται)

IMPERFECT ACTIVE INDICATIVE

Singular	*Plural*
1. ἐσταύρ ου ν (ο + ον)	ἐσταυρ οῦ μεν (ό + ομεν)
2. ἐσταύρ ου ς (ο + ες)	ἐσταυρ οῦ τε (ό + ετε)
2. ἐσταύρ ου (ο + ε)	ἐσταύρ ου ν (ο + ον)

IMPERFECT MIDDLE/PASSIVE INDICATIVE

Singular	*Plural*
1. ἐσταυρ ού μην (ο + όμην)	ἐσταυρ ού μεθα (ο + όμεθα)
2. ἐσταυρ οῦ (ό + ου)	ἐσταυρ οῦ σθε (ό + εσθε)
3. ἐσταυρ οῦ το (ό + ετο)	ἐσταυρ οῦ ντο (ό + οντο)

The following chart presents the final stem vowels in the far left vertical column. The top horizontal row has the possible variable vowel(s). A given contraction may be found at the point of intersection from the two variables.

ε	ει	η	ῃ	ο	ου	οι	ω
α	α	ᾳ	α	ᾳ	ω	ω	ῳ	ω
ε	ει	ει	η	ῃ	ου	ου	οι	ω
ο	ου	οι	ω	οι	ου	ου	οι	ω

Principal Parts of Contract Verbs

Only the first principal part of contract verbs shows the preceding contractions. The other principal parts will lengthen the vowel that ends the stem (α or ε to η; ο to ω) and add the characteristic signs of the various tenses, followed by the appropriate primary or secondary endings.[1] The reason there is little or no problem in these principal parts is that the η or ω of the stem regularly couples to a consonant—in contrast to the variable vowels of the tenses formed on the first principal part.

Consider the principal parts of the following representative verbs:

ἀγαπάω, ἀγαπήσω, ἠγάπησα, ἠγάπηκα, ἠγάπημαι, ἠγαπήθην

τηρέω, τηρήσω, ἐτήρησα, τετήρηκα, τετήρημαι, ἐτηρήθην

φανερόω, φανερώσω, ἐφανέρωσα, πεφανέρωκα, πεφανέρωμαι, ἐφανερώθην

Several verbs that are not a contract type manifest in the future tense the endings of the present tense contract verbs. ἀποθνήσκω shows a future contracted form ἀποθανεῖται (Rom. 5:7) and ἀποθανεῖσθε (Jn. 8:21, 24). In Mt. 10:29 a future form of πίπτω occurs: πεσεῖται; in Mt. 15:14 is another instance: πεσοῦνται. All of these are deponents.

A few verbs which end in -ιζω will delete the ζ and use the present contract endings of the -εω type to form their futures. Among these are the verbs ἐγγίζω, ἐλπίζω, καθαρίζω and καθίζω, all of which were introduced in Chapter 9. The future that occurs for λέγω also follows this scheme: ἐρῶ, ἐρεῖς, ἐρεῖ, ἐροῦμεν, ἐρεῖτε, ἐροῦσι(ν).

---

[1] καλέω is an exception; it retains the ε in the future and aorist tenses, but has a lengthened stem vowel in the remaining principal parts: καλέω, καλέσω, ἐκάλεσα, κέκληκα, κέκλημαι, ἐκλήθην.

Formation of Liquid Verbs

Liquid verbs (stems end in λ, λλ, ν, or ρ) show peculiarities in forming the future and the aorist tenses. So, care must be given to the second and third principal parts. Again, at issue is formation, not function. Usually the verb stem varies from the first principal part and by that variation one can identify the tense.

Future Tense Active and Middle Voices

The endings of the future tense active and middle voices (e.g., βαλῶ, βαλοῦμαι) are identical to those of the present tense active and middle/passive voices of the contract verb ποιῶ, ποιοῦμαι. These future tense forms have accent marks that differ from those of a regular present or future tense. This is one of the identifying clues that these are to be considered future forms. Observe carefully the following conjugations of βαλῶ ("I shall throw") and βαλοῦμαι ("I shall throw in my interest"). Compare them with ποιῶ and ποιοῦμαι (page 117).

	FUTURE ACTIVE		FUTURE MIDDLE	
	Singular	*Plural*	*Singular*	*Plural*
1.	βαλῶ	βαλοῦμεν	βαλοῦμαι	βαλούμεθα
2.	βαλεῖς	βαλεῖτε	βαλῇ	βαλεῖσθε
3.	βαλεῖ	βαλοῦσι(ν)	βαλεῖται	βαλοῦνται

Often both the stem and the accent will indicate which tense is being used. There are verbs, however, that only show differences of accent—and even this distinction sometimes disappears. When it does, one is completely dependent upon context (of course, the responsible exegete is always aware of this factor). One such verb is κρίνω. Compare the following:

Present: κρίνω, κρίνεις, κρίνει, κρίνομεν, κρίνετε, κρίνουσι

Future: κρινῶ, κρινεῖς, κρινεῖ, κρινοῦμεν, κρινεῖτε, κρινοῦσι

First Aorist Tense Active and Middle Voices

The third principal part of liquid verbs usually undergoes an internal lengthening of vowels (e.g., pres.: μένω; aor.: ἔμεινα) and does not use the characteristic σ of the first aorist tense. It is nevertheless considered a first aorist tense. As such it uses the typical secondary active or middle endings. The paradigms of ἔμεινα ("I remained") and ἐμεινάμην ("I remained in my interest") follow.

FIRST AORIST ACTIVE		FIRST AORIST MIDDLE	
Singular	Plural	Singular	Plural
1. ἔ μειν α	ἐ μείν α μεν	ἐ μειν ά μην	ἐ μειν ά μεθα
2. ἔ μειν ας	ἐ μείν α τε	ἐ μείν ω	ἐ μείν α σθε
3. ἔ μειν ε	ἔ μειν α ν	ἐ μείν α το	ἐ μείν α ντο

A careful reading of the vocabulary verb charts reveals that most liquid verbs have first aorists. If the verb has a second aorist, there is no problem at all in the conjugation (cf. ἔβαλον, from βάλλω). Likewise, not all present tense liquids will have the liquid verb formations in the second and/or third principal parts; cf. ἁμαρτάνω, but ἁμαρτήσω; πίνω, but πίομαι).

The Nominative to Name Someone;
Nominative Absolute

After the verb καλέω or following the term ὄνομα Greek often will use the nominative case where English would use the objective. No firm grammatical rule exists, however, as to which will occur.

A person's name may simply be introduced into the text, essentially grammatically independent of the sentence (though one could call it appositional in relation to the subject). See Jn. 1:6: Ἐγένετο ἄνθρωπος . . . ὄνομα αὐτῷ Ἰωάννης = "A man came . . . name to him John."

Sometimes an apparent subject nominative fails to be the subject of the main verb. It occurs without any grammatical relationship and is known as the nominative absolute or independent nominative. Illustrative is Acts 7:40: ὁ γὰρ Μωϋσῆς οὗτος, ὃς ἐξήγαγεν ἡμᾶς ἐκ γῆς Αἰγύπτου, οὐκ οἴδαμεν τί ἐγένετο αὐτῷ = "For this Moses, who led us out of the land of Eygpt—we do not know what happened to him."

Comparative and Superlative Degrees
of Adverbs and Ajectives

Adverbs and adjectives may simply modify an entity without reference to another person or thing, as "He swims well"; "She sees an evil man." "Well" and "evil" are said to be the positive degree and express no comparison with another person or thing. When two persons or things are compared, the comparative degree is used: "She swims better (than he [not 'him'; Remember that the understood portion of the sentence is 'than he swims.'])"; "He sees a more evil man." When more than two persons or things are compared, the superlative degree is used: "The twins swim best of all." "He sees the most evil man."

From the above illustrations one appropriately concludes that the formation of adverbs and adjectives in English shows two different patterns. One may use a different word for each degree, as "well," "better," "best." That is called an irregular adverb or adjective. Alternatively, one may simply prefix the terms "more" and "most." Such is called a regular adverb or adjective.

Greek shows both approaches to the formation of comparative and superlative degrees. The positive degree of adverbs usually ends in -ως, as δικαίως ("justly"). To form the comparative and superlative degrees one adds the endings -τερον and -τατα respectively. So, one would see δικαίως ("justly"), δικαιότερον ("more justly"), δικαιότατα ("most justly"). (The latter two vocabulary items are not found in the *GNT*.) Coupling letters are not constant, but vary depending upon the term in question. Another pattern uses endings in -τερω and -τατω, as ἄνω ("up"), ἀνωτέρω ("higher"), ἀνωτάτω ("highest"—not found in the *GNT*). Still other adverbs simply change the term when progressing from the positive to the other degrees, as μάλα ("very"—not in *GNT*), μᾶλλον ("more"), μάλιστα ("most").

An adverb is not declined.

Adjectives exhibit one of two patterns to form the comparative and superlative degrees. -τερος, -α, -ον and -τατος, -η, -ον may occur, e.g., μικρός, μικρότερος, μικρότατος—not used in the *GNT*. They decline as first and second declension adjectives. Alternatively, one will see a comparative -ιων (masculine and feminine) and -ιον (neuter, all of a third declension pattern) and a superlative in -ιστος, -η, -ον. βελτίων ("better") and ἐλάχιστος ("least") are illustrative.[2]

The superlative forms rarely appear in the *GNT*. Where English idiom would use the superlative, Greek will frequently have the comparative, as in Mt. 13:32 where the mustard seed is described as ὃ μικρότερον μέν ἐστιν πάντων τῶν σπερμάτων = "which is the least [lit. lesser] of all the seeds." When the superlative does occur it often has only a heightening or elating force, without the denotation of the English superlative. Compare Mk. 4:1 (ὄχλος πλεῖστος) with the parallel in Mt. 13:2 (ὄχλοι πολλοί); see the same phenomenon in reverse in Mt. 21:8 (πλεῖστος ὄχλος) and Mk. 11:8 (πολλοί).

Exercises

Translate the following sentences.

1. εἰ ἐμὲ ἐδίωξαν, καὶ ὑμᾶς διώξουσιν· εἰ τὸν λόγον μου ἐτήρησαν, καὶ τὸν ὑμέτερον* τηρήσουσιν.

---

[2]These infrequent terms need not be memorized now. In addition to illustrating the -ιων, -ιστος endings these words also demonstrate that stems may change in the comparative and/or superlative categories from what the student would expect. βελτίων is the comparative of ἀγαθός and ἐλάχιστος that of μικρός. Do not suppose the stems were in some fashion re-shaped to produce these words. They derived from altogether different stems in the Classical era. A paradigm for the -ιων/-ον pattern is seen in the Tables, "Adjectives" with μείζων, -ον.

2. οὐκέτι λέγω ὑμᾶς δούλους, ὅτι ὁ δοῦλος οὐκ οἶδεν τί ποιεῖ αὐτοῦ ὁ κύριος· ὑμᾶς δὲ εἴρηκα φίλους,* ὅτι πάντα ἃ ἤκουσα παρὰ τοῦ πατρός μου ἐγνώρισα* ὑμῖν.

3. Ἀπεκρίθησαν καὶ εἶπαν αὐτῷ, Ὁ πατὴρ ἡμῶν Ἀβραάμ ἐστιν. λέγει αὐτοῖς ὁ Ἰησοῦς, Εἰ τέκνα τοῦ Ἀβραάμ ἐστε, τὰ ἔργα τοῦ Ἀβραὰμ ἐποιεῖτε·

4. νῦν δὲ ζητεῖτέ με ἀποκτεῖναι,³ ἄνθρωπον ὃς τὴν ἀλήθειαν ὑμῖν λελάληκα ἣν ἤκουσα παρὰ τοῦ θεοῦ· τοῦτο Ἀβραὰμ οὐκ ἐποίησεν.

5. ὑμεῖς ποιεῖτε τὰ ἔργα τοῦ πατρὸς ὑμῶν. εἶπαν [οὖν] αὐτῷ, Ἡμεῖς ἐκ πορνείας* οὐ γεγεννήμεθα· ἕνα πατέρα ἔχομεν τὸν θεόν.

6. εἶπεν αὐτοῖς ὁ Ἰησοῦς, Εἰ ὁ θεὸς πατὴρ ὑμῶν ἦν, ἠγαπᾶτε ἂν ἐμέ, ἐγὼ γὰρ ἐκ τοῦ θεοῦ ἐξῆλθον καὶ ἥκω·* οὐδὲ γὰρ ἀπ᾽ ἐμαυτοῦ ἐλήλυθα, ἀλλ᾽ ἐκεῖνός με ἀπέστειλεν.

7. ὁ γὰρ πᾶς νόμος ἐν ἑνὶ λόγῳ πεπλήρωται, ἐν τῷ Ἀγαπήσεις τὸν πλησίον* σου ὡς σεαυτόν.

8. ὁ πιστὸς ἐν ἐλαχίστῳ καὶ ἐν πολλῷ πιστός ἐστιν, καὶ ὁ ἐν ἐλαχίστῳ ἄδικος* καὶ ἐν πολλῷ ἄδικός ἐστιν.

9. μακάριοι οἱ καθαροὶ* τῇ καρδίᾳ, ὅτι αὐτοὶ τὸν θεὸν ὄψονται.

10. καὶ ἡμεῖς μάρτυρες πάντων ὧν ἐποίησεν ἔν τε τῇ χώρᾳ* τῶν Ἰουδαίων καὶ Ἰερουσαλήμ.*

11. μακάριοι οἱ εἰρηνοποιοί,* ὅτι αὐτοὶ υἱοὶ θεοῦ κληθήσονται.

12. Ἀλλ᾽ ἐρεῖ τις, Σὺ πίστιν ἔχεις κἀγὼ ἔργα ἔχω.

13. σὺ πιστεύεις ὅτι εἷς θεός ἐστιν; καλῶς ποιεῖς· καὶ τὰ δαιμόνια πιστεύουσιν καὶ φρίσσουσιν*.

14. Ἀβραὰμ ὁ πατὴρ ἡμῶν οὐκ ἐξ ἔργων ἐδικαιώθη;

15. εἰ δέ τις ἀγαπᾷ τὸν θεόν, οὗτος ἔγνωσται ὑπ᾽ αὐτοῦ.

16. εἰ οὖν Δαυὶδ καλεῖ αὐτὸν κύριον, πῶς υἱὸς αὐτοῦ ἐστιν;

17. διὸ* ἐκλήθη ὁ ἀγρὸς* ἐκεῖνος Ἀγρὸς Αἵματος ἕως τῆς σήμερον.

18. Ἦν δὲ ἄνθρωπος ἐκ τῶν Φαρισαίων, Νικόδημος ὄνομα αὐτῷ, ἄρχων τῶν Ἰουδαίων.

---

³με is the direct object of the aorist active infinitive of ἀποκτείνω = "to kill."

CHAPTER 16

-μι VERBS

All the verbs that have been considered except the irregular verb εἰμί have belonged to the -ω conjugation. These regularly use the variable vowels o and ε as couplers. Now, the second class of Greek verbs needs to be learned, the -μι verbs. These are so named because the first person singular present active indicative has that ending.

-μι verbs have peculiar patterns in the present and imperfect tenses, all voices and moods, and in the aorist tenses, active and middle voices. In the second and fourth through sixth principal parts and the tenses built upon these parts the verbs follow patterns already encountered in -ω verbs. During the Koine period, the -μι verbs were giving way altogether to -ω verbs in the language. Thus, when one encounters a verb form that has an -ω conjugational ending, but is on a stem that has been introduced as a -μι verb, do not be surprised. Such simply reflects the gradual demise of the -μι verbs as a distinct class. Study the following principal parts, carefully noting the elements that are familiar from the previous chapters.

Vocabulary

Second Declension Adjective

διάβολος, -ον   slanderous; as a noun: the slanderer, the devil (cf. diabolical)

Verbs

ἰδού   See! Behold!

-μι Verbs

PRESENT A.	FUTURE A.	AORIST A.	PERFECT A.	PERFECT M./P.	AORIST P.
ἀπόλλυμι	ἀπολέσω	ἀπώλεσα	ἀπόλωλα		

ἀπολῶ [liquid pattern; cf. βαλῶ page 121]
Act.: I ruin, destroy, lose; Mid./Pass.: I perish, die, am ruined

ἀφίημι	ἀφήσω	ἀφῆκα	———	ἀφεῖμαι	ἀφέθην

I send away, cancel, pardon, leave, forgive

PRESENT A.	FUTURE A.	AORIST A.	PERFECT A.	PERFECT M./P.	AORIST P.
δείκνυμι δεικνύω I show	δείξω	ἔδειξα	— — —	— — —	ἐδείχθην
δίδωμι I give, yield, hand over, give up	δώσω	ἔδωκα	δέδωκα	δέδομαι	ἐδόθην

ἀποδίδωμι: I give away, pay, return, give back
παραδίδωμι: I hand over, deliver, pass on, hand down

ἵστημι	στήσω	ἔστησα ἔστην	ἔστηκα	— — —	ἐστάθην

Transitive (present, imperfect, future, 1 aorist active): I put, place, set
Intransitive (2 aorist, perfect, pluperfect active, future mid./pass., 1 aor. pass.): I stand, appear, stand still (see comments on page 129)
ἀνίστημι: I raise, raise up; rise, stand up
παρίστημι: I place beside, present, offer; stand

τίθημι I put, place, lay	θήσω	ἔθηκα	τέθεικα	τέθειμαι	ἐτέθην

ἐπιτίθημι: I lay upon, put upon

φημί: I say, affirm. Three forms occur in the *GNT*: φησίν, 3 singular and φασίν, 3 plural present active indicative (both are enclitic); ἔφη, 3 singular second aorist active indicative.

Conjugation of -μι Verbs

Second and Fourth Through Sixth Principal Parts

To conjugate the tenses of the second and fourth through sixth principal parts one simply uses the endings employed in the -ω conjugation and the principal parts. Thus, one has future active: στήσω, στήσεις, στήσει, etc.; perfect active: τέθεικα, τέθεικας, τέθεικε, etc.; aorist passive: ἐδόθην, ἐδόθης, ἐδόθη, etc.

First Principal Part

Present active indicative. Three novel things should be noted:
(1) The endings.

	Singular	Plural
1.	-μι	-μεν
2.	-ς	-τε
3.	-σι	-ασι

The singular forms and, to a lesser degree, the third plural are distinct from -ω verbs.

(2) The stem. The present stem is best thought of as not what one sees in first person singular, but, rather, the form that occurs in first person

plural. The two forms are the same except for a long/short vowel variation. The short vowel form functions as the stem most of the time.

(3) The coupler letters. There are none. Endings are coupled directly to the stems, with the final vowel of the stems lengthening only in the singular. Moreover, the stems have an unusual "reduplication" of the initial consonant or lengthening of the initial vowel of the stem. The prefixed consonant is attached to the stem by the vowel ι. This strange reduplication is a sure indication of the present stem of a -μι verb. Rely upon it and your parsing task will be greatly simplified. There follows the conjugation of the present active of δίδωμι ("I give"), τίθημι ("I put"), and ἵστημι ("I place"). Note that the third person plural allows two vowels in succession to occur in διδόασι and τιθέασι, but contracts them in ἱστᾶσι. The circumflex is an indication that contraction has occurred.

Singular

1.	δίδωμι	τίθημι	ἵστημι
2.	δίδως	τίθης	ἵστης
3.	δίδωσι	τίθησι	ἵστησι

Plural

1.	δίδομεν	τίθεμεν	ἵσταμεν
2.	δίδοτε	τίθετε	ἵστατε
3.	διδόασι	τιθέασι	ἱστᾶσι

Present middle/passive. This tense uses the primary middle endings. Like the perfect middle/passive, it neither uses a connecting variable vowel nor does it contract the second person singular.

Singular

1.	δίδομαι	τίθεμαι	ἵσταμαι
2.	δίδοσαι	τίθεσαι	ἵστασαι
3.	δίδοται	τίθεται	ἵσταται

Plural

1.	διδόμεθα	τιθέμεθα	ἱστάμεθα
2.	δίδοσθε	τίθεσθε	ἵστασθε
3.	δίδονται	τίθενται	ἵστανται

Imperfect active indicative. This tense uses the secondary active endings, but the stems show variations. The augment is regular. The stem is that of the first principal part, but the vowel of the stem's last syllable is changed in the singular through contractions that are sometimes expected and sometimes inexplicable. Still, identification is relatively straightforward because the imperfect manifests the reduplicated present stem and uses the familiar secondary active endings (N.B. the third person plural uses the alternate -σαν, rather than -ν).

IMPERFECT ACTIVE INDICATIVE

Singular

1.	ἐδίδουν	ἐτίθην	ἵστην
2.	ἐδίδους	ἐτίθεις	ἵστης
3.	ἐδίδου	ἐτίθει	ἵστη

Plural

1.	ἐδίδομεν	ἐτίθεμεν	ἵσταμεν
2.	ἐδίδοτε	ἐτίθετε	ἵστατε
3.	ἐδίδοσαν	ἐτίθεσαν	ἵστασαν

Imperfect middle/passive. The secondary middle endings are attached to the augmented stem of the first principal part without using variable vowels and without contracting second person singular—just like the pluperfect middle/passive.

Singular

1.	ἐδιδόμην	ἐτιθέμην	ἱστάμην
2.	ἐδίδοσο	ἐτίθεσο	ἵστασο
3.	ἐδίδοτο	ἐτίθετο	ἵστατο

Plural

1.	ἐδιδόμεθα	ἐτιθέμεθα	ἱστάμεθα
2.	ἐδίδοσθε	ἐτίθεσθε	ἵστασθε
3.	ἐδίδοντο	ἐτίθεντο	ἵσταντο

Third Principal Part

Aorist active tense. The aorist tense active voice is quite predictable so long as the third principal part is carefully memorized. The verbs δίδωμι and τίθημι use the secondary active endings of the -ω conjugation; however, rather than the tense stem ending in σ, it ends in κ. A similar pattern involving the deletion of σ was observed in the aorist stems of liquid verbs (e.g., ἔκρινα, ἔμεινα). Note in the following aorist paradigms that both -μι verbs use the lengthened vowel in the second syllable of the stem (pres.:

διδο-, τιθε-; aor.: εδω-, εθη-). Because the stems do not have reduplication, there should be no confusion with the perfect tenses.

FIRST AORIST ACTIVE

Singular	Plural	Singular	Plural
1. ἔδωκα	ἐδώκαμεν	ἔθηκα	ἐθήκαμεν
2. ἔδωκας	ἐδώκατε	ἔθηκας	ἐθήκατε
3. ἔδωκε(ν)	ἔδωκαν	ἔθηκε(ν)	ἔθηκαν

ἵστημι merits individual attention in the aorist tense active voice because it has both a first and a second aorist principal part. The first aorist form ἔστησα (conjugated as any other first aorist) is transitive; i.e., it takes a direct object. It means "I caused _____ to stand; I set _____"; etc. The second aorist form ἔστην (the stem ἐστη- is conjugated exactly like a second aorist passive) is intransitive; i.e., it does not take a direct object. It means "I stood; I stood firm."

Aorist middle tense. Of the three verbs just considered, only τίθημι occurs in this tense. It conjugates precisely as a second aorist middle of the -ω conjugation (cf. ἠγαγόμην on page 92). Observe that the difference between the imperfect middle/passive and this tense is—of course—the stem: ἐτιθε- and ἐθε-.

Singular	Plural
1. ἐθέμην	ἐθέμεθα
2. ἔθου (ἔθε + σο)	ἔθεσθε
3. ἔθετο	ἔθεντο

ἀφίημι, ἀπόλλυμι, δείκνυμι

These three verbs are of sufficient frequency in the *GNT* and importance to merit particular comment about their peculiarities. The rule previously stated, learn the principal parts, is especially appropriate in their cases. If the student will carefully analyze the form to be parsed so as to identify the principal parts being used, then identify the endings as to primary active, secondary active, etc., the task of parsing will be tolerable.

ἀφίημι: I cancel

In the present tense ἀφίημι occurs with a mixture of -μι and -ω verb endings. The stem ἱε- has been obscured in the Koine period. Those forms that are pertinent for study of the *GNT* follow.

	Present A.	Present M./P.	Imperfect A.

Singular

1. ἀφίημι   ἀφίεμαι
2. ἀφεῖς
3. ἀφίησι(ν)   ἀφίεται   ἤφιε

Plural

1. ἀφίομεν
2. ἀφίετε
3. ἀφίουσι(ν)   or   ἀφίονται
                 ἀφίενται [the classical Greek form which is consistent with the present stem ἱε-]

In addition to these forms built upon the first principal part the following occur: the future active (a regular form: ἀφήσω); the first aorist (ἀφῆκα [but, like ἔθηκα, having a κ instead of a σ]); a perfect passive (only the third plural form ἀφέωνται); and the aorist and future passives (ἀφέθην[1] and ἀφεθήσομαι).

ἀπόλλυμι: I ruin

Although ἀπόλλυμι is a -μι verb, no -μι forms occur in the present active tense. In fact, few forms of the various indicative mood tenses are used and only those forms that do occur will be given. Memorize the following, paying careful attention to the stem changes and the use of familiar primary and secondary endings.

Present Active 3 Singular: ἀπολλύει

Present Middle/Passive

Singular	*Plural*
1. ἀπόλλυμαι	ἀπολλύμεθα
2. ———	———
3. ἀπόλλυται	ἀπόλλυνται

Imperfect Middle/Passive 3 Plural: ἀπώλλυντο

Future Active Singular

1. ἀπολῶ   3. ἀπολέσει

---

[1]The stem in the classical period was ἀφείθην; then, the correctly unaugmented future passive would be as shown. In the *GNT* this correct aorist stem is lacking.

Future Middle

1. — — —   — — —
2. — — —   ἀπολεῖσθε
3. ἀπολεῖται   ἀπολοῦνται

First Aorist Active Singular

1. ἀπώλεσα   3. ἀπώλεσε(ν)

First Aorist Middle

Singular   *Plural*
3. ἀπώλετο   3. ἀπώλοντο

Perfect Active: ἀπόλωλα occurs only in a participial form as ἀπολωλός and ἀπολωλότα.

δείκνυμι: *I show*

Even more sketchy is the verb δείκνυμι. In the indicative mood one finds the following examples.

Present Active Singular

1. δείκνυμι   2. δεικνύεις   3. δείκνυσι(ν)

Future Active Singular

1. δείξω   3. δείξει

First Aorist Active Singular

1. ἔδειξα   3. ἔδειξε(ν)

The perfect tenses are not used, nor is the aorist passive except in a participial form δειχθέντα, from ἐδείχθην).

Exercises

Translate the following sentences.

1. οὗτος ἔσται μέγας καὶ υἱὸς ὑψίστου* κληθήσεται, καὶ δώσει αὐτῷ κύριος ὁ θεὸς τὸν θρόνον Δαυὶδ τοῦ πατρὸς αὐτοῦ.
2. καὶ βασιλεύσει* ἐπὶ τὸν οἶκον Ἰακὼβ εἰς τοὺς αἰῶνας, καὶ τῆς βασιλείας αὐτοῦ οὐκ ἔσται τέλος.

3. οὐδὲ γὰρ ὁ πατὴρ κρίνει οὐδένα,² ἀλλὰ τὴν κρίσιν πᾶσαν δέδωκεν τῷ υἱῷ.

4. εἶπεν οὖν αὐτοῖς ὁ Ἰησοῦς, Ἀμὴν ἀμὴν λέγω ὑμῖν, οὐ Μωϋσῆς δέδωκεν ὑμῖν τὸν ἄρτον ἐκ τοῦ οὐρανοῦ, ἀλλ᾽ ὁ πατήρ μου δίδωσιν ὑμῖν τὸν ἄρτον ἐκ τοῦ οὐρανοῦ τὸν ἀληθινόν.*

5. καὶ εἶπεν, Ποῦ* τεθείκατε αὐτόν;

6. τὸ ἔθνος τοῦτο σημεῖον ζητεῖ, καὶ σημεῖον οὐ δοθήσεται αὐτῷ εἰ μὴ τὸ σημεῖον Ἰωνᾶ.*

7. Ἤγαγον δὲ αὐτοὺς καὶ ἔστησαν ἐν τῷ συνεδρίῳ.* καὶ ἐπηρώτησεν αὐτοὺς ὁ ἀρχιερεύς.

8. καὶ ἔλεγε Ἰδοὺ πεπληρώκατε τὴν Ἰερουσαλὴμ* τῆς διδαχῆς ὑμῶν, καὶ βούλεσθε ἐπαγαγεῖν [aor. inf. of ἐπάγω*] ἐφ᾽ ἡμᾶς τὸ αἷμα τοῦ ἀνθρώπου τούτου.

9. ἔφη αὐτῷ ὁ Ἰησοῦς, Πάλιν γέγραπται, Οὐκ ἐκπειράσεις* κύριον τὸν θεόν σου.

10. Πάλιν παραλαμβάνει αὐτὸν ὁ διάβολος* εἰς ὄρος ὑψηλὸν* λίαν,* καὶ δείκνυσιν αὐτῷ πάσας τὰς βασιλείας τοῦ κόσμου καὶ τὴν δόξαν αὐτῶν.

11. καὶ λέγει αὐτῷ, Ταῦτά σοι πάντα δώσω.

12. καὶ ὅτε ἐστήκατε καὶ προσεύχεσθε, ἀφήσετε εἴ τι ἔχετε κατά τινος, ἀφήσει καὶ ὑμῖν ὁ πατὴρ ὑμῶν ἐν τοῖς οὐρανοῖς.

13. ὅτε ἤμην μετ᾽ αὐτῶν ἐγὼ ἐτήρουν αὐτοὺς ἐν τῷ ὀνόματί σου ᾧ δέδωκάς μοι, καὶ ἐφύλαξα, καὶ οὐδεὶς ἐξ αὐτῶν ἀπώλετο εἰ μὴ* ὁ υἱὸς τῆς ἀπωλείας.*

14. ὑμεῖς ἐστε οἱ υἱοὶ τῶν προφητῶν καὶ τῆς διαθήκης* ἧς διέθετο* ὁ θεὸς πρὸς τοὺς πατέρας ὑμῶν.

15. εἶπεν* δὲ πρὸς Ἀβραάμ, Καὶ ἐν τῷ σπέρματί σου ἐνευλογηθήσονται* πᾶσαι αἱ πατριαὶ* τῆς γῆς.

16. Ἀλλὰ ἐρεῖ τις, Πῶς ἐγείρονται οἱ νεκροί;

17. ὁ δὲ θεὸς δίδωσιν αὐτῷ σῶμα καθὼς ἠθέλησεν, καὶ ἑκάστῳ τῶν σπερμάτων ἴδιον σῶμα.

---

²Greek often uses double negatives where English idiom uses one; so, translate "For the Father judges no one."

CHAPTER 17

PARTICIPLES: THEIR FORMATION

A knowledge of participles stands on the same plane as nouns and verbs in mastering the Greek language. Without thoroughly understanding each of these areas the student will not progress to effective exegesis of the biblical texts. Two of the areas are rather well in hand now. Here the third is introduced.

Vocabulary

More -εω Contract Verbs

αἰτέω	I ask, ask for, request
ἀκολουθέω	I follow, accompany
ἀσθενέω	I am weak, am sick
βλασφημέω	I blaspheme, revile
δέω	I bind, tie
διακονέω	I wait upon, serve, care for (cf. diaconal)
δοκέω	Transitive: I think, believe
	Intransitive: I seem
ἐλεέω	I have mercy, pity
εὐλογέω	I bless, praise, speak well of (cf. eulogize)
εὐχαριστέω	I give thanks (cf. Eucharist)
θεωρέω	I behold, look at, perceive (cf. theorize)
κατοικέω	I inhabit, dwell, live
κρατέω	I hold, take into my possession, grasp
μαρτυρέω	I bear witness, confirm, testify (cf. martyr)
μετανοέω	I change my mind, repent
μισέω	I hate, abhor (cf. misogamy)
οἰκοδομέω	I build, edify
περιπατέω	I walk around, go about, walk (cf. peripatetic)
προσκυνέω	I worship, prostrate myself before
φιλέω	I love, like [only 25 times, but common to John] (cf. Philadelphia)

φοβέομαι   I am afraid, fear, am frightened [only passive
                            forms occur in the *GNT*] (cf. phobia)
φωνέω   I call, cry out, summon (cf. phonetic)

Participles: A Definition

A Greek participle is a verbal adjective. Rarely is it the main verb of an
independent sentence. It has structural and functional qualities of both a
verb and an adjective. It is a verb stem to which nominal endings are
suffixed. It may occur with or without the article. Adjectival aspects of the
participle are manifested in the endings which, of course, exhibit case,
number, and gender. Like an adjective, the word that the participle
modifies determines what the case, number, and gender will be. Given its
nominal character the participle may function as subject, object, or
modifier.

Examples of English participles in the present tense are "walking,"
"falling," "appearing." So, "He ascertained from them the time of the
appearing star" (Mt. 2:7). "Walked," "fallen," "divided" are past participles.
Consider "Every kingdom *divided* against itself is being laid waste"
(Mt. 12:25). "And when he *laid* his hands on him, he said, 'Brother Saul'"
(Acts 9:17).

Observe carefully that forms of the participles vary. *-ing*, *-en*, or *-ed* are
formational indicators, but one encounters irregular forms that can only be
identified by their context. "Laid," for example, in Mt. 12:25 is a part of
the main verb; in Acts 9:17 it is a participle in an adverbial clause.[1]

Like a verb, the participle has tense. It occurs in the present ("the new
man which *is being renewed*"; Col. 3:10), the aorist ("*having put on* the
new man"; Col. 3:10), and the perfect tenses ("Jesus, the one who *has been
crucified*"; Mt. 28:5). It even occurs—though rarely—in the future: ("the
one who *will betray* him"; Jn. 6:64). It has voice: the active ("sons of the
living God"; Rom. 9:26), the middle ("*having stripped off* the old man";
Col. 3:9), and the passive ("the one who *has* not *been loved*"; Rom. 9:25b).
It has no mood. Finally, as a verb, the participle may have both a subject
("therefore, when *many* heard"; Jn. 6:60) and/or an object ("having said
these things"; Jn. 7:9), as well as other modifiers.

Formation of Participles

Nominal Endings

The participles use two sets of endings. The following tables will be quite
familiar to you. Rejoice.

---

[1]English grammarians would label "laid" in both contexts as a participle, but in Matthew 12
it is used with auxiliaries to form the main tense; its Greek counterpart ἐρημοῦται is a present
passive indicative, not a participle.

TABLE 1

M.	F.	N.
	Singular	

	M.	F.	N.	
N.	-ν (pres.; 2 aor. act.)	-σα	-ν	(pft. = -ς)
	-ς (all other tenses)			
G.	-ντος	-σης	-ντος	
D.	-ντι	-ση	-ντι	
A.	-ντα	-σαν	-ν	(pft. = -ς)

Plural

	M.	F.	N.
N.	-ντες	-σαι	-ντα
G.	-ντων	-σων	-ντων
D.	-σι	-σαις	-σι
A.	-ντας	-σας	-ντα

TABLE 2

	M.	F.	N.
		Singular	

	M.	F.	N.
N.	-ος	-η	-ον
G.	-ου	-ης	-ου
D.	-ῳ	-η	-ῳ
A.	-ον	-ην	-ον

Plural

	M.	F.	N.
N.	-οι	-αι	-α
G.	-ων	-ων	-ων
D.	-οις	-αις	-οις
A.	-ους	-ας	-α

TABLE 1 provides the endings for the following tenses:[2]

1. Present active

2. First aorist active

3. Second aorist active

4. First aorist passive

5. Second aorist passive

---

[2]The perfect tense active voice masculine and neuter basically uses these endings, but it will delete the -ν of -ντος, -ντι, etc. Feminine will change from the δόξα to καρδία type and not use the σ. Because it may confuse the student to include this tense in TABLE 1 it is here—with reservation—relegated to a footnote.

TABLE 2 gives the endings of these tenses:

1. Present middle and passive

2. First aorist middle

3. Second aorist middle

4. Perfect middle and passive

Formation of Present Participles

Stem. The present tense stem is used in all voices. Thus, the kind of action of this tense is linear or progressive, as in the indicative mood.

Coupling vowels. In the active voice the coupling variable vowels are o in the masculine and neuter (so λυ + o) and ου in the feminine (so λυ + ου-). However, in the masculine nominative the vowel is ω, not o (so λυ + ω-). In the middle and passive voices the coupler and voice indicator is -ομεν (so λυ + ομεν-).

Paradigms. Study the following charts, carefully noting the stem, the coupling vowel(s), and the ending of each form. You will recognize that the forms of the present participle are demanding only a new configuration of old endings (specifically, those used with ἄρχων and θάλασσα).

PRESENT ACTIVE: λύων, λύουσα, λῦον: loosing

	M.	F.	N.

Singular

	M.	F.	N.
N.	λύων	λύουσα	λῦον
G.	λύοντος	λυούσης	λύοντος
D.	λύοντι	λυούσῃ	λύοντι
A.	λύοντα	λύουσαν	λῦον

Plural

	M.	F.	N.
N.	λύοντες	λύουσαι	λύοντα
G.	λυόντων	λυουσῶν	λυόντων
D.	λύουσι(ν)	λυούσαις	λύουσι(ν)
A.	λύοντας	λυούσας	λύοντα

Note that accents of the active voice participles (whatever tense) follow the typical pattern for an adjective: Where the accent falls in the nominative singular, there it stays unless the ultima requires a shift. Genitive plural feminine accents the ultima like a noun of the first declension.

PRESENT MIDDLE/PASSIVE: λυόμενος, λυομένη, λυόμενον:
loosing in one's interest; being loosed

	M.	F.	N.

Singular

	M.	F.	N.
N.	λυόμενος	λυομένη	λυόμενον
G.	λυομένου	λυομένης	λυομένου
D.	λυομένῳ	λυομένῃ	λυομένῳ
A.	λυόμενον	λυομένην	λυόμενον

Plural

	M.	F.	N.
N.	λυόμενοι	λυόμεναι	λυόμενα
G.	λυομένων	λυομένων	λυομένων
D.	λυομένοις	λυομέναις	λυομένοις
A.	λυομένους	λυομένας	λυόμενα

Accents of middle/passive participles are like those of first and second declension adjectives, even in the feminine genitive plural. Hence, the -ων is not accented.

The Present Participle of εἰμί: "being"

Compare this participle's declension with that of λύων, the present active participle given above.

	M.	F.	N.

Singular

	M.	F.	N.
N.	ὤν	οὖσα	ὄν
G.	ὄντος	οὔσης	ὄντος
D.	ὄντι	οὔσῃ	ὄντι
A.	ὄντα	οὖσαν	ὄν

Plural

	M.	F.	N.
N.	ὄντες	οὖσαι	ὄντα
G.	ὄντων	οὐσῶν	ὄντων
D.	οὖσι(ν)	οὔσαις	οὖσι(ν)
A.	ὄντας	οὔσας	ὄντα

Formation of Aorist Participles

Stem. The stem is the first or second aorist principal part of the word in question. Obviously, this means that not every verb will have a first and a second aorist participle. Never form an aorist participle on any other stems than the third or sixth principal parts.

The above instruction should evoke the inference (a valid one): The aorist participle expresses unitary kind of action. The various aspects of the *Aktionsart* will be explored subsequently, but this fundamental notion will, indeed, continue in force.

The aorist tense participle has no augment. An augmented third principal part whose unaugmented verb stem begins with a consonant will delete the prefixed ε (e.g., ἔβλεψα becomes βλεψα); one beginning with a vowel returns the lengthened form to the short form (e.g., εἶδον becomes ἰδον; ἦλθον becomes ἐλθον; ἤχθην becomes ἀχθην). Remember, these changes are due to the fact that augment does not occur except in the indicative mood.

The coupling letter(s). These letters vary with the tenses and are critical factors in identifying the voices.

First aorist active:	-α
First aorist middle	-αμεν
First aorist passive	-ει or -ε
Second aorist active:	-ω, -ο, or -ου (as in present tense participles)
Second aorist middle:	-ομεν
Second aorist passive:	-ει or -ε

Paradigms. Compare the first aorist active participles' endings with those of πᾶς, πᾶσα, πᾶν.

FIRST AORIST ACTIVE: βλέψας, βλέψασα, βλέψαν:
having seen

	M.	F.	N.
		Singular	
N.	βλέψας	βλέψασα	βλέψαν
G.	βλέψαντος	βλεψάσης	βλέψαντος
D.	βλέψαντι	βλεψάσῃ	βλέψαντι
A.	βλέψαντα	βλέψασαν	βλέψαν
		Plural	
N.	βλέψαντες	βλέψασαι	βλέψαντα
G.	βλεψάντων	βλεψασῶν	βλεψάντων
D.	βλέψασι(ν)	βλεψάσαις	βλέψασι(ν)
A.	βλέψαντας	βλεψάσας	βλέψαντα

FIRST AORIST MIDDLE: βλεψάμενος, βλεψαμένη, βλεψάμενον:
having seen in one's interest

	M.	F.	N.

Singular

	M.	F.	N.
N.	βλεψάμενος	βλεψαμένη	βλεψάμενον
G.	βλεψαμένου	βλεψαμένης	βλεψαμένου
D.	βλεψαμένῳ	βλεψαμένῃ	βλεψαμένῳ
A.	βλεψάμενον	βλεψαμένην	βλεψάμενον

Plural

	M.	F.	N.
N.	βλεψάμενοι	βλεψάμεναι	βλεψάμενα
G.	βλεψαμένων	βλεψαμένων	βλεψαμένων
D.	βλεψαμένοις	βλεψαμέναις	βλεψαμένοις
A.	βλεψαμένους	βλεψαμένας	βλεψάμενα

Because βλέπω has no aorist passive (ὁράω does duty for that tense), ὁράω will be used to illustrate the formation of the first aorist passive tense participle, although that formation does not occur in the *GNT*.

FIRST AORIST PASSIVE: ὀφθείς, ὀφθεῖσα, ὀφθέν:
having been seen

	M.	F.	N.

Singular

	M.	F.	N.
N.	ὀφθείς	ὀφθεῖσα	ὀφθέν
G.	ὀφθέντος	ὀφθείσης	ὀφθέντος
D.	ὀφθέντι	ὀφθείσῃ	ὀφθέντι
A.	ὀφθέντα	ὀφθεῖσαν	ὀφθέν

Plural

	M.	F.	N.
N.	ὀφθέντες	ὀφθεῖσαι	ὀφθέντα
G.	ὀφθέντων	ὀφθεισῶν	ὀφθέντων
D.	ὀφθεῖσι(ν)	ὀφθείσαις	ὀφθεῖσι(ν)
A.	ὀφθέντας	ὀφθείσας	ὀφθέντα

The second aorist tense active and middle voices of the participle, like those tenses of the indicative mood, use the stem of the aorist active (e.g., ἀγαγ-), but the endings of the present tense (i.e., -ων, -ουσα, -ον; -μενος, -μενη, -μενον, etc.). They will look just like a present tense formation except for the stem and the accent (in the active voice). Thus, one will have second aorist active:

Singular

N.	ἀγαγών	ἀγαγοῦσα	ἀγαγόν
G.	ἀγαγόντος	ἀγαγούσης	ἀγαγόντος
		etc.	

Second aorist middle follows the pattern.

Singular

N.	ἀγαγόμενος	ἀγαγομένη	ἀγαγόμενον
G.	ἀγαγομένου	ἀγαγομένης	ἀγαγομένου
		etc.	

The second aorist passive participle is formed precisely as the first aorist, but upon the second aorist stem. It will, then, have no θ. Simply substitute σπαρ- (from ἐσπάρην: "having been sown") in the paradigm on page 139 for the second aorist passive participle, e.g.,

Singular

N.	σπαρείς	σπαρεῖσα	σπαρέν
G.	σπαρέντος	σπαρείσης	σπαρέντος
		etc.	

Formation of Perfect Participles

As with the previous tenses, the kind of action expressed by the perfect participle corresponds to that of the perfect tense in the indicative mood.

Active voice stems. The fourth principal part, the perfect active, will be used; so, from λέλυκα form λελυκ-.

Coupling letters. To the isolated stem one adds ο for the masculine and neuter, υι for the feminine, except in the nominative masculine, where ω occurs: λελυκω/ο- (masculine), λελυκυι- (feminine), and λελυκο- (neuter).

Middle/passive voice stems. Perfect middle and passive participles are identical in form. As was the case in the indicative mood, the endings are attached directly to the stem of the fifth principal part. The indicator for the middle/passive voice is the same as in the present and aorist tenses: -μεν-, e.g., λελυμεν-, ἡγιασμεν-, εὑρημεν-. Everywhere, the accent falls on the penult.

Paradigms. The endings of the active voice closely parallel those of πᾶς, ὥρα, πᾶν, but with the following modifications:

1. the ν of -ντος, -ντι, etc. is deleted throughout;
2. the -ν of πᾶν (neuter nominative and accusative singular) is changed to -ς.

The endings of the middle/passive are identical to the present middle/passive participle: λελυμένος, λελυμένη, λελυμένον. Watch the stem in order to discriminate between the tenses.

PERFECT ACTIVE PARTICIPLE: λελυκώς, λελυκυῖα, λελυκός:
having loosed and the effect continues

	M.	F.	N.
		Singular	
N.	λελυκώς	λελυκυῖα³	λελυκός
G.	λελυκότος	λελυκυίας	λελυκότος
D.	λελυκότι	λελυκυίᾳ	λελυκότι
A.	λελυκότα	λελυκυῖαν	λελυκός
		Plural	
N.	λελυκότες	λελυκυῖαι	λελυκότα
G.	λελυκότων	λελυκυιῶν	λελυκότων
D.	λελυκόσι(ν)	λελυκυίαις	λελυκόσι(ν)
A.	λελυκότας	λελυκυίας	λελυκότα

Present Tense Participles: Contract Verbs

These verbs use the same endings as regular verbs, but follow the coupling patterns that were introduced in Chapter 15. Review the contraction chart of page 120 for the vowel formations. A synopsis of the paradigms follows.

PRESENT ACTIVE:

ποιέω: I do, make

	M.	F.	N.
Sg.N.	ποιῶν	ποιοῦσα	ποιοῦν
	(ποιέων)	(ποιέουσα)	(ποιέον)
G.	ποιοῦντος	ποιούσης	ποιοῦντος
	(ποιέοντος)	(ποιεούσης)	(ποιέοντος)

---

³The final α is considered short for purposes of accentuation, resulting in -υῖα.

ὁράω: I see

Sg.N.	ὁρῶν	ὁρῶσα	ὁρῶν
	(ὁράων)	(ὁράουσα)	(ὁράον)
G.	ὁρῶντος	ὁρώσης	ὁρῶντος
	(ὁράοντος)	(ὁραούσης)	(ὁράοντος)

σταυρόω: I crucify

Sg.N.	σταυρῶν	σταυροῦσα	σταυροῦν
	(σταυρόων)	(σταυρόουσα)	(σταυρόον)
G.	σταυροῦντος	σταυρούσης	σταυροῦντος
	(σταυρόοντος)	(σταυροούσης)	(σταυρόοντος)

PRESENT MIDDLE/PASSIVE

Sg.N.	ποιούμενος	ποιουμένη	ποιούμενον
Sg.N.	ὁρώμενος	ὁρωμένη	ὁρώμενον
Sg.N.	σταυρούμενος	σταυρουμένη	σταυρούμενον

Aorist Tense Participles of Liquid Verbs

Liquid verbs pose no problems so long as one remembers that they do not, even when they are first aorists, use the typical sign of the aorist tense: σ. Review the paradigm on page 122 for ἔμεινα. The aorist participle stem will have no augment (as always). It uses, if first aorist, the endings used with βλέψας: -ας, -ασα, -αν, etc. If a second aorist (e.g., ἔβαλον), isolate the tense stem, remove any augment, and use the present participial endings as with ἀγαγῶν (cf. page 140). A synopsis of the first and second aorist participles follows.

FIRST AORIST ACTIVE: μείνας: having remained

	M.	F.	N.
Sg.N.	μείνας	μείνασα	μεῖναν
G.	μείναντος	μεινάσης	μείναντος

FIRST AORIST MIDDLE: μεινάμενος:
having remained in one's own interest

Sg.N.	μεινάμενος	μειναμένη	μεινάμενον
G.	μειναμένου	μειναμένης	μειναμένου

SECOND AORIST ACTIVE: βαλών: having thrown

Sg.N.	βαλών	βαλοῦσα	βαλόν
G.	βαλόντος	βαλούσης	βαλόντος

SECOND AORIST MIDDLE: βαλόμενος:
having thrown in one's own interest

| Sg.N. | βαλόμενος | βαλομένη | βαλόμενον |
| G. | βαλομένου | βαλομένης | βαλομένου |

Present and Aorist Tense Participles: -μι Verbs

TABLES 1 and 2 presented earlier in the chapter continue to provide the endings. Identifying the stem of the verb continues to be the key to tense identification. After that task is completed, normal patterns are encountered. A synopsis of the verbs δίδωμι ("I give"), τίθημι ("I put"), and ἵστημι ("I stand") follows.

PRESENT PARTICIPLE: δίδωμι

	Active			Middle/Passive		
Sg.N.	διδούς	διδοῦσα	διδόν	διδόμενος,	-η,	-ον
G.	διδόντος	διδούσης	διδόντος	διδομένου,	-ης,	-ου

AORIST PARTICIPLE: δίδωμι

	Active			Middle/Passive		
Sg.N.	δούς	δοῦσα	δόν	— — —		
G.	δόντος	δούσης	δόντος			

The present tense of τίθημι looks as if it were an aorist passive—in terms of its ending -θεις, but it is not. Remember the -μι verb reduplication of the present tense and you will not err.

PRESENT PARTICIPLE: τίθημι

	Active			Middle/Passive		
Sg.N.	τιθείς	τιθεῖσα	τιθέν	τιθέμενος,	-η,	-ον
G.	τιθέντος	τιθείσης	τιθέντος	τιθεμένου,	-ης,	-ου

AORIST PARTICIPLE: τίθημι

	Active			Middle/Passive		
Sg.N.	θείς	θεῖσα	θέν	θέμενος,	-η,	-ον
G.	θέντος	θείσης	θέντος	θεμένου,	-ης,	-ου

PRESENT PARTICIPLE: ἵστημι

	Active			Middle/Passive		
Sg.N.	ἱστάς	ἱστᾶσα	ἱστάν	ἱστάμενος,	-η,	-ον
G.	ἱστάντος	ἱστάσης	ἱστάντος	ἱσταμένου,	-ης,	-ου

AORIST PARTICIPLE: ἵστημι

	Active			Middle/Passive
Sg.N.	στάς	στᾶσα	στάν	— — —
G.	στάντος	στάσης	στάντος	

Exercises

Parse the following (tense, voice, case, number, gender, and verb stem).

1. αἰτούμενος
2. σταυροῦντος
3. γεννῶσα
4. φάναντι
5. ἀποκτεινάσαις
6. ἀποστεῖλαν
7. βαλόντα
8. ἀναβαινομένους
9. ἀπαγγειλάσης
10. ἀναβεβηκότος
11. κεκριμένῳ
12. ἀπαγγελεῖσι(ν)
13. τιθέντα
14. ἱστάντων
15. δόντες
16. ἐστηκότων
17. δεδωκυίας
18. ἐληλυθότες
19. ἀγοράζουσιν
20. γνωσθέντα
21. κρατοῦντος
22. καλουμένῃ
23. πεποιηκόσιν
24. κρίναντος
25. ἀναστάντες

CHAPTER 18

FUNCTION OF PARTICIPLES:
ADJECTIVAL AND SUPPLEMENTARY

Vocabulary

Liquid Verb Stems in ρ

PRESENT A.	FUTURE A.	AORIST A.	PERFECT A.	PERFECT M/P.	AORIST P.
αἴρω	ἀρῶ	ἦρα	ἦρκα	ἦρμαι	ἤρθην
I lift, take or pick up, take away					
ἐγείρω	ἐγερῶ	ἤγειρα	———	ἐγήγερμαι	ἠγέρθην
I wake, raise or raise up, rise					
σπείρω	———	ἔσπειρα	———	———	ἐσπάρην
I sow, scatter					
φέρω	οἴσω	ἤνεγκα	-ενήνοχα [occurs only in compounds with prepositions]	———	ἠνέχθην
I bear, carry, bring					
προσφέρω: I bring (to), offer, present					
χαίρω	χαρήσομαι	———	———	———	ἐχάρην
I rejoice, am glad					

More Contract Verbs

ἀρνέομαι	I deny, repudiate
ἐπιτιμάω	I rebuke, reprove, warn
καυχάομαι	I boast, glory, pride oneself in
πλανάω	I lead astray, deceive, wander about

A Word About Translating Participles

Participles are one of the richest modes of expression in the Greek language because they carry both nominal and verbal significations. One cannot, therefore, find a simple, single word-to-word correlation between Greek and English to render all that is inherent to the Greek participle. For example, as seen in the previous chapter, a participle has tense, voice, case, number, and gender. What English term (N.B., singular) can carry all that significance? None. Therefore, do not be reluctant to have more English words in translation than in the Greek text. Use all the words and English grammatical structures needful to convey accurately to the reader everything that the Greek construction communicated to its original reader.

As an example, consider Mt. 26:25 where Judas, who betrayed Jesus, is referred to by the participle παραδιδοὺς, present active nominative singular masculine form. It would be quite inadequate to translate the term simply as "betraying" because the Greek form tells you additionally that the betrayer is a masculine, singular one and that one is the subject (nominative) of the clause. So, the translator adds for the English reader appropriate terms, e.g., "he who is betraying." A relative clause will often nicely convey the sense of the Greek participle when its adjectival aspect has the ascendancy (about which more will be said shortly).

This explanation may sound contradictory in terms of the translations provided with the paradigms of the last chapter. For simplicity's sake at the introductory level, an effort was made there to give no more than the simple verbal sense without any reflection of the adjectival value. In translating texts, however, all the data should be made known to the reader in lucid English idiom. Keeping these ideas in mind, we turn to a detailed analysis of the functions of the participle in its various tenses and cases.

Temporal Value

The participle itself is timeless; it does not have inherent time value. Nevertheless, one speaks of it as present, aorist, future, or perfect. It takes on temporal value in relation to the main verb of a given context. What is denoted by tense per se in participles is kind of action. The kinds of action are consistent with what has been found in each of the tenses which have been previously considered.

Present Tense Participles

Antecedent activity.   Romans 5:17b illustrates the present tense participle expressing action that is antecedent to the action of the main verb: "much more οἱ . . . λαμβάνοντες the abundance . . . shall reign." The participle is translated "the ones who are receiving [on-going activity]." This action is preceding that of the main verb "shall reign" [βασιλεύσουσιν].

Simultaneous activity.   The present tense participle may reflect action that is simultaneous with that of the main verb. Consider Rom. 6:13b: "but present yourselves to God as out of the dead ζῶντας," i.e., living at the time of the presentation.

Future activity. Robertson includes a category of present participles that are future oriented relative to the main verb.[1] Mark 13:26 and Mt. 24:46 are cited as illustrative. Each of these verses well demonstrates the present participle expressing action that is to occur in the future, a fact that is shown by the principal verb in each context. In Mk. 13:26, "They will see [ὄψονται] the Son of Man coming [ἐρχόμενον]," the future ὄψονται orients the action of the present participle ἐρχόμενον to a yet-to-be experienced time. Matthew 24:46, "Blessed is that servant whom his master will find [εὑρήσει] doing [ποιοῦντα] thus when he returns," derives its temporal perspective from εὑρήσει, a future; ποιοῦντα, a present participle, is future oriented by virtue of the main verb.

In each of the above examples the student might demur, suggesting instead that the participles are simply expressing time that is simultaneous with the main verb. There are grammarians who would agree. The unequivocal thing to note is that the time factor of each participle is determined by the main verb and in these contexts the temporal orientation is not present, but future.

Aorist Tense Participles

Antecedent activity. Most frequently the aorist participle expresses action that is prior to the action of the main verb. Note Rom. 6:9a: "Knowing that since Christ was raised [ἐγερθεὶς] out of the dead, he will never again die [ἀποθνῄσκει]." ἐγερθεὶς, an aorist passive participle, precedes ἀποθνῄσκει in time.[2]

Observe Mt. 25:20: "And when the one who had received the five talents came [προσελθὼν], he presented five other talents." The aorist participle προσελθὼν conveys the notion of action that precedes that of the main verb—προσήνεγκεν. Likewise, ὁ ... λαβών, "the one who had received," expresses antecedent action. In this instance note that an English past perfect tense has been used in order to reflect the sequential character expressed in the tenses of the Greek verbs. Do not, however, import Greek perfect tense significance into the English translation.[3]

Simultaneous activity. At times the aorist participle expresses action that is essentially occurring at the same time as the main verb. One of the most common of these is the idiom "He answered and said," ἀποκριθεὶς εἶπεν (cf. Lk. 5:5). A translation that aptly conveys the thought of the Greek is "by way of response he said."

---

[1] *Robertson*, p. 891, 5(b).

[2] Note that ἀποθνῄσκει and κυριεύει of v. 9 provide excellent illustrations of the futuristic sense occurring in a present tense verb.

[3] On the use of the perfect participle see the discussion of Mt. 25:24 on p. 148.

An often cited illustration of this category is Mt. 27:4 where Judas says, "I have sinned [Ἥμαρτον] in betraying [παραδοὺς] innocent blood." Both verbs are aorist: the first, the main verb, which surely has a completed force to it (and so the English perfect tense translation); and the second, the participle, whose action was simultaneous with the main verb. Indeed, Judas's sin was the betrayal.

Future Tense Participles

Future participles are rarely encountered. They, contrary to the other tenses, do carry a time value, namely, the future. Examples may be found in *Robertson*,[4] but need not be pursued by the beginning student.

Perfect Tense Participles

Antecedent activity. The action of the perfect participle precedes that of the main verb and the effect of the action continues in force. See Jn. 5:10a: "Therefore, the Jews said to the man who had been healed [τῷ τεθεραπευμένῳ]; Mt. 25:24a: "But when the man who had received [ὁ . . . εἰληφὼς] the one talent came, he said." The contrast between the aorist and perfect participles in terms of the kind of action is seen in comparing Mt. 25:20 and 24. In the former the aorist indicates simple action: He received. In the latter the perfect tense indicates precisely what the context expresses: He had received and he had continued to hold what he had received.

The Adjectival Participle

To speak of a category of participles as "adjectival" is, in a sense, misleading, because all participles per se have adjectival qualities, just as all have adverbial. Nevertheless, sufficient enhancement of the student's grasp of these forms should be derived from this organization to warrant the categories.

Attributive Participles

With the article. Like its adjective counterpart the participle will occur with the article to modify a noun. One finds both attributive positions:

article, participle, noun: e.g., Lk. 7:9: τῷ ἀκολουθοῦντι αὐτῷ ὄχλῳ, (lit., "to the following him crowd")

article, noun, article, participle: e.g., Jn. 5:12: ὁ ἄνθρωπος ὁ εἰπών σοι (lit., "the man the one who said to you"); Col. 1:5: τὴν ἐλπίδα τὴν ἀποκειμένην (lit., "the hope the one which is laid up")

---

[4]See pp. 877f.

Observe the agreement in each instance between the noun and the participle in gender, number, and case.

Without the article. Contrary to typical adjectival constructions the participle may have an attributive relation without the article. See Lk. 6:48: "He is like a man who builds [ἀνθρώπῳ οἰκοδομοῦντι] a house." The participle clearly is modifying "man," and is best translated by a relative clause. Indeed, in Matthew's parallel version (7:24) a relative pronoun is used rather than the participial construction: ἀνδρὶ . . . ὅστις ᾠκοδόμησεν αὐτοῦ τὴν οἰκίαν.

Matthew 26:7 is another illustration of the anarthrous (without the article) construction: "A woman who had [γυνὴ ἔχουσα] an alabastar jar of very expensive ointment came to him and she poured it on his head as he was reclining [ἐπὶ τῆς κεφαλῆς αὐτοῦ ἀνακειμένου]." That the last participle is describing "him" is clear from the agreement in case, number, and gender. As noted earlier, an aspect of the participle's genius lies in the fact that it is not either adjectival or else adverbial; it is both. The last participle highlights this truth. One could have translated ἀνακειμένου as "who was reclining," since the word is describing a pronoun—a clear adjectival function. However, there is an adverbial temporal force present in the context that is expressed by the translation "as he was reclining."[5]

As a substantive. Just as the adjective may be coupled with the article and used for a substantive, so can the participle. Any form of the participle may have this function. In Lk. 6:47 ὁ ἐρχόμενος ["he who comes"], ἀκούων ["he who hears"], and ποιῶν ["he who does"] illustrate the substantive being used as subject. Further illustrations are abundant.

It was mentioned earlier that the participle may have objects. Colossians 1:8 and Lk. 6:47 display this relationship with the participle. Colossians 1:8: [Epaphras is a faithful servant] "who also made known to us your love in the spirit" [ὁ καὶ δηλώσας ἡμῖν τὴν ὑμῶν ἀγάπην ἐν πνεύματι]. ἡμῖν is the indirect object of the substantival participle, while τὴν ἀγάπην is the direct object.

In Lk. 6:47 πᾶς ὁ ἐρχόμενος ("everyone who comes") is a substantival nominative with a modifying prepositional phrase: πρὸς με ("to me"). καὶ ἀκούων μου τῶν λόγων ("and hears my words") is a continuation of the substantival nominative participle that has a genitive "direct" object as its complement (remember, ἀκούω may take for its object the genitive). καὶ ποιῶν αὐτούς ("and does them") concludes the substantival participial construction with its direct object. Now, observe that all this clause from

---

[5]See Chapter 19 concerning the adverbial participle expressing time. Further illustrations of attributive participles without the article are Rom. 8:24: ἐλπὶς δὲ βλεπομένη οὐκ ἔστιν ἐλπίς ("But hope that is seen is not hope") and Mk. 5:36: τὸν λόγον λαλούμενον ("the word that is being spoken").

πᾶς to αὐτούς is, in effect, the subject of ἐστὶν in the next clause: hence, "I will show to you to what everyone . . . is like." Yes, it is a complicated sentence, but it is typical Greek.[6]

Matthew 25:20 (ὁ τὰ πέντε τάλαντα λαβὼν) is another illustration of the substantival participle. Note the attributive position in which the direct object of λαβὼν stands: "he who received the five talents."

The Supplementary Participle

A division between adjectival and supplementary participles should not be taken to deny the adjectival character of the latter. Although supplementary participles are adjectival, they do not occur in the attributive position. They are regularly in the predicate position—without the article—and they are used with certain classes of verbs.

Complements of the Main Verb

Verbs of sense perception and cognition. Verbs such as βλέπω, ὁράω, γινώσκω, οἶδα, εὑρίσκω, etc. frequently have the participle following them in the clause/phrase that completes the verb idea. For example, study Heb. 2:8b: "But now we are not yet seeing everything having been subjected to him" [νῦν δὲ οὔπω ὁρῶμεν αὐτῷ τὰ πάντα ὑποτεταγμένα]. "Everything" is the object of ὁρῶμεν, but the thought of the writer is incomplete without the following participle that delineates more precisely the meaning of ὁρῶμεν. The distinction being made in this category is one of logical relationship. The verbal idea of the participle is necessary to complete the statement as it concerns that which is being perceived, known, etc. So, it is in this sense of supplying information that the participle is a complement to the main verb, but not as a grammatically essential structural element.

Verbs of ceasing, completing, etc. Perhaps a clearer illustration of the complementary participle is with verbs of ceasing or finishing. "And as he

---

[6]Luke 6:47 well illustrates what H. E. Dana and Julius R. Mantey (in *A Manual Grammar of the Greek New Testament* [Toronto: The Macmillan Company, 1927], p. 147) designate as "Sharpe's Rule":

> When the copulative καί connects two nouns of the same case, if the article ὁ or any of its cases precedes the first of the said nouns or participles, and is not repeated before the second noun or participle, the latter always relates to the same person that is expressed or described by the first noun or participle; i.e., it denotes a farther description of the first-named person.

Here three participles, all of which are nominative singular masculine, are connected by καί. The second and third are additional modifiers of πᾶς ὁ ἐρχόμενος. Thus, one appropriately translates the clause: "Everyone who is coming to me and is hearing my words and doing them" and understands by the Greek construction that part and parcel of "coming to me" is "hearing and doing."

"When a second article does occur [as in Rev. 1:17], it accents sharply a different aspect of the person or phase of the subject," (*Robertson*, p. 785).

ceased speaking [ἐπαύσατο λαλῶν]" (Lk. 5:4) shows the participle completing the thought of the main verb.

Periphrastic Participles.

When forming the third person plural of the perfect and pluperfect middle or passive verb of the indicative mood a perfect participle and the verb εἰμί were used. At that time little explanation was offered for the form. It was the periphrastic construction; that is to say, it is a circumlocution (a roundabout maneuver) for another form. In those cases, it replaced forms that were unacceptable for euphonic reasons. Not only in these two instances, but in a variety of places the Greeks used the verb εἰμί or ὑπάρχω with either the present or the perfect tense participle to express a number of forms. In these instances the construction is not necessary, but is often used for some contextual emphasis. Close scrutiny is often needed. Six categories are identifiable in the *GNT*.[7]

The present periphrastic tense. This consists of the verb εἰμί and the present participle. When it occurs the author is usually emphasizing either customary action or a general truth. See 2 Cor. 2:17: "For we are not, as many, peddling the word of God [ἐσμεν . . . καπηλεύοντες]"; Col. 1:6: "just as in all the world it [the gospel] is bearing fruit and increasing [ἐστὶν καρποφορούμενον καὶ αὐξανόμενον]."

The imperfect periphrastic tense. This construction uses the imperfect of εἰμί and the present participle. Examples are Gal. 1:23: "only they were hearing [ἀκούοντες ἦσαν]" (N.B., the reversal of the participle and the verb); Jn. 13:23: "One of his disciples was reclining [ἦν ἀνακείμενος]." Observe how the periphrastics enhance the continuing nature of the activity. Compare Mk. 14:4 with Mt. 26:8, the imperfect periphrastic and the simple imperfect tense.

The future periphrastic tense. One encounters the future of εἰμί and the present participle. Luke 21:24b ("And Jerusalem will be trampled upon [ἔσται πατουμένη] by the Gentiles" and 22:69 ("But from now on the Son of Man will be seated [ἔσται . . . καθήμενος]" are both illustrative. The continuative force of the activity is enhanced with the use of the present participle.

The perfect periphrastic tense. The present tense of εἰμί and the perfect participle are used so as to emphasize either the existing state or the continuation of the results of an action. John 3:28 illustrates this: John says "I am not the Messiah, but I have been sent [Ἀπεσταλμένος εἰμί] before

---

[7]The following largely follows Burton, *Moods*, §§ 20, 34, 71, 84, 91, 94.

that one." Literally, this would be translated "I am having been sent with the effect continuing." Only by commentary can the translator hope to convey the full force of the Greek construction to an English audience. Consider v. 21: "But the one doing the truth is coming to the light, in order that the fact that his works have been wrought [ἐστιν εἰργασμένα] in God may be manifested." The works have been worked in God and the effect continues—they are divinely inspired works.

The pluperfect periphrastic tense. This construction uses the perfect participle and the imperfect tense of εἰμί. It, like the regular pluperfect tense, simply makes past the perfect tense. As noted earlier, it is the common way of forming the third person plural of the pluperfect tense. Examples are Jn. 3:24: "For John had not yet been cast into prison [ἦν βεβλημένος]" and Lk. 2:26: "And that he would not see death before he saw the Lord's Messiah had been revealed [ἦν κεχρηματισμένον] to him by the Holy Spirit."

The future perfect periphrastic tense. This tense (using the future tense of εἰμί and the perfect participle) occurs rarely in the *GNT*, but the student will do well to be familiar with it. Consider Mt. 16:19 (two examples) and 18:18 (two examples): "Whatever you bind on the earth will have been bound [ἔσται δεδεμένον] in heaven and whatever you loose on the earth will have been loosed [ἔσται λελυμένον] in heaven." The construction declares that a completed heavenly action and its continuing results will come to exist on earth upon the completion of a future earthly event.

Exercises

Translate the following sentences.

1. οὐδέπω* γὰρ ἦν ἐπ' οὐδενὶ αὐτῶν ἐπιπεπτωκός,* μόνον δὲ βεβαπτισμένοι ὑπῆρχον εἰς τὸ ὄνομα τοῦ κυρίου Ἰησοῦ.

2. Οἱ μὲν* οὖν διαμαρτυράμενοι* καὶ λαλήσαντες τὸν λόγον τοῦ κυρίου ὑπέστρεφον εἰς Ἱεροσόλυμα, πολλάς τε κώμας* τῶν Σαμαριτῶν εὐηγγελίζοντο.

3. καὶ οἱ εἴκοσι* τέσσαρες πρεσβύτεροι οἳ ἐνώπιον τοῦ θεοῦ κάθηνται ἐπὶ τοὺς θρόνους αὐτῶν ἔπεσεν ἐπὶ τὰ πρόσωπα αὐτῶν καὶ προσεκύνησαν τῷ θεῷ.

4. λέγοντες,
Εὐχαριστοῦμέν σοι, κύριε ὁ θεὸς ὁ παντοκράτωρ,
ὁ ὢν καὶ ὁ ἦν,
ὅτι εἴληφας τὴν δύναμίν σου τὴν μεγάλην
καὶ ἐβασίλευσας.*

5. Πολλὰ μὲν* οὖν καὶ ἄλλα σημεῖα ἐποίησεν ὁ Ἰησοῦς ἐνώπιον τῶν μαθητῶν αὐτοῦ, ἃ οὐκ ἔστιν γεγραμμένα ἐν τῷ βιβλίῳ τούτῳ.

6. Εἰ δὲ Χριστὸς κηρύσσεται ὅτι ἐκ νεκρῶν ἐγήγερται, πῶς λέγουσιν ἐν ὑμῖν τινες ὅτι ἀνάστασις νεκρῶν οὐκ ἔστιν;

7. ἔχοντες δὲ τὸ αὐτὸ πνεῦμα τῆς πίστεως, κατὰ τὸ γεγραμμένον, ᾿Επίστευσα, διὸ* ἐλάλησα, καὶ ἡμεῖς πιστεύομεν, διὸ* καὶ λαλοῦμεν,

8. εἰδότες ὅτι ὁ ἐγείρας τὸν κύριον ᾿Ιησοῦν καὶ ἡμᾶς σὺν ᾿Ιησοῦ ἐγερεῖ καὶ παραστήσει σὺν ὑμῖν.

9. καὶ ὁ πέμψας με πατὴρ ἐκεῖνος μεμαρτύρηκεν περὶ ἐμοῦ. οὔτε φωνὴν αὐτοῦ πώποτε* ἀκηκόατε οὔτε εἶδος* αὐτοῦ ἑωράκατε,

10. καὶ τὸν λόγον αὐτοῦ οὐκ ἔχετε ἐν ὑμῖν μένοντα, ὅτι ὃν ἀπέστειλεν ἐκεῖνος τούτῳ ὑμεῖς οὐ πιστεύετε.

11. ᾿Εγόγγυζον* οὖν οἱ ᾿Ιουδαῖοι περὶ αὐτοῦ ὅτι εἶπεν, ᾿Εγώ εἰμι ὁ ἄρτος ὁ καταβὰς ἐκ τοῦ οὐρανοῦ.

12. Σοφίαν δὲ λαλοῦμεν ἐν τοῖς τελείοις, σοφίαν δὲ οὐ τοῦ αἰῶνος τούτου οὐδὲ τῶν ἀρχόντων τοῦ αἰῶνος τούτου τῶν καταργουμένων·*

13. ἀλλὰ λαλοῦμεν θεοῦ σοφίαν ἐν μυστηρίῳ, τὴν ἀποκεκρυμμένην*, ἣν προώρισεν* ὁ θεὸς πρὸ τῶν αἰώνων εἰς δόξαν ἡμῶν.

14. καὶ ὤφθησαν αὐτοῖς διαμεριζόμεναι* γλῶσσαι ὡσεὶ* πυρός, καὶ ἐκάθισεν ἐφ᾿ ἕνα ἕκαστον αὐτῶν.

15. ὁ φυτεύων* δὲ καὶ ὁ ποτίζων* ἕν εἰσιν, ἕκαστος δὲ τὸν ἴδιον μισθὸν* λήμψεται κατὰ τὸν ἴδιον κόπον.*

16. ῏Ησαν δὲ ἐν ᾿Ιερουσαλὴμ κατοικοῦντες ᾿Ιουδαῖοι, ἄνδρες εὐλαβεῖς* ἀπὸ παντὸς ἔθνους τῶν ὑπὸ τὸν οὐρανόν.

17. τότε παραδώσουσιν ὑμᾶς εἰς θλῖψιν καὶ ἀποκτενοῦσιν ὑμᾶς, καὶ ἔσεσθε μισούμενοι ὑπὸ πάντων τῶν ἐθνῶν διὰ τὸ ὄνομά μου· ὁ δὲ ὑπομείνας* εἰς τέλος οὗτος σωθήσεται.

CHAPTER 19

FUNCTION OF PARTICIPLES (CONT.):
ADVERBIAL-CIRCUMSTANTIAL.
ADVERBS

Vocabulary

Adverbs of Place

ἐγγύς	near
ἐκεῖ	there, in that place, to that place
ὀπίσω	behind; as a preposition of time or place (gen.): behind, after
ὅπου	where, whither
ποῦ	where
ὧδε	here, in this place; to this place; fig.: in this case

Adverb of Comparison

ὁμοίως	likewise, so, similarly, in the same way

Adverbs of Time

ἄρτι	now, just now
εὐθύς, εὐθέως	immediately, at once
ἤδη	now, already, by this time
οὐκέτι	no longer
πάντοτε	always, at all times
σήμερον	today

Adverb of Manner

καλῶς	well, beautifully

Adverb Used as an Adversative Conjunction

πλήν	but, however, only, nevertheless; as a preposition (gen.): except

Adverbial-Circumstantial Participles

Because the participle is a verbal adjective, one may have a category called "adverbial" or "circumstantial." However, the previously mentioned tension prevails in making any division between adverbial and adjectival participles. Be aware that although the adverbial aspect of the participle is being highlighted, the adjectival is not lost. It is simply not being emphasized.

Definition of Circumstantial Participle

This participle occurs in a predicate construction and expresses a thought that is grammatically unessential to the rest of the sentence. "The circumstantial participle may be removed and the sentence will not bleed."[1] The reader will simply not gain certain information by its omission. The circumstantial participle will be in grammatical agreement (i.e., case, number, gender) with the noun or noun substitute which it modifies. This modified element may be the subject of the verb (whether expressed separately from the verb or only in the verb's personal ending), the object of the verb, or any other noun or noun substitute in the sentence. An exception to this is the genitive absolute which is considered later in this chapter.

The circumstantial participle is one way of expressing various adverbial ideas in relation to nouns and/or noun substitutes in a sentence: e.g., cause, condition, concession, manner, means, purpose, and time. It cannot be overemphasized that these notions are not inherent in the participle per se. Rather, they are derived from the context in which the participles occur.[2] It is only by careful analysis of the context with all its various parts that the student can deduce which of the functions or significances is present in the given instance. The following analysis and illustrations will demonstrate that there are situations where the sense is clear, but there are ample places where ambiguity certainly exists. It is also quite possible for more than one of the adverbial senses to be present in a given situation.

Types of Circumstantial Participles

Cause

The participle may express the reason or basis for an action. (Another way would be to use a ὅτι clause.) Mark 5:33a shows this: "And the woman, with fear and trembling—because she knew [εἰδυῖα] what had happened to her—came." "Having known" would hardly capture the force of the Greek; the woman's subsequent state of being healed and her knowledge of

---

[1] *Robertson*, p. 1124.
[2] Ibid., pp. 1124–25; see also *BDF* § 417.

this (cf. v. 29), motivated her to respond. Consider Col. 3:9 and 10: "Do not continue lying to one another, since you stripped off [ἀπεκδυσάμενοι] the old nature." The basis for the exhortation is the event of the stripping off.

Concession

A circumstance named by a participle could have thwarted or negated another action. English idiom frequently uses "although" or "in spite of" for such thoughts. See Jn. 9:25: "Therefore, that one responded, 'Whether he is a sinner, I do not know; one thing I do know, although I was blind [τυφλὸς ὢν], now I am seeing.'"

Condition

The circumstantial participle expresses the condition under which something prevails or may prevail. Hebrews 2:3 is illustrative: "How shall we escape, if we ignore [ἀμελήσαντες] so great a salvation?" The participle clearly expresses the contingency upon which the question is to be decided.

Which class of condition is being conveyed is not clear. Grammarians agree that contrary to fact conditions are not expressed by the participle. However, both simple or logical and future more probable (a yet-to-be introduced category) protases may be the sense of a given participle. This is not a common function of the participle.

Manner

This category, sometimes called "mode" or "modal," indicates how something exists or occurs. In Mk. 5:33a (considered under "cause") "with fear and trembling" [φοβηθεῖσα καὶ τρέμουσα] expresses the manner in which the woman with the flow of blood came. Hebrews 13:13 uses the participle to express the manner of "going out": "Let us go out to Him, . . . bearing [φέροντες] his reproach."

Means

The distinction between "manner" and "means" is not always clear-cut. Whereas "manner" indicates how an action occurs, "means" indicates that whereby the action is performed. So, in Mk. 15:30 Jesus is commanded "Save yourself by coming down [καταβὰς] from the cross." Not by calling down angels to deliver Him, but by his own coming down is He to give proof to the crowds of his power and profession (note the jeer of v. 29).

The reader may have felt an imperatival force in καταβὰς. *RSV* translates it so. Another possibility would have been to coordinate the two verbs, supply καί, and read "Save yourself and come down." *NIV* chose that option. But the force of the context suggests choosing in favor of means. One additional observation: the aorist participle translated "by coming down" could be taken as indicating a present tense. On the contrary, the aorist should be taken to express a simultaneous unitary activity which is viewed from the vantage point of a completed event.

Purpose

Infrequently the participle expresses the intention for which an action occurs. When this is so, the present or future participle will be encountered. Acts 3:26 demonstrates this function: "After God had raised up his servant, He sent him to you first in order to bless [εὐλογοῦντα] you."

Time

Probably the most common significance of the circumstantial participle is that of time. It is precisely equivalent to a temporal clause. Matthew 26:7, mentioned earlier, has this function. "As Jesus was reclining" is the sense of ἀνακειμένου. In v. 8 ἰδόντες has temporal force. Being an aorist tense with a main verb which is aorist also, it may be translated "When the disciples saw [what happened], they were indignant." Review Mt. 25:20 where the aorist participle expresses antecedent time: "When [or "after"] the man who had received the five talents came [προσελθὼν]." Colossians 1:3 illustrates the present participle expressing simultaneous time: "We give thanks to God . . . as we are praying [προσευχόμενοι] for you."

Attendant Activity

There are occasions when the participle simply defies categorization in terms of the above. When that occurs one might consider calling it a participle expressing "attendant activity." It stands in a logical relationship to the main verb of the sentence, but does not quite express one of the adverbial notions. It may precede or follow the main verb and may be present or aorist tense. This participle is not, like the genitive absolute below, grammatically independent; it is merely adding an additional bit of information to the main construction. Consider Acts 13:11: "And now, behold, the hand of the Lord is upon you, and you shall be blind, not seeing [μὴ βλέπων] the sun for a time."

Genitive Absolute

A noun or noun substitute in the genitive case may serve as subject of a participle that is also in the genitive case. This is the genitive absolute, a clause that is grammatically independent from the remainder of the sentence. Although it is unnecessary from the standpoint of sentence integrity, the genitive absolute adds information that would be otherwise lost. Such clauses often translate aptly as temporal clauses. There are instances of other adverbial senses, however; e.g., explanatory (Acts 7:5), concessive (Acts 18:20), or an attendant circumstance that is not really covered by any of the previously listed adverbial categories (Eph. 2:20). When translating genitive absolutes, the English preposition "of," so often associated with the genitive case, is not to be used.

Luke 8:49 illustrates the genitive absolute with the present tense: "While he is still speaking [αὐτοῦ λαλοῦντος] someone comes [ἔρχεταί]." Ἔτι, together with the present participle, indicates the action is simultaneous and on-going. (In other words, context plus basic tense significance are the keys.)

Compare Mt. 26:6 with the Lucan example: "Now when Jesus was [Τοῦ δὲ Ἰησοῦ γενομένου] in Bethany . . . , a woman came." Note the aorist participle's action in this instance is simultaneous with that of the main verb. However, in Acts 26:14 the aorist participle expresses antecedent time: "And when we had all fallen [πάντων τε καταπεσόντων ἡμῶν] to the ground I heard a voice."

The genitive case per se does not indicate that a participle is a genitive absolute. In Mt. 26:7 the genitive participle ἀνακειμένου is grammatically related to the pronoun in the genitive case: αὐτοῦ; for this reason it is the genitive. Yet, it is not the genitive absolute. The clause is very much an integral part of the grammatical structure.

Exercises

Translate the following sentences.

1. Καὶ μεθ᾿ ἡμέρας ὀκτὼ* πάλιν ἦσαν ἔσω* οἱ μαθηταὶ αὐτοῦ καὶ Θωμᾶς μετ᾿ αὐτῶν. ἔρχεται ὁ Ἰησοῦς τῶν θυρῶν* κεκλεισμένων,* καὶ ἔστη εἰς τὸ μέσον καὶ εἶπεν, Εἰρήνη ὑμῖν.
2. λέγει αὐτῷ ὁ Ἰησοῦς, Ὅτι ἑώρακάς με πεπίστευκας; μακάριοι οἱ μὴ* ἰδόντες καὶ πιστεύσαντες.
3. βλέπεις ὅτι ἡ πίστις συνήργει τοῖς ἔργοις αὐτοῦ καὶ ἐκ τῶν ἔργων ἡ πίστις ἐτελειώθη,*
4. καὶ ἐπληρώθη ἡ γραφὴ ἡ λέγουσα, Ἐπίστευσεν δὲ Ἀβραὰμ τῷ θεῷ, καὶ ἐλογίσθη αὐτῷ εἰς δικαιοσύνην, καὶ φίλος* θεοῦ ἐκλήθη.
5. ὁμοίως δὲ καὶ Ῥαὰβ ἡ πόρνη* οὐκ ἐξ ἔργων ἐδικαιώθη, ὑποδεξαμένη* τοὺς ἀγγέλους καὶ ἑτέρᾳ ὁδῷ ἐκβαλοῦσα;
6. γενομένης δὲ τῆς φωνῆς ταύτης συνῆλθεν τὸ πλῆθος καὶ συνεχύθη,* ὅτι ἤκουον εἷς ἕκαστος τῇ ἰδίᾳ διαλέκτῳ* λαλούντων αὐτῶν.
7. ἐξίσταντο* δὲ καὶ ἐθαύμαζον λέγοντες, Οὐκ ἰδοὺ ἅπαντες οὗτοί εἰσιν οἱ λαλοῦντες Γαλιλαῖοι;
8. καὶ πῶς ἡμεῖς ἀκούομεν ἕκαστος τῇ ἰδίᾳ διαλέκτῳ ἡμῶν ἐν ᾗ ἐγεννήθημεν;
9. ἕτεροι δὲ διαχλευάζοντες* ἔλεγον ὅτι Γλεύκους* μεμεστωμένοι* εἰσίν.
10. καὶ ἐλθὼν πάλιν εὗρεν αὐτοὺς καθεύδοντας,* ἦσαν γὰρ αὐτῶν οἱ ὀφθαλμοὶ βεβαρημένοι.*

11. καὶ ἀφεὶς αὐτοὺς πάλιν ἀπελθὼν προσηύξατο ἐκ τρίτου* τὸν αὐτὸν λόγον εἰπὼν πάλιν.

12. Ἀκούσαντες δὲ οἱ ἐν Ἱεροσολύμοις ἀπόστολοι ὅτι δέδεκται ἡ Σαμάρεια τὸν λόγον τοῦ θεοῦ ἀπέστειλαν πρὸς αὐτοὺς Πέτρον καὶ Ἰωάννην.

13. ἐλήλυθεν γὰρ Ἰωάννης ὁ βαπτιστὴς* μὴ* ἐσθίων ἄρτον μήτε* πίνων οἶνον, καὶ λέγετε, Δαιμόνιον ἔχει.

14. Ταῦτα εἶπεν ἐν συναγωγῇ διδάσκων ἐν Καφαρναούμ.*

15. ἔστιν γεγραμμένον ἐν τοῖς προφήταις, Καὶ ἔσονται πάντες διδακτοὶ θεοῦ· πᾶς ὁ ἀκούσας παρὰ τοῦ πατρὸς καὶ μαθὼν ἔρχεται πρὸς ἐμέ.

16. Καὶ διαπεράσαντες* ἦλθον ἐπὶ τὴν γῆν εἰς Γεννησαρέτ.*

17. Καὶ ἐπιγνόντες αὐτὸν οἱ ἄνδρες τοῦ τόπου ἐκείνου ἀπέστειλαν εἰς ὅλην τὴν περίχωρον* ἐκείνην, καὶ προσήνεγκαν αὐτῷ πάντας τοὺς κακῶς ἔχοντας.

CHAPTER 20

THE SUBJUNCTIVE MOOD

Vocabulary

First and/or Second Declension Adjectives

ἀκάθαρτος, -ον	unclean
ἁμαρτωλός, -όν	sinful; as a noun with the masculine or feminine article: the sinner (cf. hamartialogy)
ἄξιος, -α, -ον	worthy (cf. axiom)
δυνατός, -ή, -όν	powerful, possible (cf. dynamic)
ἐχθρός, -ά, -όν	hating; as a noun: an enemy
ἱκανός, -ή, -όν	sufficient, able, considerable
καινός, -ή, -όν	new
κακός, -ή, -όν	bad, evil (cf. cacophony)
μικρός, -ά, -όν	small, little (cf. micrometer)
ὀλίγος, -η, -ον	little, few (cf. oligarchy)
πτωχός, -ή, -όν	poor; as a noun: a poor man or woman
τυφλός, -ή, -όν	blind

Numerals

δεύτερος, -α, -ον	second (cf. Deuteronomy)
δώδεκα	twelve (cf. duodecimal)
ἕπτα	seven
πέντε	five (cf. pentagon)
τρίτος, -η, -ον	third (cf. triangle)

Terms Used with the Subjunctive Mood

ἐάν	if
ἵνα	in order that, that
μή	not, lest; μήτε: and not μήτε . . . μήτε: neither . . . nor
ὅπως	in order that, that

161

ὅστις, ἥτις, ὅ τι	whoever, whichever, whatever. Plural nominative forms: οἵτινες, αἵτινες, ἅτινα. Only the nominative occurs.
ὅταν	whenever

Interjection

οὐαί	woe! alas!

Particles That Intensify, Emphasize, or Contrast

μέν	Postpositive: on the one hand, in fact, indeed. Context determines if it expresses contrast or agreement.
γέ	indeed, at least, really, even
ἤ	or

English and the Subjunctive Mood

The subjunctive mood expresses contingency, e.g., "If he *were* you"; a non-realized state, e.g., "*May* he *finish* the course"; or a possibility, e.g., "You *may comprehend*," as opposed to a reality. When speaking with uncertainty about something, one should most likely use the subjunctive mood, rather than the indicative. One uses the subjunctive to express a wish, an exhortation (but not a positive command), a conditional thought that has a questionable likelihood of being fulfilled, or a variety of subordinate clauses.

In contemporary American English one seldom hears the subjunctive mood, not because it is useless, but because the vernacular is nevertheless coping without it. The writers of the Greek New Testament had not "progressed" so far; it is a frequent mood there.

Tenses in the Subjunctive Mood

Future Orientation

The subjunctive mood has two tenses that need concern the first year student: the present (in the active and middle/passive voices) and the aorist (in all three voices and first and second aorist forms).[1] Tenses in the subjunctive mood do not indicate time of action in and of themselves. Like the participle (and the infinitive and imperative mood), tenses in the subjunctive mood adopt a time of action that must be ascertained from the context within which they occur. This much may be said regarding the time

---

[1]*Robertson*, p. 360, cites the few instances of the perfect tense subjunctive mood in the *GNT*.

of the action of the subjunctive per se: Because it is a mood of contingency or possibility, it does bear a *futuristic* orientation. For example, one utters an exhortation (a function of this mood) only with respect to the future. To say, "Let us think yesterday" is nonsense. Even to say: "Let us think today" demands a future perspective—from the vantage point of the one who is speaking. So, there is a future time orientation, but that springs from the mood, not the tense.

Aktionsart *of Tenses*

Remember that tense functions to express kind of action regardless of the mood. Hence, in the subjunctive the present tense denotes an on-going, linear, or repetitive kind of activity. The aorist tense denotes an act, whether it be viewed from the perspective of its beginning (inceptive), its totality (constative), or its completed state (culminative).[2] As may be surmised, the subjunctive mood aorist tense does not have any augment.

A final note regarding tense: Because the aorist subjunctive does not express past time, an appropriate translation will be different from that of the indicative mood. The goal of the translator will be to convey the kind of activity in the mind of the speaker when he chose to use the aorist instead of the present.

Formation of the Subjunctive Mood Tenses

Tense Endings

The primary active and middle endings are those used in forming all the tenses of the subjunctive mood. Only one modification is made: The variable or coupling vowels are lengthened: ο/ε to ω/η; ει to ῃ; ου to ω. The endings are shown in the following chart.

	PRIMARY ACTIVE		PRIMARY MIDDLE	
	Singular	*Plural*	*Singular*	*Plural*
1.	-ω	-ωμεν	-ωμαι	-ωμεθα
2.	-ῃς	-ητε	-ῃ	-ησθε
3.	-ῃ	-ωσι(ν)	-ηται	-ωνται

Tense Stems

The stem is absolutely critical in determining the tense of the subjunctive forms (remember, the same is true of the participle). The present tense (whatever voice) is formed on the first principal part (e.g., λυ-); the aorist

---

[2] *Robertson*, p. 849, observes that "the aorist, subj.[unctive] . . . is used as a matter of course unless durative (linear) action is to be emphasized."

active and middle use the third (e.g., λυσ- or λιπ-); the aorist passive the sixth (e.g., λυθ- or σπαρ-).

Paradigms of the Present Tense

	PRESENT A.			PRESENT M/P.	
Singular	*Plural*		*Singular*	*Plural*	
1. λύω	λύωμεν		λύωμαι	λυώμεθα	
2. λύῃς	λύητε		λύῃ	λύησθε	
3. λύῃ	λύωσι(ν)		λύηται	λύωνται	

The forms of the first person singular present active indicative and subjunctive are the same. So are those of the third person singular present active and the second person singular present middle/passive of the subjunctive. Context or some other consideration must guide the student when seeking to parse these terms.

A literal translation of these paradigms would be, respectively, "I, you, he/she/it be loose; we, you, they be loose"; "I, you, he/she/it be loose in my, your, his/her/its own interest; we, you, they be loose in our, your, their own interest": "I, you, he/she/it be loosed; we, you, they be loosed." This translation has been set forth in an atypical format precisely because, although the student should be aware of the English literal equivalent, this pattern ought not be learned as the translation for the subjunctive mood. Rather, idiomatic translations that must be derived in the context of translation should be learned. Hence, pay careful attention to the examples in subsequent sections.

Paradigms of the Aorist Tenses

FIRST AORIST A.		FIRST AORIST M.		FIRST AORIST P.	
Singular	*Plural*	*Singular*	*Plural*	*Singular*	*Plural*
1. λύσω	λύσωμεν	λύσωμαι	λυσώμεθα	λυθῶ	λυθῶμεν
2. λύσῃς	λύσητε	λύσῃ	λύσησθε	λυθῇς	λυθῆτε
3. λύσῃ	λύσωσι(ν)	λύσηται	λύσωνται	λυθῇ	λυθῶσι(ν)

SECOND AORIST A.		SECOND AORIST M.		SECOND AORIST P.	
Singular	*Plural*	*Singular*	*Plural*	*Singular*	*Plural*
1. λίπω	λίπωμεν	λίπωμαι	λιπώμεθα	σπαρῶ	σπαρῶμεν
2. λίπῃς	λίπητε	λίπῃ	λίπησθε	σπαρῇς	σπαρῆτε
3. λίπῃ	λίπωσι(ν)	λίπηται	λίπωνται	σπαρῇ	σπαρῶσι(ν)

Note the following differences from the indicative mood: The α that was used as a coupler letter and tense indicator of the first aorist is missing;

none of the aorists subjunctive has an augment; the aorist does not use secondary endings in the subjunctive.

The aorist passive stem has the circumflex accent throughout because a contraction has occurred. This stem, in the subjunctive, is said to be λυθε-, σπαρε-, with η shortened to ε. When the primary endings are attached, ε contracts with the following ω or η and receives the circumflex in keeping with previously observed rules of contract verb accentuation.

Paradigm of εἰμί (Only in the Present Tense)

PRESENT SUBJUNCTIVE: εἰμί

	Singular	Plural
1.	ὦ	ὦμεν
2.	ᾖς	ἦτε
3.	ᾖ	ὦσι(ν)

Paradigms of the -μι Verbs

Observe the repeated use of the forms of εἰμί, except for the use of ω in δίδωμι where other patterns use η.

τίθημι

PRESENT (No Middle/Passives)

	Singular	Plural
1.	τιθῶ	τιθῶμεν
2.	τιθῇς	τιθῆτε
3.	τιθῇ	τιθῶσι(ν)

	AORIST A.			AORIST M.	
	Singular	Plural		Singular	Plural
1.	θῶ	θῶμεν		θῶμαι	θώμεθα
2.	θῇς	θῆτε		θῇ	θῆσθε
3.	θῇ	θῶσι(ν)		θῆται	θῶνται

ἵστημι (No Middle/Passives)

	PRESENT A.			SECOND AORIST A.	
	Singular	Plural		Singular	Plural
1.	ἱστῶ	ἱστῶμεν		στῶ	στῶμεν
2.	ἱστῇς	ἱστῆτε		στῇς	στῆτε
3.	ἱστῇ	ἱστῶσι(ν)		στῇ	στῶσι(ν)

δίδωμι (No Middle/Passives)

PRESENT A.		AORIST A.	
Singular	Plural	Singular	Plural
1. διδῶ	διδῶμεν	δῶ	δῶμεν
2. διδῷς	διδῶτε	δῷς	δῶτε
3. διδῷ	διδῶσι(ν)	δῷ	δῶσι(ν)

Paradigms of Liquid Verbs

Only the aorist active and middle should raise a question. These use the same endings as λίπω and λίπωμαι (see page 164). Simply attach the endings to the aorist stem; remember there will be neither a σα/ε to denote aorist (because liquid stems reject that σ) nor an augment. Consider μείνω and μείνωμαι from μένω ("I remain").

AORIST A.		AORIST M.	
Singular	Plural	Singular	Plural
1. μείνω	μείνωμεν	μείνωμαι	μεινώμεθα
2. μείνῃς	μείνητε	μείνῃ	μείνησθε
3. μείνῃ	μείνωσι(ν)	μείνηται	μείνωνται

Paradigms of Contract Verbs

Using the endings of λίπω and λίπωμαι, follow the contraction patterns set forth on pages 117–120. Illustrative are the following present active and middle or passive verbs.

Singular

1. ποιῶ	ποιῶμαι	ὁρῶ	ὁρῶμαι	σταυρῶ	σταυρῶμαι
2. ποιῇς	ποιῇ	ὁρᾷς	ὁρᾷ	σταυροῖς	σταυροῖ
3. ποιῇ	ποιῆται	ὁρᾷ	ὁρᾶται	σταυροῖ	σταυρῶται

Plural

1. ποιῶμεν	ποιώμεθα	ὁρῶμεν	ὁρώμεθα	σταυρῶμεν	σταυρώμεθα
2. ποιῆτε	ποιῆσθε	ὁρᾶτε	ὁρᾶσθε	σταυρῶτε	σταυρῶσθε
3. ποιῶσι	ποιῶνται	ὁρῶσι	ὁρῶνται	σταυρῶσι	σταυρῶνται

Uses of the Subjunctive Mood

Hortatory Subjunctive

The first person plural is used regularly to urge the listener(s) and the speaker to engage in an action; thus, in Jn. 14:31b Jesus says, "Arise, let us go [ἄγωμεν] hence." The present subjunctive is used to indicate "Let us be going" or "Let us be going on our way."

The aorist subjunctive, signifying a unitary kind of action, contrasts with the linear or durative character of the present subjunctive. Note Mk. 12:7 where the wicked tenants urge one another "Come, let us kill [ἀποκτείνωμεν] him." The aorist emphasizes their action is but an act, rather than a process.[3] Consider Lk. 2:15, the statement by the shepherds, "Let us go [Διέλθωμεν] then, to Bethlehem and let us see [ἴδωμεν] this word." An action not currently happening is to commence. The unitary aspect focuses upon the commencement of the events—ingressive. Both verbs' lexical meaning suggests activities that will be on-going, but not so with regard to their inception. Cf. Acts 15:36.

Subjunctive Expressing Prohibition

When a Greek wished to forbid an action, the aorist tense of the subjunctive mood and the negative particle μή were used rather than the imperative mood (the mood for positive commands). The subjunctive, being the mood of contingency, is well-suited to express this thought because the prohibition—however strongly it may be expressed—is still only an entreaty. It does not carry non-negotiable force or an inherent assurance of realization.

The unitary quality of the aorist expresses itself in that the action is forbidden to occur—period. So, Jesus says, "Do not give [δῶτε] the holy thing to the dogs, neither cast [βάλητε] your pearls before swine" (Mt. 7:6a). "Do not begin to . . ." is the force of the prohibition. Second Timothy 1:8 well illustrates the matter: "Therefore, do not begin to be ashamed of [ἐπαισχυνθῇς] witnessing about our Lord." From the remainder of the letter, one can be sure Timothy was not being ashamed; the prohibition was to deny its possible beginning.[4]

The present tense subjunctive is not used to express prohibitions. Instead, the present tense of the imperative and the negative μή are used. This will be considered with the imperative mood.

Deliberative Subjunctive

Whereas the hortatory subjunctive exhorts one to perform, etc., the deliberative asks the question, "What should one perform?" It may occur in any number (though the first person plural most frequently occurs) and is closely related to the future indicative in terms of its function. Although it may occur in the present (signifying linear activity), the aorist (signifying

---

[3]The Greek form per se may be either present or aorist, but the verb's lexical sense is hardly progressive.

[4]"[There are exceptions] but, as a rule, it is the ingressive aorist subj.[unctive] used in prohibitions to forbid a thing not yet done." *Robertson*, p. 852.

unitary activity) is the common tense. Mark 12:14 conveys its sense with both a positive and negative query: As regards giving tax to Caesar, the question is raised: δῶμεν ἢ μὴ δῶμεν—"Should we give or should we not give?"

Luke 3:7ff. compared with Jn. 6:28 and context illustrate the significance of the change of tenses. In Luke persons who are not bearing acceptable "fruit" question John the Baptist (in v. 10), after he (in v. 8) has exhorted the listeners to begin to bear fruit (ποιήσατε; aorist imperative): Τί οὖν ποιήσωμεν; (lit., "What, therefore, should we do?"). By the use of the aorist Luke suggests "What work should we *commence* to do to bear fruit that befits repentance?" In contrast to this Lucan interchange Jesus (in Jn. 6:28) is asked Τί ποιῶμεν ("What should we *continue* doing?") by people who are working, but for the wrong thing. This query is made in response to Jesus' present imperative command of v. 27: ἐργάζεσθε ("Continue in the process of working").

Subordinate Clauses and the Subjunctive

In the previous categories the subjunctive is in the main clause. A number of particles will introduce subordinate clauses that will use the subjunctive mood. The following are among the more important.

Ἵνα or ὅπως with the subjunctive to introduce purpose clauses. Anytime ἵνα is encountered, think "Subjunctive is following." Rarely will you be in error. An excellent illustration of the purpose clause and the *Aktionsarten* of the tenses is found in Jn. 10:38: "And if I am doing [ποιῶ = present indicative] [the works of my Father (cf. v. 37)], even if you be not believing [πιστεύητε = present subjunctive] in me, be in the process of believing [πιστεύετε = present imperative] in my works, in order that [ἵνα] you may begin to know [γνῶτε = aorist subjunctive] and may continue in the process of knowing [γινώσκητε = present subjunctive] that the Father is in me and I am in the Father." The context indicates that v. 38a expresses a first class condition: "If I do, and I am doing." On that basis the following subjunctives and imperatives are to be understood. First is the concession that the listeners may not be believing—present subjunctive. Then, the present imperative commands that they begin having another lifestyle—not just a one-time experience. The aorist subjunctive couched within a purpose clause gives the outcome of the new lifestyle: that they commence having a new knowledge. The last present subjunctive expresses the purpose in terms of its on-going nature.

ὅπως likewise introduces purpose clauses. The two styles are synonymous. Compare Mt. 1:22 (ἵνα πληρωθῇ τὸ ῥηθὲν) and Mt. 2:23 (ὅπως πληρωθῇ τὸ ῥηθὲν), illustrations of the stylistic variation.

John 10:38 and 6:28 contrasted with Mt. 14:36 offer guidance regarding the appropriate English auxiliary verbs to use in translating the subjunctive in these subordinate clauses. Matthew translates "And they were beseeching [imperfect] him in order that they *might* only touch [ἵνα . . . ἅψωνται] the edge of his garment." John 6:28 reads, "What should we continue doing that we *may* be performing [ἵνα ἐργαζώμεθα] the works of God?" John 10:38, in part, has "*may* begin to know and *may* continue in the process." Note the use of *may* and *might. May* acts as an auxiliary to translate the subjunctive in contexts of present or future time as indicated by the main verb. *Might* translates the subjunctive in contexts of past time as indicated by the main verb. To express the matter another way, remember the main verb is that which determines the time factor of the subordinate verbs in any given sentence.

ὅταν with the subjunctive to express indefinite time. The present subjunctive is used with ὅταν, a contraction of ὅτε and ἄν, to express indefinite time that is simultaneous with the action of the main verb. The present tense indicates that a repetitive kind of action is in mind. For example, Jesus teaches his listeners on the mountain with a series of these constructions: Mt. 6:2: "Whenever you give alms [Ὅταν ποιῇς]; 6:5: "And whenever you pray" [ὅταν προσεύχησθε]; 6:16: "And whenever you fast" [Ὅταν δὲ νηστεύητε]. In each instance the thought is that at sometime one may do these things. When one does, the terms expressed in the remainder of the verses are the conditions under which they are to be done.

The aorist subjunctive is used with ὅταν to express an indefinite time that will precede the action of the main verb. The parables concerning seeds (Mk. 4:15, 16, 29, 31, and 32) illustrate this construction; e.g., v. 15: "And these are the ones along the way where the word is sown; καὶ ὅταν ἀκούσωσιν εὐθὺς ἔρχεται ὁ Σατανᾶς = and whenever they hear, immediately, Satan comes." The subjunctive mood expresses an aspect of contingency; the aorist tense that a single experience prior to the main verb is in mind; and the ὅταν that the time element is indefinite.

ἐάν with the subjunctive to introduce conditional sentences that are quite likely to be fulfilled. This is the third class of conditional sentences introduced in the text. Earlier the following were presented: First class or Type I: the condition assumed to be real from the vantage point of the speaker;[5] Second class or Type II: the condition assumed as unreal or contrary to fact.[6] In the Third class the structure is the following:

Protasis	Apodosis
ἐάν + subjunctive	future, present, or aorist indicative, or even an imperative

---

[5]See above, p. 33.
[6]See above, pp. 59f., 78.

Because the subjunctive is used, some uncertainty exists as to the future fulfillment of the condition, but that is tempered by a distinct expectation that the condition will be realized. The present or the aorist tense may occur in the protasis of a third class condition, although the aorist is more common. Remember: the present tense in dependent moods indicates durative action, i.e., on-going or repeated; the aorist indicates the simple act's occurrence. The following examples are representative.

Present tense in the protasis. John 5:31: "If I testify [ἐὰν ἐγὼ μαρτυρῶ] concerning myself, my testimony is not true." One could become confused with this example because one might think "But Jesus did testify concerning himself." Context, specifically the next verse, makes it clear that in Jesus' mind he did not bear witness to himself. The Father did. Another confusion might occur from οὐκ in the apodosis: is this a second class type? No, it is not. The structure is plainly ἐάν with the subjunctive, not the indicative mood.

John 8:16: "But even if I am judging [ἐὰν κρίνω], my judgment is true." Again, the context tells whether or not He is; this verse itself does not. The structure, however, clearly indicates a high degree of probability that He does judge.

John 13:17: "If you know these things [εἰ . . . οἴδατε, N.B., First Class], blessed are you if you do [ἐὰν ποιῆτε] them." The initial condition gives basis for thinking one is blessed since it is a first class. The apodosis, "Blessed are you," is, however, also the apodosis (in a reversal of the protasis-apodosis order) of a third class condition. Thus, one is blessed indeed only upon the fulfillment of doing these things—which it is likely one will do.

Aorist tense in the protasis. John 8:36: "If therefore the Son set you free [ἐὰν . . . ἐλευθερώσῃ], truly you will be free." The aorist tense indicates a process is not in mind, but an act. Given its future fulfillment, which, according to the Greek structure, is quite likely, the apodosis is sure to follow.

Romans 10:9: "If you confess [ἐὰν ὁμολογήσῃς] . . . and if you believe [πιστεύσῃς] . . . , you will be saved." Again the single acts are viewed as the contingencies. Given their fulfillment, the conclusion will follow without question.

Indefinite relative clauses expressing a conditional thought. The relative pronoun ἄν or ἐάν may express a conditional thought that precisely parallels the third class condition.[7] Whereas the examples in the preceding section had definite subjects expressed either in the verb or as a noun, pronoun, or substantive, this group uses the relative pronoun and either ἄν,

---

[7]So *BDF* § 380 (1). *Robertson*, pp. 956ff., rejects this analysis.

usually preceded by δ' (a contraction of δέ), or ἐάν (the two terms are used interchangeably) to express the subject. The terms translate as "whoever," "whatever," "whichever." Consider Mt. 12:32a and b: καὶ ὃς ἐὰν εἴπῃ λόγον . . . ὃς δ' ἂν εἴπῃ. . . . *NIV* translates this "Anyone who speaks a word . . . , but anyone who speaks. . . ." Such a translation captures the indefinite character of the subject, but fails to reflect the tentative element of the subjunctive. Communicate in your translation or in your exegetical analysis of the text the information that is contained in the Greek. For example, one might render it: "Should anyone speak a word . . . , but should anyone. . . ."

The phrases ὃς ἄν and ὃς ἐάν also occur in the oblique cases with a subjunctive mood verb following. Luke 10:8 has ὃς ἄν functioning as the object of the preposition εἰς: "And into whatever [εἰς ἣν ἄν] city you may enter and they receive you." Note that what is uncertain is not so much the verbal activity as the location where the entry will occur: which city will you enter? In the oblique cases a conditional force is not to the fore in the use of ἄν or ἐάν as it is in the nominative case. The indefinite quality shifts to the phrase with which ἄν or ἐάν is used and the conditional element recedes from view. It is precisely this shift in sense that undelies Robertson's rejection of the analysis herein endorsed.

Anticipated Answers to Questions

The questioner may indicate whether an affirmative or negative response is expected by the manner in which the query is posed. If the anticipated or desired response is affirmative, the question will begin with οὐ; e.g., Jn. 6:70: Οὐκ ἐγὼ ὑμᾶς τοὺς δώδεκα ἐξελεξάμην, καὶ ἐξ ὑμῶν εἷς διάβολός ἐστιν, = "I have chosen you twelve, and one of you is a devil, are you not?" If the anticipated response is negative, the question will begin with μή; e.g., 1 Cor. 12:29f.: μὴ πάντες ἀπόστολοι, etc. = "Not all are apostles, are they?" Observe these are often rhetorical questions.

Exercises

Translate the following sentences.

1. ἀπεκρίθη ὁ Ἰησοῦς καὶ εἶπεν αὐτοῖς, Τοῦτό ἐστιν τὸ ἔργον τοῦ θεοῦ, ἵνα πιστεύητε εἰς ὃν ἀπέστειλεν ἐκεῖνος.
2. εἶπον οὖν αὐτῷ, Τί οὖν ποιεῖς σὺ σημεῖον, ἵνα ἴδωμεν καὶ πιστεύσωμέν σοι; τί ἐργάζῃ;
3. οἱ πατέρες ἡμῶν τὸ μάννα ἔφαγον ἐν τῇ ἐρήμῳ, καθώς ἐστιν γεγραμμένον, Ἄρτον ἐκ τοῦ οὐρανοῦ ἔδωκεν αὐτοῖς.
4. καὶ ἀγοράσας σινδόνα* καθελὼν* αὐτὸν ἐνείλησεν* τῇ σινδόνι καὶ ἔθηκεν αὐτὸν ἐν μνημείῳ* ὃ ἦν λελατομημένον* ἐκ πέτρας, καὶ προσεκύλισεν* λίθον ἐπὶ τὴν θύραν* τοῦ μνημείου.

5. ἠτήσατο παρ' αὐτοῦ ἐπιστολὰς εἰς Δαμασκὸν πρὸς τὰς συναγωγάς, ὅπως ἐάν τινας εὕρῃ τῆς ὁδοῦ ὄντας, ἄνδρας τε καὶ γυναῖκας, δεδεμένους ἀγάγῃ εἰς Ἰερουσαλήμ.

6. καθὼς ἐμὲ ἀπέστειλας εἰς τὸν κόσμον, κἀγὼ ἀπέστειλα αὐτοὺς εἰς τὸν κόσμον· καὶ ὑπὲρ αὐτῶν ἐγὼ ἁγιάζω ἐμαυτόν, ἵνα ὦσιν καὶ αὐτοὶ ἡγιασμένοι ἐν ἀληθείᾳ.

7. καὶ ἐδίδασκεν καὶ ἔλεγεν αὐτοῖς, Οὐ γέγραπται ὅτι Ὁ οἶκός μου οἶκος προσευχῆς κληθήσεται πᾶσιν τοῖς ἔθνεσιν; ὑμεῖς δὲ πεποιήκατε αὐτὸν σπήλαιον* λῃστῶν.*

8. καὶ ἤκουσαν οἱ ἀρχιερεῖς καὶ οἱ γραμματεῖς, καὶ ἐζήτουν πῶς αὐτὸν ἀπολέσωσιν· ἐφοβοῦντο γὰρ αὐτόν, πᾶς γὰρ ὁ ὄχλος ἐξεπλήσσετο* ἐπὶ τῇ διδαχῇ αὐτοῦ.

9. καὶ ὅταν ὀψὲ* ἐγένετο, ἐξεπορεύοντο ἔξω τῆς πόλεως.

10. ἐὰν δὲ ἐν τῷ φωτὶ περιπατῶμεν ὡς αὐτός ἐστιν ἐν τῷ φωτί, κοινωνίαν ἔχομεν μετ' ἀλλήλων καὶ τὸ αἷμα Ἰησοῦ τοῦ υἱοῦ αὐτοῦ καθαρίζει ἡμᾶς ἀπὸ πάσης ἁμαρτίας.

11. ὃς δ' ἂν ἔχῃ τὸν βίον* τοῦ κόσμου καὶ θεωρῇ τὸν ἀδελφὸν αὐτοῦ χρείαν* ἔχοντα καὶ κλείσῃ* τὰ σπλάγχνα* αὐτοῦ ἀπ' αὐτοῦ, πῶς ἡ ἀγάπη τοῦ θεοῦ μένει ἐν αὐτῷ;

12. Τεκνία,* μὴ ἀγαπῶμεν λόγῳ μηδὲ τῇ γλώσσῃ ἀλλὰ ἐν ἔργῳ καὶ ἀληθείᾳ.

13. ἐὰν εἴπῃ ὁ πούς, Ὅτι οὐκ εἰμὶ χείρ, οὐκ εἰμὶ ἐκ τοῦ σώματος, οὐ παρὰ τοῦτο οὐκ ἔστιν ἐκ τοῦ σώματος;

14. νυνὶ δὲ ὁ θεὸς ἔθετο τὰ μέλη, ἓν ἕκαστον αὐτῶν, ἐν τῷ σώματι καθὼς ἠθέλησεν. εἰ δὲ ἦν τὰ πάντα ἓν μέλος, ποῦ τὸ σῶμα;

15. Ἐν ἐκείνῃ τῇ ἡμέρᾳ προσῆλθον αὐτῷ Σαδδουκαῖοι,* καὶ ἐπηρώτησαν αὐτὸν λέγοντες, Διδάσκαλε, Μωϋσῆς εἶπεν, Ἐάν τις ἀποθάνῃ μὴ ἔχων τέκνα, ἐπιγαμβρεύσει* ὁ ἀδελφὸς αὐτοῦ τὴν γυναῖκα αὐτοῦ καὶ ἀναστήσει σπέρμα τῷ ἀδελφῷ αὐτοῦ.

16. ἀποκριθεὶς δὲ ὁ Ἰησοῦς εἶπεν αὐτοῖς, Πλανᾶσθε μὴ εἰδότες τὰς γραφὰς μηδὲ τὴν δύναμιν τοῦ θεοῦ.

17. χρηματισθεὶς* δὲ κατ' ὄναρ* ἀνεχώρησεν* εἰς τὰ μέρη τῆς Γαλιλαίας,* καὶ ἐλθὼν κατῴκησεν εἰς πόλιν λεγομένην Ναζαρέτ,* ὅπως πληρωθῇ τὸ ῥηθὲν* διὰ τῶν προφητῶν ὅτι Ναζωραῖος* κληθήσεται.

18. ταῦτα δὲ γέγραπται ἵνα πιστεύσητε ὅτι Ἰησοῦς ἐστιν ὁ Χριστὸς ὁ υἱὸς τοῦ θεοῦ, καὶ ἵνα πιστεύοντες ζωὴν ἔχητε ἐν τῷ ὀνόματι αὐτοῦ.

19. Ἀπῆλθεν δὲ Ἀνανίας καὶ εἰσῆλθεν εἰς τὴν οἰκίαν, καὶ ἐπιθεὶς ἐπ' αὐτὸν τὰς χεῖρας εἶπεν, Σαοὺλ* ἀδελφέ, ὁ κύριος ἀπέσταλκέν με, Ἰησοῦς ὁ ὀφθείς σοι ἐν τῇ ὁδῷ ᾗ ἤρχου, ὅπως ἀναβλέψῃς* καὶ πλησθῇς* πνεύματος ἁγίου.

20. ἔπεμψα δὲ τοὺς ἀδελφούς, ἵνα μὴ τὸ καύχημα* ἡμῶν τὸ ὑπὲρ ὑμῶν κενωθῇ* ἐν τῷ μέρει τούτῳ, ἵνα καθὼς ἔλεγον παρεσκευασμένοι* ἦτε, μή πως* ἐὰν ἔλθωσιν σὺν ἐμοὶ Μακεδόνες* καὶ εὕρωσιν ὑμᾶς ἀπαρασκευάστους* καταισχυνθῶμεν* ἡμεῖς.

CHAPTER 21

INFINITIVES, INDIRECT DISCOURSE

Vocabulary

Conjunctions

ἄρα	inferential particle: so then, consequently
διό	inferential particle: therefore, for this reason
ὥστε	inferential (sometimes called "consecutive") particle introducing dependent clauses: so that; introducing independent clauses: for this reason, therefore

Interrogative Pronoun

ποῖος, -α, -ον	of what kind? which, what?

Negative Particles

μήδε	and not, but not, nor, not even
οὐχί	not, no

Prepositions

ἔμπροσθεν	(gen.): in front of, before; as an adverb: in front of, ahead
χωρίς	(gen.): without, apart from

Adjectives

μείζων, -ονος	larger, greater
πλείων, -ονος	more

Adverb

μᾶλλον	more, rather

173

Verbs

PRESENT A.	FUTURE A.	AORIST A.	PERFECT A.	PERFECT M./ P.	AORIST P.

ἄρχομαι   ἄρξομαι   ἠρξάμην
I begin (infinitive usually follows, though a finite verb is possible)

βούλομαι   — — —   — — —   — — —   — — —   ἐβουλήθην
I wish, am willing (infinitive usually follows, though the deliberative subjunctive may occur.
No difference in meaning from θέλω in the Koine period.)

δεῖ (3 singular present active indicative of δέω, used as an impersonal verb)
(it) is necessary; one must, one ought

δύναμαι   δυνήσομαι   — — —   — — —   — — —   ἠδυνήθην
I can, am able (usually followed by the infinitive)

ἔξεστι(ν) (an impersonal verb, 3 singular present of ἔξειμι)
(it) is permitted, is possible, proper

θέλω   θελήσω   ἠθέλησα
ἤθελον, the imperfect, and the aorist reflect ἔθελω of the classical period
I wish, want, will (followed by an infinitive or the subjunctive, with or without ἵνα, as an
object clause)

μέλλω   μελλήσω
I am about to, am on the point of; intend, propose (usually followed by an infinitive)

Infinitives: A Definition

An infinitive is a verbal noun, having characteristics of both the verb and
the noun. An English infinitive is formed, usually, by placing "to" before
the simple present tense form or past participle of a verb, e.g., "to go," "to
think," "to have gone," "to have thought," etc.

Tenses of the Infinitive

Verbal aspects of the infinitive are tense and voice. The Greek infinitive
occurs in the present, future, aorist, and perfect tenses. As in the subjunctive mood and the participle, tense does *not* indicate time of action, except
the future, where an anticipation of action is to be felt.[1] Rather, tense in the
infinitive indicates kind of action.

Present tense.   The present infinitive indicates that the action is on-
going or linear. The action may occur in present, past, or future time, a
matter to be ascertained from the given context. Consider Mt. 14:4, where
John the Baptist is said to have kept on saying to Herod, "For you *to have*

---

[1]As only six examples of the future infinitive occur in the *GNT*, further comment about this
tense is omitted. See *Robertson*, pp. 1081f. for additional notes.

her [Herodias] is not lawful." The present infinitive indicates not just a single occurrence; he is keeping her. A matter of a lifestyle is precisely the problem.

Aorist tense. The aorist infinitive, by contrast, expresses action that is unitary in some sense. It may be a single event, as in Mt. 14:5: "And although he [Herod] was wanting *to kill* him [John]." Alternatively, the action may have an ingressive nature, as in Mt. 14:16: "And [Jesus] said to them, 'They do not need *to go away*; you give them [something] *to eat.*'" Both "to go away" and "to eat" are aorists, but neither expresses an activity that is of a simple unit nature. Rather, the focus falls upon the inception of the departing or the eating.

The student will have noticed that the present and the aorist tenses are translated alike. Some grammars suggest using a phrase such as "to be in the process of" or "to perform the act of" as a means of distinguishing between the two tenses. Whether one uses those phrases or others, some avenue is needed to make clear that a significant difference exists in the Greek text as regards kind of action.

Perfect tense. The perfect tense is used to express, as in the indicative mood, the continuation of a state or the existing results of an activity. Although the idiomatic English translations of the infinitives in Mk. 5:4 mask their infinitival structure, they still show their perfect tense nature: "No one was able to bind him because many times he *had been bound* with shackles and chains and the chains *had been torn apart* by him and the shackles *had been shattered* and no one was able to subdue him." The precise Greek structure will be discussed in a later paragraph, but the perfect tense force is apparent in the italicized words.

Voice and the Infinitive

All three voices, the active, middle, and the passive, occur and function as in the other moods and the participles.

Noun Characteristics of the Infinitive

Nominal characteristics are not observable in terms of the lexical forms of the infinitive. In fact Robertson suggested that one treat it "as an indeclinable substantive."[2] This is appropriate because a case aspect only becomes clear as the infinitive is used in composition, in contrast to appearing in a table that gives the conjugated forms.

Like any noun the infinitive may be used with an article. It will only use the neuter gender and only the singular number. Any case may occur. Do

---

[2]*Robertson*, p. 1058.

not assume that the nominal aspect has disappeared if the article is not present. Like the participle, the infinitive is always conveying both nominal and verbal aspects.

Formation of Infinitives

Four endings are employed, three of which are new: -ειν,[3] -σθαι, -ναι. The fourth, -σαι, has been encountered as a primary middle ending. Remember, a present infinitive must use a present stem; a first or second aorist infinitive, the same first or second aorist stem, etc. Because the infinitive is not of the indicative mood, no augment will occur (cf. the subjunctive and the participle). Variable vowels and/or tense indicators will continue their identifying roles: ε = present/second aorist; σα = first aorist active and/or middle; θη/η = first or second aorist passive; normal reduplication = perfect active or middle or passive; κ = perfect active connecting letter, etc.

-ω Conjugation

Regular verbs.

	PRESENT (λύω)	FIRST AORIST (ἔλυσα)	SECOND AORIST (ἔλιπον; ἐχάρην)	PERFECT (λέλυκα)
Active	λύ-ειν	λῦ-σαι[4]	λιπ-εῖν	λελυ-κέ-ναι
Middle	λύ-ε-σθαι	λύ-σα-σθαι	λιπ-έ-σθαι	λελύ-σθαι
Passive	λύ-ε-σθαι	λυ-θῆ-ναι	χαρ-ῆ-ναι	λελύ-σθαι

Contract verbs. Recall that only the present tense contracts. Thus, as aorists, one encounters, e.g., ποιῆσαι (act.); ποιήσασθαι (mid.); ἀγαπη- θῆναι (pass.); etc.

PRESENT A.	PRESENT M./P.
ποι-εῖν (ε + ειν)	ποι-εῖσθαι (ε + εσθαι)
ὁρ-ᾶν[5] (α + ειν)	ὁρ-ᾶσθαι (α + εσθαι)
σταυρ-οῦν[5] (ο + ειν)	σταυρ-οῦσθαι (ο + εσθαι)

---

[3]-ειν is a contraction of an original -εν with the variable vowel ε.

[4]All first aorist active and passive, second aorist middle and passive, and perfect (all voices) infinitives accent the penult. Final -αι is still considered short. Recall that the circumflex will only occur as the accent when the penult is long.

[5]N.B., this is an exception to the usual pattern. In these forms the original infinitive ending -εν (cf. note 3 above) has contracted with the stem vowel to yield the present tense formation with its circumflex on the ultima. This is also what happened in the second aorist active, except the contraction was with a variable vowel (not a stem vowel).

Liquid verbs: aorist tenses. Recall that these are subject to question only in the aorist tenses. The stem continues to provide the distinction between the present and the second aorist tense. As in the indicative mood of the liquids, so in the infinitive: there is no σ as a "sign of the first aorist."

	FIRST AORIST	SECOND AORIST
Act.	μεῖν-αι	βαλ-εῖν
Mid.	μείν-ασθαι	βαλ-έσθαι

-μι *Verbs*

The active voice of the present infinitive uses the ending that was introduced for an aorist passive: -ναι. The aorist passive infinitive of the -μι verbs will also use this ending, but since it is formed on the sixth principal part (e.g., ἐδόθην = δοθῆναι), no confusion between the tenses should occur.

PRESENT INFINITIVES

Act.	διδό-ναι	τιθέ-ναι	ἱστά-ναι
M./P.	δίδο-σθαι	τίθε-σθαι	ἵστα-σθαι

Note that no variable vowel is used in these forms.

AORIST INFINITIVES

Act.	δοῦ-ναι⁶	θεῖ-ναι	στῆ-ναι
Mid.	— — —	θέ-σθαι	— — —

ἀπόλλυμι occurs in an aorist active form ἀπολέσαι (Mt. 2:13; Jas. 4:12) and an aorist middle form ἀπολέσθαι (Lk. 13:33; 2 Pet. 3:9).

ἀφίημι has a present active infinitive ἀφιέναι (Mt. 9:6; 23:23; Mk. 2:7, 10; Lk. 5:24; 1 Cor. 7:11) and an aorist active ἀφεῖναι (Lk. 5:21). δείκνυμι (δεικνύω) occurs in a present infinitive form δεικνύειν (Mt. 16:21). The verb εἰμί forms its present infinitive as the -μι verbs: εἶναι.

Functions of the Infinitive

No translations of the preceding forms have been provided because of the difficulty that confronts one who seeks to provide one or two word equivalencies. As suggested on page 175 "to be in the process of" and "to perform the act of" are rough non-idiomatic translations of the present and

---

⁶δοῦναι, θεῖναι, and ἀφεῖναι all have contracted forms. An explanation of them may be found in *G.G.*, ¶798.

aorist infinitives. Only in its context can one begin to appreciate the richness of the infinitive. The functions of the infinitive are divided into substantival and verbal categories by Robertson[7] and according to their being with or without the article by Burton.[8] Neither of these is a particularly helpful organizational scheme. Instead, there follows a survey of the most clear-cut, common uses with which the beginning exegete needs to be conversant.

Subjects

Impersonal verbs. ἔξεστι(ν), δεῖ and like verbs commonly use the infinitive as their subjects. English translators regularly will use the idiom "It is lawful" or "It is necessary," but this approach does not identify "it." The infinitive, being the subject of the verb, will provide that information. Consider Mt. 12:10b: Εἰ ἔξεστιν τοῖς σάββασιν θεραπεῦσαι; θεραπεῦσαι is the subject. Thus, translate it "Is to heal on the sabbath lawful?" Εἰ is introducing a direct question, rather than a condition. In this context leave it untranslated. If this were an indirect question, Εἰ would be translated "whether."

Consider Mk. 3:4 where infinitives are the subject of ἔξεστιν, but have the added feature of having their own direct objects: Ἔξεστιν τοῖς σάββασιν ἀγαθὸν ποιῆσαι ἢ κακοποιῆσαι, ψυχὴν σῶσαι ἢ ἀποκτεῖναι; Translate it "Is to do good on the sabbath or to do evil lawful, to save a soul or to kill?" The aorist tense infinitives suggest only an act is in mind.

Subject accusatives of infinitives. Mark 8:31b and parallels (Mt. 16:21 and Lk. 9:22) illustrate the infinitives both being used as the subject of δεῖ and having their own "subject." Study this verse carefully. The Son of Man is the one who is to suffer, to be rejected, to be killed, and to be raised; he is the subject of these infinitives. Robertson objects to using the label "subject" in this context, preferring to call this the "accusative of general reference."[9] This is an apt label in that the term "Son" is in the accusative and is expressing the one with reference to whom the activity occurs. He strains the point, however, when he seeks to deny any subjective force to the accusative because τὸν υἱὸν is precisely the subject of the actions. Hence, I would opt for the label "subject accusative" or "infinitival subject" or some such phrase that reflects both the grammatical function and form. (That subjects may be expressed in cases other than the nominative will be recalled from the use of the genitive in the genitive absolute.)

---

[7] *Robertson*, pp. 1058ff.

[8] *Moods and Tenses*, pp. 146ff.

[9] *Robertson*, p. 1083.

Always expect the word expressing the doer (if with an active voice infinitive) or the recipient (if with a passive voice infinitive) of the activity, i.e., the "subject," to be in the accusative case, never anything else. This means that the predicate adjective or predicate noun following the infinitive εἶναι with a subject accusative will also be in the accusative. Contrast Mk. 9:5 and 35. In v. 35 the predicate nominative (πρῶτος) is used with εἶναι since the subject of εἶναι is the same as the subject of its governing verb θέλει. However, in v. 5 ἡμᾶς is subject accusative of the infinitive. Therefore, καλόν must be in the accusative case.

Subject of finite verbs.   The article may be prefaced to the infinitive and used as the subject of sentences that do not use impersonal verbs. Philippians 1:21 (without a principal verb expressed; supply ἔστιν) illustrates the matter: ἐμοὶ γὰρ τὸ ζῆν Χριστὸς καὶ τὸ ἀποθανεῖν κέρδος. Literally this would require a rather awkward English sentence: "For to me the to be in the process of living is Christ, etc." Do not translate it literally. τό is in each instance a pointer, almost a demonstrative, drawing attention to the two infinitives and indicating that they are to be considered as subjects in the nominative case. A more adequate translation might be as follows: "For the matter of continuing living is—so far as I am concerned—Christ and the experience of death is gain."

Objects

The infinitive as complementary object after verbs of mental activity, intentionality, or ability.   See Mk. 10:38b: δύνασθε πιεῖν . . . , ἢ . . . βαπτισ-θῆναι; ("Are you able to drink . . . , or . . . to be baptized?") The infinitive simply fills out the thought expressed by the main verb. In this sense it is a complement, not in a grammatical sense.

Object of a verb.   The infinitive may be a simple direct object of the verb, whether that verb is in the indicative (as Lk. 16:3: ἐπαιτεῖν αἰσχύνομαι = "I am ashamed to beg") or a participle (as Phil. 2:13: θεὸς γάρ ἐστιν ὁ ἐνεργῶν ἐν ὑμῖν καὶ τὸ θέλειν καὶ τὸ ἐνεργεῖν ὑπὲρ τῆς εὐδοκίας = "For He who is working in you both the 'to be wishing' and the 'to be accomplishing' for his good pleasure is God.") Note in these two examples that the present tense of the infinitive is used. The activities envisioned by them are linear in nature. Observe, too, the use of the article in the Philippians verse. Again, it has a diluted demonstrative force, pointing to what the subject (ὁ ἐνεργῶν) is doing. One might leave τό untranslated and use single quotation marks or even do both, thereby drawing attention to the objects and highlighting them.

Secondary object. This category is called an "indirect object" by Burton,[10] an "epexegetical infinitive" by Robertson,[11] and the "explanatory (epexegetical) infinitive" by *BDF*.[12] Robertson also observes that this category is no different from the "appositional infinitive."[13] Perhaps this last label will provide an adequate clue to the function of the infinitive in this cateogry: It expresses an action that limits or gives coloration to the main verb or to a noun (or other substantive to which it is related). It is epexegetical when with verbs, appositional when with nouns.

Luke 7:40 and 11:1 illustrate the epexegetical force with verbs. In the former one has ἔχω σοί τι εἰπεῖν. τι is the direct object of ἔχω; σοί is the indirect object after εἰπεῖν; εἰπεῖν is the infinitive functioning as a secondary object to limit further the main assertion ἔχω. In Lk. 11:1 the relevant clause is δίδαξον ἡμᾶς προσεύχεσθαι = "Teach [an imperative; see next chapter] us to pray." The direct object is clearly "us"; the secondary object is "to pray."

The appositional infinitive may or may not be an "object." In Rom. 14:13 it is: τοῦτο κρίνατε μᾶλλον, τὸ μὴ τιθέναι πρόσκομμα = "Rather, let your judgment be this, [namely] not to be placing an obstacle." In the appositional structure, however, one may just as likely encounter the infinitive related to a term in some other grammatical position than an object. First Thessalonians 4:3f. is illustrative: "For the will of God is this: your sanctification, namely ἀπέχεσθαι ὑμᾶς . . . , εἰδέναι ἕκαστον . . . = for you to be abstaining . . . , for each of you to be knowing. . . ." All of these infinitives are in apposition to τοῦτο, the predicate of ἐστιν.

Complement to a noun, adjective, or substantive. The infinitive may be used in relation to a noun, adjective, or other substantive in such a way as to complement that term—usually a word expressing ability, authority, need, etc. The infinitive shows how, to what extent, in what way, etc. the matter exists or is the case. See Mk. 2:10: "The Son of Man has authority to forgive sins" = ἐξουσίαν ἔχει ὁ υἱὸς τοῦ ἀνθρώπου ἀφιέναι ἁμαρτίας. ἀφιέναι explains the sense in which authority is held. In this function the infinitive has an adjectival force that modifies the substantive. Again it needs to be noted that although these infinitives many times are modifying an object, that is not always the case (cf. Rom. 11:23b).

Although one may initially think this category duplicates the appositional/epexegetical category, it does not. The infinitive complement cannot stand in lieu of the noun to which it refers. An appositional infinitive can.

---

[10] *Moods and Tenses*, p. 147.

[11] *Robertson*, p. 1086.

[12] *BDF*, § 394.

[13] *Robertson*, pp. 1078, 1086.

Purpose

There are four different constructions in which the infinitive may be used to express purpose, i.e., the reason for which something occurs.

The simple infinitive. This quite common pattern is illustrated in Mk. 10:45: "For the Son of Man came not to be served [διακονηθῆναι], but to serve [διακονῆσαι], and to give [δοῦναι] his life a ransom for many." The infinitives tell the purpose of his coming. Cf. Lk. 16:3: "I am not able to dig" = σκάπτειν οὐκ ἰσχύω.

The student may well be asking, "Is this not an extension of the epexegetical infinitive or infinitive as a secondary object?" Such could be rightly thought. There is frequently an overlap between categories. No attempt is being made to draw exclusive boundaries around various "territories." The language will not allow such to be done. One category merges into another with no more than a shift of emphasis. Be alert to this phenomenon and prepared to use more than one label to exegete a particular construction in its context.

The infinitive with τοῦ. See Mt. 2:13b: "For Herod is about to seek the child in order to destroy [τοῦ ἀπολέσαι] him." Do not try to translate the τοῦ. As this is an idiomatic expression, it has no English equivalent.

εἰς τό and the infinitive. First Thessalonians 4:9b illustrates this category: "For you yourselves are taught by God that you are to be loving [εἰς τὸ ἀγαπᾶν] one another." As in the previous category, this is simply a Greek idiom that expresses purpose. There is no English word-for-word equivalent. The clause "that you ..." is an attempt to capture the progressive character of the present infinitive.

πρὸς τό and the infinitive. Much less frequently one may see this idiom expressing purpose. Consider Mt. 6:1: "Take care not to be doing your act of piety before men in order to be seen by them" = Προσέχετε [δὲ] τὴν δικαιοσύνην ὑμῶν μὴ ποιεῖν ἔμπροσθεν τῶν ἀνθρώπων πρὸς τὸ θεαθῆναι αὐτοῖς. Observe that ποιεῖν is a complementary infinitive with προσέχετε (another imperative).

Time

Although infinitives per se express no specific time, in conjunction with various prepositions they become idiomatic phrases having the following time significances.

Simultaneous time. ἐν τῷ and the infinitive have this task 55 times. The introductory words of Lk. 11:1 are typical: Καὶ ἐγένετο ἐν τῷ εἶναι αὐτὸν ἐν τόπῳ τινὶ προσευχόμενον = "And it came to pass[14] while He was in a certain place praying." The present infinitive is translated as if it were a past tense because of the time of the main verb of the sentence: εἶπεν. Always determine the temporal setting of the main verb. Then cast that of the idiom accordingly.

Antecedent or subsequent time. Antecedent time is expressed by πρίν or πρὶν ἤ (either means "before") and the infinitive (cf. Mt. 26:34). Subsequent time may be expressed by μετὰ τό and the infinitive (cf. Acts 1:3). Neither of these occurs more than 15 times. They may be readily understood when encountered in texts.

Cause

διὰ τό and the infinitive express cause. John 2:24, where one finds an infrequent use of πιστεύω meaning "entrust," is illustrative: "But Jesus himself did not entrust himself to them because he was understanding [διὰ τὸ αὐτὸν γινώσκειν] all men." In v. 25 ὅτι expresses cause with no difference in significance. The passage earlier cited on page 175 (Mk. 5:4) to illustrate the perfect tense infinitive is also an example of this construction.

Use of ὥστε

The construction ὥστε introduces either independent or dependent clauses that basically express result. This function is not always maintained and instances will be encountered where the clause seems to be more expressive of purpose.[15] Where the text suggests purpose, one may perceive there was only an intended result conveyed by the ὥστε clause. Such is clear in Lk. 4:29. There the typical construction, ὥστε followed by the infinitive κατακρημνίσαι (= "to throw down from a cliff"), expresses the townpeople's intended result, but v. 30 makes clear their failure to succeed. Note that, as usual, context becomes a critical aspect of an adequate analysis.

Though ὥστε, the infinitive, and its usual "subject accusative" may express intended result, this construction also may express actual result; e.g., Mt. 15:30f.: "And many crowds approached . . . and he healed them so that the crowd marveled (ὥστε τὸν ὄχλον θαυμάσαι)." Both of these functions are in dependent clauses.

ὥστε may introduce real or possible result in independent clauses that use the indicative, imperative, or subjunctive mood; e.g., Mt. 19:6: ὥστε

---

[14]See Walter Bauer, *A Greek-English Lexicon of the New Testament and Other Early Christian Literature*, trans. and ed. by W. F. Arndt and F. W. Gingrich. 2nd edition rev. and augmented by F. W. Gingrich and F. W. Danker (Chicago: The University of Chicago Press, 1979), γίνομαι 3f regarding καὶ ἐγένετο.

[15]Cf. *BDF*, § 391(3).

οὐκέτι εἰσὶν δύο ἀλλὰ σὰρξ μία = "Therefore, they are no longer two, but one flesh." Consider 1 Cor. 5:8 for the hortatory subjunctive using this construction; Phil. 2:12 for an imperative.

Indirect Discourse

One could treat this topic as a subcategory of object clauses using the infinitive, but because indirect discourse more frequently occurs in another form it is treated as a separate topic.

Grammarians differ as to the range of verbs that introduce indirect discourse. Students sometimes conclude that only verbs of verbal expression (e.g., λέγω, ἀπαγγέλλω, etc.) introduce indirect discourse. Robertson[16] has made it abundantly clear, however, that numerous other verbs may be included in this category. Such are those of saying, reporting, proclaiming or some other verbal and/or mental activity, e.g., ἀγνοέω, γινώσκω, δοκέω, δηλόω, ἐλπίζω, θαυμάζω, etc. The grammatical construction is either (a) the accusative case together with an infinitive (e.g., Mk. 12:18) or (b) ὅτι followed by an appropriate tense of the indicative mood (e.g., Jn. 1:50).

Direct discourse is simply the precise quotation of a statement; e.g., "He heard, 'Archelaus reigns over Judea.'" In indirect discourse this would be "He heard that Archelaus reigned over Judea." Indirect discourse may be a declarative statement, as this example, or either a reported question (e.g., Mk. 5:14) or a reported command (e.g., Mt. 14:7). In indirect discourse Greek will retain the original tense—and, usually, mood—used in the original statement, whereas English modifies the tense used in the indirect discourse when reporting the past tenses. The following patterns appear.

Present time for both the report and the original speech or thought. Consider Mt. 16:13ff. In vv. 13, 14, 15, 16, and 17 one has repeated examples of direct discourse. One notes in the *GNT* the uncial letters introducing portions of each verse—those sections deemed to be direct discourse by the editors of the *GNT*. Contained in v. 13b and within v. 15 are examples of indirect discourse. Verse 13b reads, literally, "Who do men say that the Son of Man is?" This entire question is direct discourse [N.B. the Τίνα], but within it Τίνα and εἶναι τὸν υἱὸν τοῦ ἀνθρώπου form an example of the accusative and the infinitive expressing indirect discourse— in the form of a question. The direct question would have been "Who is the Son of Man?" The same structure is found in v. 15: "But you, whom do you say me to be?" (lit.) "The indirect discourse portion is τίνα με . . . εἶναι. An English free rendering of the verse is "But who do you say that I am?" The direct question is "Who am I?"

---

[16] *Robertson*, pp. 1033–36.

Rather than accusative and infinitive, the Greek will more frequently use ὅτι and the indicative mood. This is exemplified in Jn. 9:31a: "We know that God does not hear sinners." Here one has a verb of mental perception [οἴδαμεν] introducing the indirect discourse, but this is precisely the typical pattern. A direct statement would have been "God does not hear sinners." In both of these structures there has been no change of verb tense.

Past time for the report; present time for the original thought or speech. Matthew 21:45 reports that "When the chief priests and the Pharisees heard his parables, they perceived that he was speaking about them" (*RSV*). The latter part of the verse in *GNT* has ἔγνωσεν ὅτι περὶ αὐτῶν λέγει. Note that λέγει is in the present tense. This is the tense used in the original statement and retained in the Greek to preserve faithfully the form of the original discourse. Consider Mk. 6:49b: "they thought it was a ghost" (*RSV*) = ἔδοξαν ὅτι φάντασμά ἐστιν. The same rationale is being used for the tense.

Past time for the report; past time for the original speech or thought. "Not from the beginning of the world has it been heard that someone has opened the eyes of one who had been born blind" (Jn. 9:32). The direct report would be "Someone has opened the eyes of the one who had been born blind." *GNT* uses aorists, ἠκούσθη and ἠνέῳξεν, but English shifts the tenses in order to portray the time sequences of the activities.

Remember that ὅτι may signal one is reading indirect discourse or it may introduce direct speech (usually followed by a word beginning with an uncial [cf. Jn. 9:41]) or it may introduce a causal clause (e.g., Jn. 10:4f.).

Exercises

Translate the following sentences.

1. τόν τε ἄνθρωπον βλέποντες σὺν αὐτοῖς ἑστῶτα τὸν τεθεραπευμένον οὐδὲν εἶχον ἀντειπεῖν.*
2. κελεύσαντες δὲ αὐτοὺς ἔξω τοῦ συνεδρίου ἀπελθεῖν συνέβαλλον* πρὸς ἀλλήλους
3. λέγοντες, Τί ποιήσωμεν τοῖς ἀνθρώποις τούτοις, ὅτι μὲν γὰρ γνωστὸν* σημεῖον γέγονεν δι᾽ αὐτῶν πᾶσιν τοῖς κατοικοῦσιν Ἰερουσαλὴμ φανερόν,* καὶ οὐ δυνάμεθα ἀρνεῖσθαι.
4. ὕστερον* δὲ προσελθόντες δύο εἶπαν, Οὗτος ἔφη, Δύναμαι καταλῦσαι* τὸν ναὸν τοῦ θεοῦ καὶ διὰ τριῶν ἡμερῶν οἰκοδομῆσαι.
5. Τότε παραγίνεται ὁ Ἰησοῦς ἀπὸ τῆς Γαλιλαίας ἐπὶ τὸν Ἰορδάνην πρὸς τὸν Ἰωάννην τοῦ βαπτισθῆναι ὑπ᾽ αὐτοῦ.
6. Καὶ ἐγένετο ἐν μιᾷ τῶν ἡμερῶν καὶ αὐτὸς ἦν διδάσκων, καὶ ἦσαν καθήμενοι Φαρισαῖοι καὶ νομοδιδάσκαλοι* οἳ ἦσαν ἐληλυθότες ἐκ

πάσης κώμης τῆς Γαλιλαίας καὶ Ἰουδαίας καὶ Ἰερουσαλήμ· καὶ δύναμις κυρίου ἦν εἰς τὸ ἰᾶσθαι* αὐτόν.

7. Ἰδοὺ ἀναβαίνομεν εἰς Ἱεροσόλυμα,* καὶ ὁ υἱὸς τοῦ ἀνθρώπου παραδοθήσεται τοῖς ἀρχιερεῦσιν καὶ γραμματεῦσιν, καὶ κατακρινοῦσιν αὐτὸν θανάτῳ,

8. καὶ παραδώσουσιν αὐτὸν τοῖς ἔθνεσιν εἰς τὸ ἐμπαῖξαι* καὶ μαστιγῶσαι* καὶ σταυρῶσαι, καὶ τῇ τρίτῃ ἡμέρᾳ ἐγερθήσεται.

9. Λοιπὸν οὖν, ἀδελφοί, ἐρωτῶμεν ὑμᾶς καὶ παρακαλοῦμεν ἐν κυρίῳ Ἰησοῦ, ἵνα καθὼς παρελάβετε παρ᾽ ἡμῶν τὸ πῶς δεῖ ὑμᾶς περιπατεῖν καὶ ἀρέσκειν* θεῷ, καθὼς καὶ περιπατεῖτε, ἵνα περισσεύητε μᾶλλον.

10. οἱ δὲ Φαρισαῖοι ἰδόντες εἶπαν αὐτῷ, Ἰδοὺ οἱ μαθηταί σου ποιοῦσιν ὃ οὐκ ἔξεστιν ποιεῖν ἐν σαββάτῳ.

11. ὁ δὲ εἶπεν αὐτοῖς, Οὐκ ἀνέγνωτε τί ἐποίησεν Δαυὶδ ὅτε ἐπείνασεν* καὶ οἱ μετ᾽ αὐτοῦ;

12. πῶς εἰσῆλθεν εἰς τὸν οἶκον τοῦ θεοῦ καὶ τοὺς ἄρτους τῆς προθέσεως* ἔφαγον, ὃ οὐκ ἐξὸν ἦν αὐτῷ φαγεῖν οὐδὲ τοῖς μετ᾽ αὐτοῦ, εἰ μὴ τοῖς ἱερεῦσιν μόνοις;

13. καὶ οὐδεὶς ἐδύνατο ἀποκριθῆναι αὐτῷ λόγον, οὐδὲ ἐτόλησέν* τις ἀπ᾽ ἐκείνης τῆς ἡμέρας ἐπερωτῆσαι αὐτὸν οὐκέτι.

14. ἐγὼ γὰρ ὑποδείξω* αὐτῷ ὅσα δεῖ αὐτὸν ὑπὲρ τοῦ ὀνόματός μου παθεῖν.

CHAPTER 22

THE IMPERATIVE MOOD. THE OPTATIVE MOOD.
FOURTH CLASS CONDITIONS

Vocabulary

First Declension Nouns

γενεά, -ᾶς, ἡ	generation
διαθήκη, -ης, ἡ	covenant, will
διακονία, -ας, ἡ	waiting at tables; service, ministry
διδαχή, -ῆς, ἡ	teaching
ἐπιθυμία, -ας, -ἡ	desire, passion
θύρα, -ας, ἡ	door, entrance
μαρτυρία, -ας, ἡ	testimony, evidence
ὀργή, -ῆς, ἡ	anger, wrath, indignation
παρρησία, -ας, ἡ	boldness, confidence
περιτομή, -ῆς, -ἡ	circumcision
προσευχή, -ῆς, ἡ	prayer
σωτηρία, -ας, ἡ	salvation
τιμή, -ῆς, ἡ	honor, price
ὑπομονή, -ῆς, ἡ	steadfast endurance
φυλακή, -ῆς, ἡ	guard, prison, watch
φυλή, -ῆς, ἡ	tribe
χρεία, -ας, ἡ	need

Second Declension Nouns

ἀγρός, -οῦ, ὁ	field (cf. agronomy)
ἄνεμος, -ου, ὁ	wind (cf. anemometer)
ἥλιος, -ου, ὁ	sun (cf. helioscope, helium)
ναός, -οῦ, ὁ	temple
οἶνος, -ου, ὁ	wine
φόβος, -ου, ὁ	fear, terror (cf. phobia)
ἀρνίον, -ου, τό	lamb
βίβλιον, -ου, τό	book (cf. bibliography)
θηρίον, -ου, τό	wild beast

μνημεῖον, -ου, τό	tomb, monument
ποτήριον, -ου, τό	cup
πρόβατον, -ου, τό	sheep

The Imperative Mood in English

The imperative mood is used to express a command, e.g., "*Go!*"; a request, e.g., "*Will you* please *go*" (N.B., no question mark occurs in this construction); or to give instructions, e.g., "In your junior year, *take* Greek." Imperatives do not express affirmations, as the indicative, nor possibility, as the subjunctive. They simply express the action that is expected of the addressee. English has only the present tense second person singular and plural of the imperative. Both active and passive voices occur. So, one may say either "See!" or "Be seen!" In either case the listener understands that the subject is "you."

The Imperative Mood and Tenses in Greek

Greek has two tenses in the imperative: the present and the aorist. Like the subjunctive, these refer not to time of action, but to kind of action. Again, the present expresses linear, on-going, or repeated type of activity. The aorist denotes the simple unitary act itself with nothing implied or asserted regarding the duration or the completion of the event. It does not refer to past time. Not being the indicative mood, there will be no augment.

Greek imperatives are used in the second and third person singular and plural and in all three voices, all of which have the same significances as in any other mood. The first person is not used. Instead, the hortatory subjunctive is used for first person plural. When one commands oneself (first person), one speaks as if to another, saying, for example, "Soul, (you [second person]) arise!" In translating the third person use the added English term "let" with the objective case in the appropriate gender and number, e.g., "Let him/her/them go!"

Formation of the Imperative Mood Tenses

Personal Endings

A little similarity exists between the endings of the imperative mood and some of the previously learned primary and secondary endings, but not in such a pattern as to make it useful for purposes of memorization to cross reference them. The following two sets of endings are used repeatedly.

GROUP 1		GROUP 2	
Active or Aorist Passive		Middle and/or Passive	
Singular	*Plural*	*Singular*	*Plural*
2. -θι (-τι); -ον or nothing	-τε	-σο/αι	-σθε
3. -τω	-τωσαν	-σθω	-σθωσαν

The present, first and second aorist active, and the first and second aorist passive tenses use Group 1. The present middle/passive and both first and second aorist middle tenses use Group 2. The tenses faithfully are formed on the appropriate stems. The variable vowel/tense sign indicators are used. Second singular is best learned simply by rote.[1]

Accents

The recessive pattern is normally followed. However, there are exceptions. The following second aorist verbs will accent the ultima: εἰπέ, ἐλθέ, εὑρέ, λαβέ, ἰδέ. In addition the second aorist middle has a circumflex on the ultima. This, however, is not an exception, but due to the vowel contractions noted in the previous footnote.

Regular -ω Conjugation Verb

ACTIVE VOICE

Present		First Aorist		Second Aorist	
Singular	*Plural*	*Singular*	*Plural*	*Singular*	*Plural*
2. λῦε	λύετε	λῦσον	λύσατε	λίπε	λίπετε
3. λυέτω	λυέτωσαν	λυσάτω	λυσάτωσαν	λιπέτω	λιπέτωσαν

---

[1]The following notes account for second person singular (insofar as one can). Present and second aorist active use no personal ending; only the variable vowel occurs. First aorist active and second aorist middle are inexplicable. Present middle/passive and second aorist middle are due to a contraction of the variable vowel ε with the ending σο where the σ has deleted and ε + ο become ου. The aorists passive ending θι may appear as τι if the penult contains a rough consonant (φ, χ, θ), e.g., φάνηθι ("Appear!"), but πορεύθητι ("Go!"). Where two successive syllables occur with rough consonants the second (in this case the θ) was replaced by the corresponding smooth consonant τ.

190 New Testament Greek

MIDDLE VOICE

Present		First Aorist		Second Aorist	
Singular	Plural	Singular	Plural	Singular	Plural
2. λύου	λύεσθε	λῦσαι	λύσασθε	λιποῦ	λίπεσθε
3. λυέσθω	λυέσθωσαν	λυσάσθω	λυσάσθωσαν	λιπέσθω	λιπέσθωσαν

PASSIVE VOICE

Present		First Aorist		Second Aorist	
Singular	Plural	Singular	Plural	Singular	Plural
2. λύου	λύεσθε	λύθητι	λύθητε	γράφητι	γράφητε
3. λυέσθω	λυέσθωσαν	λυθήτω	λυθήτωσαν	γραφήτω	γραφήτωσαν

Present Tense Contract Verbs

-ετω, etc. and -εσθω, etc. contract with the α, ε, or o of the contract verb's stem according to the patterns on pages 117–120. The second person singular active is a contraction of the final vowel of the stem and the variable vowel ε. The second person singular middle/passive is a contraction of the final stem vowel and o of -σο, after σ has been deleted.

ACTIVE VOICE

Singular	Plural	Singular	Plural	Singular	Plural
2. ὅρα	ὁρᾶτε	ποίει	ποιεῖτε	σταύρου	σταυροῦτε
3. ὁράτω	ὁράτωσαν	ποιείτω	ποιείτωσαν	σταυρούτω	σταυρούτωσαν

MIDDLE/PASSIVE VOICE

Singular	Plural	Singular	Plural	Singular	Plural
2. ὁρῶ	ὁρᾶσθε	ποιοῦ	ποιεῖσθε	σταυροῦ	σταυροῦσθε
3. ὁράσθω	ὁράσθωσαν	ποιείσθω	ποιείσθωσαν	σταυρούσθω	σταυρούσθωσαν

-μι Verbs

Imperatives of the -μι verbs are infrequent in the *GNT*. Of the verbs presented in this text only the following forms will occur. Present tense of δίδωμι has the present active second person singular (δίδου; cf. Lk. 6:30) and plural (δίδοτε; cf. Lk. 6:38; Eph. 4:27). The aorist active second person singular (δός; cf. Mt. 5:42) and plural (δότε; cf. Mt. 10:8) also occur. ἵστημι occurs in the second aorist active second person singular (στῆθι; cf. Lk. 6:8; Acts 26:16) and plural (στῆτε; cf. Eph. 6:14). τίθημι has the aorist active second person plural (θέτε; cf. Lk. 21:14) and the aorist middle second person plural (θέσθε; cf. Lk. 9:44). ἀφίημι has the aorist active second person singular and plural (ἄφες, ἄφετε; cf. Mt. 5:24; 13:30). The present tense of εἰμί has second and third person singular ἴσθι and ἔστω and the third person plural ἔστωσαν.

Liquid Verbs

These verbs present no problems. The aorist simply uses neither the augment nor the σ of the first aorist regular verbs. The stem continues to be the key.

	Aorist Active		Aorist Middle	
	Singular	*Plural*	*Singular*	*Plural*
2.	μεῖνον	μείνατε	μεῖναι	μείνασθε
3.	μεινάτω	μεινάτωσαν	μεινάσθω	μεινάσθωσαν

Functions of the Imperative Mood

Commands and Entreaties

Grammarians discriminate between commands, i.e., statements that order someone to do or be something, and entreaties, i.e., petitions made with urgency—often from an inferior person to a superior one. Although this is a valid distinction, to classify the imperative mood into these groups is so much a contextual matter that the two categories are simply acknowledged and the task of differentiation is left to the exegete. Illustrations of the general classification abound. See, for example, Mt. 14:27–30: θαρσεῖτε, μὴ φοβεῖσθε, κέλευσόν με, Ἐλθέ, σῶσόν με.

The Matthew 14 passage demonstrates the significance of textual shifts from the present to the aorist tense. An affirmative command that is in the present tense will in some way designate linear activity. Consider in Mt. 14:27 θαρσεῖτε. The disciples were hard pressed from a night of rowing into a headwind (v. 24). They were terrified by their Master's ghostly appearance (v. 26). They certainly were not a cheerful lot. But what they were to begin being, Jesus wished to continue. So, He commands with a present tense that might be paraphrased, "Have a cheerful mood!"

Another significance the present imperative may bear is that action in progress is commanded to continue, as in Mk. 11:24 (πιστεύετε = "Keep on believing"). Still another possibility is that the action is to be repeated, as in 1 Cor. 14:20 (τῇ κακίᾳ νηπιάζετε = "with respect to evil consistently be a child"). The one petitioning God is—in the Marcan context—a follower of Christ. Therefore, he is not exhorted to begin, but to continue in the process of believing. In the Corinthian context, when the addressees are confronted with evil, then they need be children.

The aorist imperative views the action from the unitary perspective. As in the indicative mood, this may be from any of three vantages. A commanded action may be to begin to occur in contrast to what has been happening. This is an ingressive type of aorist. Matthew 14:28 κέλευσόν μὲ and v. 29 ἐλθέ are both illustrative. Peter wishes to come, but only at the Lord's bidding. We have, then, the entreaty, "Command me" and the instruction, "Come!"

The constative flavor of an aorist is evident in σῶσόν με (Mt. 14:30). Peter had no desire for Jesus just to begin saving; the nature of Peter's wish is expressed in the tense: "Rescue me!"

A culminative or effective aspect to the aorist imperative also occurs. The commanded activity is viewed from the perspective of envisioned results. See, for example, Jn. 2:19: λύσατε τὸν ναὸν τοῦτον. Jesus is focusing on neither the beginning nor the component parts of the action, but rather the finished work: "Destroy this temple."

John 2:19 and Mt. 26:39 illustrate yet another important consideration about Greek imperatives. In the Matthean passage Jesus asks the Father concerning the cup παρελθάτω ἀπ᾽ ἐμοῦ, if it should be the Father's will. From this passage and from information in other texts one knows the entreaty was not granted. So, note well, nothing is implied in the imperative per se either as to when or whether the command or entreaty will be granted. Dana and Mantey quoted Winer, saying that "When the aorist imperative is used it denotes *summary* [their italics] action—'an action that is either transient or instantaneous, . . . or to be undertaken at once.'"[2] This should not be construed to mean that where this tense and mood occur there follows inevitably a fulfillment of the command. That may or may not have happened, but it is the context and not the tense—nor the mood—that will tell.

The student will doubtlessly encounter instances where the above discriminations seem to be impossible to apply consistently. Nevertheless, careful analysis of the context and the lexical significances of the vocabulary being used often will yield insight into why the writer chose one or another tense. The writers of the *GNT* were very aware that present tense denoted linear and aorist tense unitary kind of action. The exegete of today should never assume that the different tenses were chosen haphazardly. Look to discern the rationale in each context, although there may come times when it will elude you (test yourself on ἔγειρε in Lk. 8:54).

Prohibitions

Present imperative.   μή regularly is the negative particle with the imperative. Two structures occur. Again, tense is the discriminating factor. The present tense imperative negated indicates that an action in progress is to

---

[2] *Grammar,* ¶ 288 (2).

cease or else that one is not from time to time to do some action. Luke 8:49–52 illustrates the matter: μηκέτι σκύλλε = "Do not bother any longer" (v. 49); Μὴ φοβοῦ = "Do not continue fearing" (v. 50); Μὴ κλαίετε = "Cease your weeping" (v. 52). The context makes it clear that Jairus was bothering Jesus; he is told not to continue fearing. The crowd that was weeping is forbidden to continue such. All the commands are concerned to halt on-going activities. (Cf. Jesus' contrasting affirmative command in v. 50: μόνον πίστευσον [aorist] "Only get to believing!"

Aorist subjunctive. The *GNT* uses the aorist subjunctive, not imperative, to forbid the occurrence of an act that is not in progress. It denotes "Do not commence!" The prohibition is future in its orientation, so, quite naturally, this is an ingressive type of activity. The *point* of the action is the moment of inception. See 2 Tim. 1:8: μὴ οὖν ἐπαισχυνθῇς ("Do not be ashamed").

Formation of the Optative Mood

The letters οι, αι, and ει stand out when one surveys a paradigm of the optative mood. A complete set of tenses is not provided since only 67 instances of the optative occur in the *GNT*. The following examples will enable the student to cope with these. Note the frequent appearance of secondary endings, the continuing discriminatory relevance of the stems, and, because this is a dependent mood, the lack of augment in the aorist.

PRESENT TENSE 3 sg. of εἰμί = εἴη (Acts 8:20)

PRESENT ACTIVE

Singular	Plural
	2. πάσχοιτε (1 Pet. 3:14)
3. θέλοι (Acts 17:18)	3. ἔχοιεν (Acts 24:19)

PRESENT DEPONENTS

Singular	Plural
1. δυναίμην (Acts 8:31)	
3. βούλοιτο (Acts 25:20)	3. δύναιντο (Acts 27:39)

FIRST AORIST ACTIVE

Singular	Plural
3. παρακαλέσαι³ (2 Thess. 2:17)	3. ποιήσαιεν (Lk. 6:11)
	or
	ψηλαφήσειαν (Acts 17:27)

---

³Contrast this with the aorist infinitive which accents the antepenult, e.g., παρακάλεσαι.

FIRST AORIST PASSIVE 3 sg. = λογισθείη (2 Tim. 4:16)

SECOND AORIST ACTIVE

Singular	*Plural*
3. φάγοι (Mk. 11:14)	3. εὕροιεν (Acts 17:27)

FIRST AORIST DEPONENT 1 sg. of εὔχομαι = εὐξαίμην (Acts 26:29)

SECOND AORIST DEPONENT 3 sg. of γίνομαι = γένοιτο (Rom. 9:14)

AORIST TENSE ACTIVE 3 sg. of δίδωμι = δῴη (Rom. 15:5)

Functions of the Optative Mood

Whatever the function or tense, the optative mood is the one most removed from actuality. The indicative asserts or declares; the subjunctive expresses itself in view of contingencies, but with expectation of realization; the imperative commands. In contrast to these, the optative expresses a polite request without any connotation of anticipated realization; it has an air of perplexity or possibility; it always has a remoteness with regard to whether or not the action might come into being. This remoteness is conveyed in translation by the use of "may," "can," "might," "should," "would," "could," or the like. Three areas of use occur in the *GNT.*

The Optative of Wishing

The following illustrate the optative of wish. Romans 15:13 "*May* the God of hope *fill* [πληρώσαι] you with all joy"; 1 Thess. 5:23: "*May* the God of peace himself *sanctify* [ἁγιάσαι] you." The aorist tense is always used except in Acts 8:20.[4] It signifies simply the wish or prayer that the actions might occur. By using the aorist the speaker makes no suggestion of a continuation or repetition of the action. The time frame of the verbs is regularly future from the point of view of the speaker, but it is undetermined, i.e., not made specific by the tense. Only context can assist in this regard. All three kinds of action occur in the aorist optatives: the ingressive (e.g., Philm. 20); the constative (e.g., 2 Thess. 3:5); the culminative (e.g., 1 Pet. 1:2).

In the optatives of wish (the mood being the most removed from reality) the petitioner is in no wise presuming upon the one (usually God) to whom the request is made. Whether or not the request will be honored hangs altogether unresolved in the balance.

---

[4]εἴη occurs. There being no aorist tense for εἰμί, nothing else—saying what Peter said—could be used. He could have shifted to ἀπόλλυμι and have used the aorist. Cf. Mk. 11:14, the other instance of a curse, where the aorist does occur.

In the expression μὴ γένοιτο the most remote possibility is being negated; hence, commentators can say of the phrase that it is one of the strongest negations of an idea that the speaker may make (examples include Rom. 6:2, 15; 7:7; Gal. 2:17).

The Potential Optative

The potential optative expresses perplexity (note Lk. 1:61f.; 3:15; 8:9; 15:26; 22:23; Acts 5:24; 8:31; 10:17; 21:33) or possibility (see Lk. 1:29; 6:11; 9:46; Acts 17:18, 27; 25:16 [twice]). It occurs once to express a potential prayer (Acts 26:29). Both the present and the aorist tenses occur with their usual significances. Note again that time of action depends on context.

Fourth Class Conditions (Future Less Probable)

This condition, the least likely to be fulfilled, uses εἰ with a tense of the optative mood in the protasis and ἄν with a tense of the optative in the apodosis. It should not, however, be considered a condition of unreality; the sense is remoteness. There is no complete example of this condition in the *GNT*, although instances of either an apodosis or a protasis do occur. For a complete example, consider the following from Aeschylus' *Prometheus*, 979: εἴης φορητὸς οὐκ ἄν, εἰ πράσσοις καλῶς = "You would not be bearable, if you should fare well."

Examples of the protasis in the *GNT* are the following: 1 Pet. 3:14: ἀλλ᾽ εἰ καὶ πάσχοιτε = "But if you should suffer" and v. 17: εἰ θέλοι τὸ θέλημα τοῦ θεοῦ = "if the will of God should will."

An example of the apodosis is in Acts 8:31: Πῶς γὰρ ἂν δυναίμην = "How, [pray tell me,] can I be [understanding]?"[5]

Exercises

Translate the following sentences.

1. Ἀλλ᾽ ἐρεῖ τις, Σὺ πίστιν ἔχεις κἀγὼ ἔργα ἔχω. δεῖξόν μοι τὴν πίστιν σου χωρὶς τῶν ἔργων, κἀγώ σοι δείξω ἐκ τῶν ἔργων μου τὴν πίστιν.
2. Μὴ οὖν βασιλευέτω* ἡ ἁμαρτία ἐν τῷ θνητῷ* ὑμῶν σώματι εἰς τὸ ὑπακούειν* ταῖς ἐπιθυμίαις αὐτοῦ,
3. μηδὲ παριστάνετε τὰ μέλη ὑμῶν ὅπλα* ἀδικίας τῇ ἁμαρτίᾳ, ἀλλὰ παραστήσατε ἑαυτοὺς τῷ θεῷ ὡσεὶ* ἐκ νεκρῶν ζῶντας καὶ τὰ μέλη ὑμῶν ὅπλα δικαιοσύνης τῷ θεῷ.
4. οἱ δὲ λοιποὶ ἔλεγον, Ἄφες ἴδωμεν εἰ ἔρχεται Ἠλίας σώσων αὐτόν.
5. Οὕτως οὖν προσεύχεσθε ὑμεῖς·
   Πάτερ ἡμῶν ὁ ἐν τοῖς οὐρανοῖς,

---

[5]For a complete list and comments see *Robertson*, pp. 1020ff.

ἁγιασθήτω* τὸ ὄνομά σου,
ἐλθέτω ἡ βασιλεία σου,
γενηθήτω τὸ θέλημά σου,
ὡς ἐν οὐρανῷ καὶ ἐπὶ γῆς.

6. καὶ τότε ἐάν τις ὑμῖν εἴπῃ, Ἴδε ὧδε ὁ Χριστός, Ἴδε ἐκεῖ, μὴ πιστεύετε.

7. μὴ ψεύδεσθε* εἰς ἀλλήλους, ἀπεκδυσάμενοι* τὸν παλαιὸν* ἄνθρωπον σὺν ταῖς πράξεσιν* αὐτοῦ, καὶ ἐνδυσάμενοι* τὸν νέον* τὸν ἀνακαινούμενον* εἰς ἐπίγνωσιν* κατ᾽ εἰκόνα* τοῦ κτίσαντος* αὐτόν.

8. ἔλεγον οὖν οἱ Ἰουδαῖοι τῷ τεθεραπευμένῳ, Σάββατόν ἐστιν, καὶ οὐκ ἔξεστίν σοι ἆραι τὸν κράβαττόν* σου. ὁ δὲ ἀπεκρίθη αὐτοῖς, Ὁ ποιήσας με ὑγιῆ* ἐκεῖνός μοι εἶπεν, Ἆρον τὸν κράβαττόν σου καὶ περιπάτει.

9. Καὶ εἶπεν ὁ καθήμενος ἐπὶ τῷ θρόνῳ. Ἰδοὺ καινὰ ποιῶ πάντα. καὶ λέγει, Γράψον, ὅτι οὗτοι οἱ λόγοι πιστοὶ καὶ ἀληθινοί* εἰσιν.

10. Καὶ τὸ πνεῦμα καὶ ἡ νύμφη* λέγουσιν, Ἔρχου. καὶ ὁ ἀκούων εἰπάτω, Ἔρχου. καὶ ὁ διψῶν ἐρχέσθω, ὁ θέλων λαβέτω ὕδωρ ζωῆς δωρεάν.

11. ὁ δὲ κύριος πρὸς αὐτόν, Ἀναστὰς πορεύθητι ἐπὶ τὴν ῥύμην* τὴν καλουμένην Εὐθεῖαν* καὶ ζήτησον ἐν οἰκίᾳ Ἰούδα Σαῦλον ὀνόματι Ταρσέα· ἰδοὺ γὰρ προσεύχεται.

12. εἶπεν δὲ πρὸς αὐτὸν ὁ κύριος, Πορεύου, ὅτι σκεῦος ἐκλογῆς ἐστίν μοι οὗτος τοῦ βαστάσαι* τὸ ὄνομά μου ἐνώπιον ἐθνῶν τε καὶ βασιλέων υἱῶν τε Ἰσραήλ.

13. εἶτα* λέγει τῷ Θωμᾷ, Φέρε τὸν δάκτυλόν* σου ὧδε καὶ ἴδε τὰς χεῖράς μου, καὶ φέρε τὴν χεῖρά σου καὶ βάλε εἰς τὴν πλευρὰν* μου, καὶ μὴ γίνου ἄπιστος ἀλλὰ πιστός.

14. Τίμα τὸν πατέρα καὶ τὴν μητέρα, καί, Ἀγαπήσεις τὸν πλησίον* σου ὡς σεαυτόν.

15. ἔφη αὐτῷ ὁ Ἰησοῦς, Εἰ θέλεις τέλειος εἶναι, ὕπαγε πώλησόν* σου τὰ ὑπάρχοντα καὶ δὸς τοῖς πτωχοῖς,* καὶ ἕξεις θησαυρὸν ἐν οὐρανοῖς, καὶ δεῦρο ἀκολούθει μοι.

16. Ἀδελφοί, μὴ παιδία γίνεσθε ταῖς φρεσίν, ἀλλὰ τῇ κακίᾳ νηπιάζετε, ταῖς δὲ φρεσὶν τέλειοι γίνεσθε.

17. Ἀγαπητοί, μὴ παντὶ πνεύματι πιστεύετε, ἀλλὰ δοκιμάζετε* τὰ πνεύματα εἰ ἐκ τοῦ θεοῦ ἐστιν, ὅτι πολλοὶ ψευδοπροφῆται* ἐξεληλύθασιν εἰς τὸν κόσμον.

18. καὶ εἰσελθὼν πρὸς αὐτὴν εἶπεν, Χαῖρε, κεχαριτωμένη,* ὁ κύριος μετὰ σοῦ. ἡ δὲ ἐπὶ τῷ λόγῳ διεταράχθη* καὶ διελογίζετο* ποταπὸς* εἴη ὁ ἀσπασμὸς* οὗτος. καὶ εἶπεν ὁ ἄγγελος αὐτῇ, Μὴ φοβοῦ, Μαριάμ, εὗρες γὰρ χάριν παρὰ τῷ θεῷ.

19. κεκρίκει γὰρ ὁ Παῦλος παραπλεῦσαι* τὴν Ἔφεσον, ὅπως μὴ γένηται αὐτῷ χρονοτριβῆσαι*ἐν τῇ Ἀσίᾳ, ἔσπευδεν γὰρ εἰ δυνατὸν εἴη αὐτῷ τὴν ἡμέραν τῆς πεντηκοστῆς* γενέσθαι εἰς Ἱεροσόλυμα.

CHAPTER 23

USES OF THE GENITIVE, DATIVE, AND ACCUSATIVE CASES

Vocabulary

ἤ	than (comparative particle)
ὅμοιος, -α, -ον	like
ὥσπερ	just as, even as

The Genitive Case

The genitive case is used to add more definiteness than the substantive, adjective, verb, or preposition would otherwise have. It will tell the kind, specify, define, limit, or designate something about the word to which it is related that the bare word itself would not convey. Although translations suggested in the following pages will be appropriate, given certain contexts, all the English words used are not inherent to the case itself. Remember the root idea and find words that express the idea within the given context and the given vocabulary items.

Adjectival Genitive

The student will quickly discover that labels per se are not important. Indeed, various grammars use different labels to designate the same function. The important thing is to understand the function being expressed by the word in the genitive.

Description. Some grammars label this the "qualitative" or "attributive" genitive or the genitive of "reference." The word in the genitive simply provides description. Examples include Mk. 1:4: "John came preaching a baptism μετανοίας" = "of repentance" or "a baptism characterized by repentance"; 1 Pet. 1:14: "As children ὑπακοῆς, do not be being conformed" = "as obedient children"; Heb. 1:3: "bearing all things by His word τῆς δυνάμεως" = "by His powerful word."

After the linking verbs, the genitive may be used as a predicate adjective describing the subject. Sometimes, the description, in terms of English idioms, is simply an expression of possession. Consider 1 Cor. 14:33: "For

God is not ἀκαταστασίας [= One characterized by confusion], but εἰρήνης [= One characterized by peace]"; 1 Cor. 1:12: "I am Παύλου [= belonging to Paul], . . . and I Χριστοῦ [= am belonging to Christ]."

Possession. Used far more regularly than the above predicate genitive to express possession is the simple genitive following or preceding the substantive. Hebrews 1:3, cited above, illustrates the matter: "by the word of power αὐτοῦ [= of Him]"; cf. 1 Thess. 1:2f.: "in the prayers ἡμῶν [= of us]"; "ὑμῶν the work [= your work]"; "the Lord ἡμῶν Jesus [= our Lord Jesus]."

Relationship. The specific relation must be determined by the context. It may be that of a son to his father or mother, e.g., Σίμων Ἰωάννου = "Simon, son of John" (Jn. 21:15); a wife to her husband, e.g., Μαρία ἡ τοῦ Κλωπᾶ = "Mary, the wife of Cleopas" (Jn. 19:25); a mother to her child(ren), e.g., Μαρία ἡ Ἰωσῆτος = "Mary, the mother of Joses" (Mk. 15:47).

Apposition. The word in the genitive may be substituted for another word, thereby gaining the signification of the prior term. Some grammars will call this the "genitive of definition." Note the following: "sign περιτομῆς = consisting of circumcision" (Rom. 4:11); "the down payment τοῦ πνεύματος = that is the Spirit" (2 Cor. 5:5); "fruit δικαιοσύνης = consisting of righteousness" (Heb. 12:11).

Contents. Quite close to the sense of apposition is the genitive expressing contents. It is, however, distinct. See Heb. 5:12: "Having need γάλακτος = of milk"; Mk. 14:3: "an alabaster flask μύρου = containing ointment." Note this verse carefully because the next word νάρδου is the appositional genitive that identifies the ointment.

Subjective. Nouns that connote activity, e.g., forgiveness, circumcision, resurrection, work, desire, etc., may be followed by a word in the genitive that identifies the actor of the implied activity. That word in the genitive is called the "subjective genitive." Examples are Heb. 1:10b: "The heavens are works τῶν χειρῶν σού = made by your hands"; 1 Jn. 2:16: "The desire τῆς σαρκὸς = that the flesh expresses"; 1 Thess. 1:3: "Remembering your work τῆς πίστεως = that faith evokes and your labor τῆς ἀγάπης = that love produces and your steadfastness τῆς ἐλπίδος = that hope evokes." Let the student be aware: the additional words "made," "expresses," "evokes," etc., reflect one interpreter's efforts to express how the genitive specifies. The words themselves are not in the Greek text, but are implicit in the genitive case used in conjunction with nouns of action.

Objective. The obverse of "subjective genitive" occurs with nouns of action when the word in the genitive receives the implied activity of that noun. Observe the wide latitude in the use of English prepositions and other grammatical constructions to communicate the sense of the Greek context and the basic idea of the genitive case as the specifying item. Matthew 12:31b: "But the τοῦ πνεύματος blasphemy = blasphemy against the Spirit"; Jn. 17:2: "Just as you gave to Him authority πάσης σαρκός = over all flesh"; 1 Cor. 1:18: "For the message τοῦ σταυροῦ = about the cross"; Mk. 11:22: "Have faith θεοῦ = in God"; Rom. 3:25b: "in order to show forth τῆς δικαιοσύνης αὐτοῦ = His righteousness" [N.B. "in order to show forth" is the prepositional phrase εἰς ἔνδειξιν]; Rom. 3:25c: "on account of the passing over [another not-so-obvious noun in a prepositional phrase] τῶν προγεγονότων [attributive adjectival participle] ἁμαρτημάτων = the sins that were committed in former times."

Partitive. This is an ineptly named category because one would surmise that the term in the genitive is the "part." Not so. That is, in fact, the whole. Thus, a better label might be "genitive expressing the whole." See Rom. 15:26: "poor τῶν ἁγίων = among the saints"; Lk. 18:11: "the rest τῶν ἀνθρώπων = of men."

Comparison. A word in the genitive may specify the category within which the relative value or excellence of an item named in an assertion (or question) is to be understood. Matthew 12:6: "Something greater τοῦ ἱεροῦ is here = than the temple"; Mt. 12:12: "By how much more is a man worth προβάτου = than a sheep"; Jn. 15:13a: "No one has greater love ταύτης = than this"; Jn. 14:28b: "because the Father is greater μού = than I."

The English signal word for a comparison, "than," is not expressed by the Greek in these examples. Rather, it is supplied on the basis of the context. When Jesus says, "The Father is greater μού" one knows from μού specifically with reference to whom Jesus—in that context—perceived the Father to be greater. Note proper English idiom dictates that one translate the Greek genitive, not with an objective case, but a nominative, understanding an elliptical clause to follow; so, "The Father is greater than *I* [am great]." The word "than" may occur in Greek comparative sentences. It is ἤ. In such cases the genitive is unnecessary. Cf. Lk. 15:7; Mt. 18:8, 13.

The Adverbial Genitive

Kind of time. The noun in the genitive may indicate the type of time within which an activity occurs. This is distinct from the dative, which expresses a particular point of time, or the accusative, which expresses the extent of time that an activity occurs. First Thessalonians 2:9 well illustrates the descriptive flavor: "working night and day [νυκτὸς καὶ ἡμέρας] in order not to burden anyone of you." This neither identifies a terminus (accusative) nor a precise time (dative).[1]

Source, authorship, or separation.　The source from which something has come, the idea of separation between two entities, or the author of something may be indicated by the genitive. At times this closely parallels the subjective genitive, but is not restricted to nouns of action. Consider Acts 26:12: "As I journeyed to Damascus with the authority and commission τῶν ἀρχιερέων = from the high priests." Compare this with v. 10 where the idea of source is made explicit by τὴν παρὰ τῶν ἀρχιερέων ἐξουσίαν. See 1 Thess. 1:6: "You received the word . . . with joy πνεύματος ἁγίου = from the Holy Spirit." Note Rom. 1:4 as an example where separation is clearly the force of the genitive: "designated Son of God . . . by His resurrection νεκρῶν = from the dead ones."

Romans 1:4 is a good place to see how easily a Greek statement may be construed in different ways and only resolved by context. "Resurrection" is a noun of action. Hence, the isolated phrase ἐξ ἀναστάσεως νεκρῶν could be understood to mean "because of resurrecting dead ones" (objective genitive) or "because dead ones resurrect" (a patently absurd subjective genitive). Although the Gospels record several instances of resuscitation, no other instance of resurrection is recorded. In this particular context, since it is making pointed comments about Jesus who is the Lord, one can be quite sure that νεκρῶν should be understood as separation.

The genitive as the object complement of certain verbs.　In the *GNT* whether the genitive, the dative, or the accusative case is used following a transitive verb does not seem to be antecedently determined by strictly followed canons of Greek grammar. However, the choice is not left to whim. Usually the writers show regard for the essential ideas of each case and choose their object case accordingly. The exegete's task, then, is to pay careful attention to the context; to note the nuances of possible lexical meanings for a given verb; to remember that the genitive case specifies or expresses kind; and to seek to ascertain whether or not a noun in the genitive following a verb may be expressing one of the notions just set forth under "The Adjectival Genitive." The exegete then should seek to articulate the significance underlying the writer's choice of case in relation to the given verb in fluent English idiom. The following is a list of more common categories of verbs that frequently have the genitive as their object.

Verbs of sensation.　Verbs expressing tasting, hearing, touching, but not seeing, are often followed by the genitive. See Heb. 6:4, but cf. v. 5.

---

[1]Cf. Exercise 11, page 79 and note 7.

Verbs of emotion/mental activity. These are verbs of remembering, forgetting, desiring, etc. See Heb. 10:17; Jn. 15:20.

Verbs of sharing, partaking, filling. See Heb. 5:13; Lk. 1:15; contrast Heb. 2:14 (gen.) with Phil. 4:15 (dat.).

Verbs expressing ideas of departing, lacking, asking, abstaining. See 1 Tim. 4:1; Lk. 22:35; 10:2; Acts 8:22; 15:29.

The Dative Case

In analyzing the uses of the third inflectional form one should bear in mind this form may convey any one of three distinct notions: (1) personal interest (the basic idea of the dative case); (2) location (in an eight-case system the idea of the locative case); or (3) means (in an eight-case system the basic notion of the instrumental case). These categories may be subdivided to appreciate better the variegated hues that each displays in the *GNT*.

Dative Expressing Personal Interest

Indirect object. This is the most frequent expression of personal interest. The word in the dative simply tells to or for whom something is or occurs. The student has already encountered this function. For review, consider 1 Cor. 11:22: τί εἴπω ὑμῖν; = "What should I say to you?"

Advantage or disadvantage. In expressing personal interest the dative often bears a positive or negative aspect in the light of its context. Consider Mt. 23:31: μαρτυρεῖτε ἑαυτοῖς = "you are testifying against yourselves." "Against" is an appropriate English expression of the Greek's sense of personal interest within that context. Examine Lk. 15:30: ἔθυσας αὐτῷ τὸν σιτευτὸν μόσχον = "You sacrificed for him the fattened calf." "For him" certainly has an advantageous ring to it.

Possession. With the linking verbs εἰμί, γίνομαι, and ὑπάρχω Greek will express personal interest that is, in effect, possession. See Jn. 13:35: γνώσονται πάντες ὅτι ἐμοὶ μαθηταί ἐστε = "All will know that for me you are disciples." By the use of the dative the Greek's emphasis falls on the possessor.

Reference or sphere. The dative may define or express the limits within which a noun, an adjective, or a verb is to be understood. Often the dative expresses the logical sphere within which something is. Consider "the poor τῷ πνεύματι [= in spirit]" (Mt. 5:3); "the pure τῇ καρδίᾳ [= in heart]" (Mt. 5:8); "givers of offense Ἰουδαίοις . . . καὶ Ἕλλησιν καὶ τῇ ἐκκλησίᾳ τοῦ θεοῦ [= to Jews and to Greeks and to the church of God]" (1 Cor. 10:32); "we died τῇ ἁμαρτίᾳ [= to sin]" (Rom. 6:2). In this category one is only remotely concerned with personal interest.

The Locative Dative

Dative of place where. The simple dative used in a local (locative) sense expressing the place where is rarely encountered in the *GNT*. Together with a preposition that specifies place, the dative is quite common, e.g., ἐν, παρά, ἐπί. Illustrative of the local dative are Heb. 12:22 ("But you have come Σιὼν ὄρει [= to Mount Zion]") and Lk. 7:12 ("And as He drew near τῇ πύλῃ [= to the gate]").

Dative of time when (point of time). The student will find it instructive to compare νύξ in Mt. 25:6 (gen.); Mk. 14:30 (dat.); Acts 26:7 (acc.). Note Rev. 18:10b: "Woe, woe, O great city, O Babylon the mighty city, because μιᾷ ὥρᾳ [= in one hour] your judgment has come."

The Instrumental Dative

Means. See page 87 for a discussion.

Cause. The instrumental dative may express the motive, the basis, or the impetus that gives rise to a situation. See Lk. 15:17b: "But I am perishing here λιμῷ [= because of hunger]"; 2 Cor. 2:7b: "lest such a one be overwhelmed τῇ περισσοτέρᾳ λύπῃ [= by excessive sorrow]"; Rom. 11:20: "They were broken off τῇ ἀπιστίᾳ [= because of unbelief] and you stand τῇ πίστει [= because of faith]."

Manner. Still another shade of the instrumental spectrum is manner, the way in which something is performed. The word in the dative may function like an adverb, as in Jn. 3:29: χαρᾷ χαίρει = "he rejoices joyfully [lit. = with joy]." Note the intensification that this dative adds. See Phil. 1:18: παντὶ τρόπῳ, εἴτε προφάσει εἴτε ἀληθείᾳ, Χριστὸς καταγγέλλεται = "In every way, whether in pretext or in truth, Christ is being proclaimed"—three instances of manner.

Association. The dative is frequently used to name a thing or person that has some relationship to the subject of a verb. The relationship will be expressed usually by the verb. Examples are Eph. 2:5: συνεζωοποίησεν τῷ Χριστῷ = "He made [us] alive with Christ"; Jn. 11:31: οἱ οὖν Ἰουδαῖοι . . . ἠκολούθησαν αὐτῇ = "Therefore the Jews . . . followed her."

Direct object. The dative case may function with many verbs to express the direct object; in particular, word groups that express a "close personal relation like trust, distrust, envy, please, satisfy, serve, etc."[2] Consider Rev. 22:3: "His servants will serve him [αὐτῷ]"; Rom. 8:8: "The ones who are in the flesh are not able to please God [θεῷ]."

The Accusative Case

Types of Accusatives

Direct Object. See page 18 for a discussion.

Cognate accusative. This is but a particular subcategory of the direct object. One frequently finds in the *GNT* constructions in which the verb and its object are related etymologically. The accusative repeats the idea that is expressed by the verb. Matthew 22:11 is illustrative: "He saw there a man who was not clothed with clothing [ἐνδεδυμένον ἔνδυμα] of a wedding celebration." Note how English idiom needs "with" where Greek has the simple accusative case. Cf. 1 Jn. 5:16; Mt. 2:10; 2 Tim. 4:7.

Accusatives expressing time and space. These functions of the accusative are adverbial in sense. The temporal notion is extent of time or time during which something occurs. For example, Jn. 11:6 says of Jesus "He remained in the place in which he was two days [δύο ἡμέρας]." With verbs of activity the accusative may tell how far or the extent to which a motion is to be understood. Consider Mk. 14:35: προελθὼν μικρὸν = "having gone forth a short distance." Cf. Lk. 24:13.

Double accusative. Another variation of the simple direct object is the accusative used twice to express two objects, one answering the question "Whom?," the other the question "What?" after a host of verbs. Among them are those of naming, saying, calling, making, teaching, clothing, etc. Examples are Jn. 14:26: "That one will teach you all things [ὑμᾶς . . . πάντα]"; Mt. 22:43: "He calls him lord [αὐτὸν κύριον]."

Exercises

Translate the following sentences.

1. ἀμὴν λέγω ὑμῖν, οὐκ ἐγήγερται ἐν γεννητοῖς* γυναικῶν μείζων Ἰωάννου τοῦ βαπτιστοῦ· ὁ δὲ μικρότερος ἐν τῇ βασιλείᾳ τῶν οὐρανῶν μείζων αὐτοῦ ἐστιν.

2. τὸ δὲ πλοῖον ἤδη σταδίους* πολλοὺς ἀπὸ τῆς γῆς ἀπεῖχεν,* βασανιζό-μενον* ὑπὸ τῶν κυμάτων,* ἦν γὰρ ἐναντίος* ὁ ἄνεμος.

---

[2] *Robertson*, p. 539.

3. τετάρτῃ* δὲ φυλακῇ τῆς νυκτὸς ἦλθεν πρὸς αὐτοὺς περιπατῶν ἐπὶ τὴν θάλασσαν.
4. ἐδύνατο γὰρ τοῦτο πραθῆναι πολλοῦ καὶ δοθῆναι πτωχοῖς.
5. γνοὺς δὲ ὁ Ἰησοῦς εἶπεν αὐτοῖς, Τί κόπους* παρέχετε* τῇ γυναικί; ἔργον γὰρ καλὸν ἠργάσατο εἰς ἐμέ.
6. ταῦτα εἶπαν οἱ γονεῖς* αὐτοῦ ὅτι ἐφοβοῦντο τοὺς Ἰουδαίους, ἤδη γὰρ συνετέθειντο* οἱ Ἰουδαῖοι ἵνα ἐάν τις αὐτὸν ὁμολογήσῃ Χριστόν, ἀποσυνάγωγος* γένηται.
7. ἦν δὲ Μαριὰμ ἡ ἀλείψασα* τὸν κύριον μύρῳ* καὶ ἐκμάξασα* τοὺς πόδας αὐτοῦ ταῖς θριξὶν* αὐτῆς, ἧς ὁ ἀδελφὸς Λάζαρος ἠσθένει.
8. Ἐλθὼν οὖν ὁ Ἰησοῦς εὗρεν αὐτὸν τέσσαρας ἤδη ἡμέρας ἔχοντα ἐν τῷ μνημείῳ.
9. ἐξῆλθεν ὁ τεθνηκὼς* δεδεμένος τοὺς πόδας καὶ τὰς χεῖρας κειρίαις,* καὶ ἡ ὄψις* αὐτοῦ σουδαρίῳ* περιεδέδετο.* λέγει αὐτοῖς ὁ Ἰησοῦς, Λύσατε αὐτὸν καὶ ἄφετε αὐτὸν ὑπάγειν.*
10. χάρις δὲ τῷ θεῷ διὰ Ἰησοῦ Χριστοῦ τοῦ κυρίου ἡμῶν. ἄρα οὖν αὐτὸς ἐγὼ τῷ μὲν νοΐ δουλεύω* νόμῳ θεοῦ, τῇ δὲ σαρκὶ νόμῳ ἁμαρτίας.
11. Λέγω οὖν, μὴ ἔπταισαν* ἵνα πέσωσιν; μὴ γένοιτο· ἀλλὰ τῷ αὐτῶν παραπτώματι* ἡ σωτηρία τοῖς ἔθνεσιν, εἰς τὸ παραζηλῶσαι* αὐτούς.
12. πᾶσα δὲ γυνὴ προσευχομένη ἢ προφητεύουσα ἀκατακαλύπτῳ* τῇ κεφαλῇ καταισχύνει* τὴν κεφαλὴν αὐτῆς.
13. οὐ γὰρ ἑαυτοὺς κηρύσσομεν ἀλλὰ Ἰησοῦν Χριστὸν κύριον, ἑαυτοὺς δὲ δούλους ὑμῶν διὰ Ἰησοῦν.
14. ὅτι ὁ θεὸς ὁ εἰπών, Ἐκ σκότους φῶς λάμψει,* ὃς ἔλαμψεν ἐν ταῖς καρδίαις ἡμῶν πρὸς φωτισμὸν* τῆς γνώσεως τῆς δόξης τοῦ θεοῦ ἐν προσώπῳ Χριστοῦ.
15. Μὴ γίνεσθε ἑτεροζυγοῦντες* ἀπίστοις· τίς γὰρ μετοχὴ* δικαιοσύνῃ καὶ ἀνομίᾳ; ἢ τίς κοινωνία φωτὶ πρὸς σκότος;
16. ἐμοὶ δὲ μὴ γένοιτο καυχᾶσθαι εἰ μὴ ἐν τῷ σταυρῷ τοῦ κυρίου ἡμῶν Ἰησοῦ Χριστοῦ, δι᾽ οὗ ἐμοὶ κόσμος ἐσταύρωται κἀγὼ κόσμῳ.
17. καὶ ὄντας ἡμᾶς νεκροὺς τοῖς παραπτώμασιν* συνεζωοποίησεν* τῷ Χριστῷ—χάριτί ἐστε σεσῳσμένοι.
18. καὶ ἐστὲ ἐν αὐτῷ πεπληρωμένοι, ὅς ἐστιν ἡ κεφαλὴ πάσης ἀρχῆς καὶ ἐξουσίας,
19. ἐν ᾧ καὶ περιετμήθητε* περιτομῇ* ἀχειροποιήτῳ* ἐν τῇ ἀπεκδύσει* τοῦ σώματος τῆς σαρκός, ἐν τῇ περιτομῇ τοῦ Χριστοῦ.
20. τελείων* δέ ἐστιν ἡ στερεὰ* τροφή,* τῶν διὰ τὴν ἕξιν* τὰ αἰσθητήρια* γεγυμνασμένα* ἐχόντων πρὸς διάκρισιν* καλοῦ τε καὶ κακοῦ.

ἡ χάρις μετὰ πάντων ὑμῶν.

For supplementary exercises that offer a review of a considerable amount of the beginning and intermediate grammar, the student may wish to consider Gal. 3:21–29 and/or Acts 8:14–25.

TABLES

TABLE 1: FIRST DECLENSION NOUNS

The nouns (ἡ) χρεία "need," (ἡ) δόξα "glory," (ἡ) τιμή "honor," and (ὁ) προφήτης "prophet" are declined as follows:

Singular

N.	χρεία	δόξα	τιμή	προφήτης
G.	χρείας	δόξης	τιμῆς	προφήτου
D.	χρείᾳ	δόξῃ	τιμῇ	προφήτῃ
A.	χρείαν	δόξαν	τιμήν	προφήτην
V.	χρεία	δόξα	τιμή	προφῆτα

Plural

N.V.	χρεῖαι	δόξαι	τιμαί	προφῆται
G.	χρειῶν	δοξῶν	τιμῶν	προφητῶν
D.	χρείαις	δόξαις	τιμαῖς	προφήταις
A.	χρείας	δόξας	τιμάς	προφήτας

TABLE 2: SECOND DECLENSION NOUNS

The nouns (ὁ) θεός "God," (ὁ) νόμος "law," (ὁ) ἄνθρωπος "human being," (ὁ) οἶκος "house," and (τὸ) ἔργον "work" are declined as follows:

Singular

N.	θεός	νόμος	ἄνθρωπος	οἶκος	ἔργον
G.	θεοῦ	νόμου	ἀνθρώπου	οἴκου	ἔργου
D.	θεῷ	νόμῳ	ἀνθρώπῳ	οἴκῳ	ἔργῳ
A.	θεόν	νόμον	ἄνθρωπον	οἶκον	ἔργον
V.	θεέ	νόμε	ἄνθρωπε	οἶκε	ἔργον

Plural

N.V.	θεοί	νόμοι	ἄνθρωποι	οἶκοι	ἔργα
G.	θεῶν	νομῶν	ἀνθρώπων	οἴκων	ἔργων
D.	θεοῖς	νομοῖς	ἀνθρώποις	οἴκοις	ἔργοις
A.	θεούς	νόμους	ἀνθρώπους	οἴκους	ἔργα

TABLE 3: THE ARTICLE

The article ὁ, ἡ, τό "the" is declined as follows:

		Masculine		Feminine		Neuter	
		Singular	*Plural*	*Singular*	*Plural*	*Singular*	*Plural*
N.		ὁ	οἱ	ἡ	αἱ	τό	τά
G.		τοῦ	τῶν	τῆς	τῶν	τοῦ	τῶν
D.		τῷ	τοῖς	τῇ	ταῖς	τῷ	τοῖς
A.		τόν	τούς	τήν	τάς	τό	τά

A table giving an overview of nouns in the third declension is presented on page 108.

TABLE 4: ADJECTIVES

The first and second declension adjective ἅγιος, ἁγία, ἅγιον—"holy" declines as follows:

	Singular			*Plural*		
	M.	F.	N.	M.	F.	N.
N.	ἅγιος	ἁγία	ἅγιον	ἅγιοι	ἅγιαι	ἅγια
G.	ἁγίου	ἁγίας	ἁγίου	ἁγίων	ἁγίων	ἁγίων
D.	ἁγίῳ	ἁγίᾳ	ἁγίῳ	ἁγίοις	ἁγίαις	ἁγίοις
A.	ἅγιον	ἁγίαν	ἅγιον	ἁγίους	ἁγίας	ἅγια
V.	ἅγιε	ἁγία	ἅγιον	ἅγιοι	ἅγιαι	ἅγια

The first and second declension adjective ἄλλος, ἄλλη, ἄλλο—"other, another" declines as follows:

	Singular			*Plural*		
	M.	F.	N.	M.	F.	N.
N.	ἄλλος	ἄλλη	ἄλλο	ἄλλοι	ἄλλαι	ἄλλα
G.	ἄλλου	ἄλλης	ἄλλου	ἄλλων	ἄλλων	ἄλλων
D.	ἄλλῳ	ἄλλῃ	ἄλλῳ	ἄλλοις	ἄλλαις	ἄλλοις
A.	ἄλλον	ἄλλην	ἄλλο	ἄλλους	ἄλλας	ἄλλα
V.	ἄλλε	ἄλλη	ἄλλο	ἄλλοι	ἄλλαι	ἄλλα

Third declension adjectives are represented by ἀσθενής, -ές (stem = ἀσθενε-)—"weak" and μείζων, -ον, (stem = μειζον-)—"greater."

	Singular				*Plural*	
	M.F.	M.F.N.	N.	M.	M.F.N.	N.
N.	ἀσθενής		ἀσθενές	ἀσθενεῖς (ἀσθενέες)*		ἀσθενῆ (ἀσθενέα)
G.		ἀσθενοῦς (ἀσθενέος)			ἀσθενῶν (ἀσθενέων)	
D.		ἀσθενεῖ (ἀσθενέϊ)			ἀσθενέσι(ν)	
A.	ἀσθενῆ		ἀσθενές	ἀσθενεῖς		ἀσθενῆ
V.		ἀσθενές		ἀσθενεῖς		ἀσθενῆ

N.	μείζων		μεῖζον	μείζονες		μείζονα
G.		μείζονος			μειζόνων	
D.		μείζονι			μειζόνοσι	
A.	μείζονα		μεῖζον	μείζονας		μείζονα
V.				μείζονες		μείζονα

*The uncontracted forms of this pattern are shown in parentheses.

TABLE 5: PRESENT AND FUTURE STEMS OF εἰμί—"I AM"

Indicative Mood

	Present		Imperfect		Future	
	Singular	*Plural*	*Singular*	*Plural*	*Singular*	*Plural*
1.	εἰμί	ἐσμέν	ἤμην	ἦμεν	ἔσομαι	ἐσόμεθα
2.	εἶ	ἐστέ	ἦς	ἦτε	ἔσῃ	ἔσεσθε
3.	ἐστί(ν)	εἰσί(ν)	ἦν	ἦσαν	ἔσται	ἔσονται

Subjunctive Mood

1.	ὦ	ὦμεν
2.	ᾖς	ἦτε
3.	ᾖ	ὦσι

Imperative Mood

2.	ἴσθι	ἔστε
3.	ἔστω	ἔστωσαν

Infinitive

εἶναι   ἔσεσθαι

*Participle

ὤν, οὖσα, ὄν   ἐσόμενος, -η, -ον

*The full declension of ὤν is found on page 137.

TABLE 6: CONTRACT VERB ENDINGS WHEN CONTRACTED*

Primary Endings

Pres. Act. Indic.   Pres. Mid./Pass. Indic.

	α	ε	ο			α	ε	ο
ω	ῶ	ῶ	ῶ	ομαι	ῶμαι	οῦμαι	οῦμαι
εις	ᾷς	εῖς	οῖς	ῃ	ᾷ	ῇ	οῖ
ει	ᾷ	εῖ	οῖ	εται	ᾶται	εῖται	οῦται
ομεν	ῶμεν	οῦμεν	οῦμεν	ομεθα	ώμεθα	ούμεθα	ούμεθα
ετε	ᾶτε	εῖτε	οῦτε	εσθε	ᾶσθε	εῖσθε	οῦσθε
ουσι	ῶσι	οῦσι	οῦσι	ονται	ῶνται	οῦνται	οῦνται

Secondary Endings

Impft. Act. Indic.   Impft. Mid./Pass. Indic.

	α	ε	ο			α	ε	ο
ον	ων	ουν	ουν	ομην	ώμην	ούμην	ούμην
ες	ας	εις	ους	ου	ῶ	οῦ	οῦ
ε	α	ει	ου	ετο	ᾶτο	εῖτο	οῦτο
ομεν	ῶμεν	οῦμεν	οῦμεν	ομεθα	ώμεθα	ούμεθα	ούμεθα
ετε	ᾶτε	εῖτε	οῦτε	εσθε	ᾶσθε	εῖσθε	οῦσθε
ον	ων	ουν	ουν	οντο	ῶντο	οῦντο	οῦντο

*Accents have been shown where they will occur.

TABLE 7: CONDITIONAL SENTENCES

Condition Assumed To Be Real, Although It May Not Be

Protasis ("if" clause)	*Apodosis* (main clause)
εἰ (rarely ἐάv) + any tense of the indicative mood	any tense of the indicative; subjunctive or imperative may occur

Cf. Mt. 12:27f.; Rom. 6:8; 1 Cor. 15:1–15; Gal. 5:25

Condition Assumed As Unreal or Contrary to Fact

Protasis	*Apodosis*
εἰ + a past tense of the indicative	only past tenses, often with ἄv, indicating contingency

Cf. Jn. 15:19, 22; Acts 26:32; 1 Cor. 2:8

Future More Probable Condition

Protasis	*Apodosis*
ἐάv + subjunctive (present or aorist)	present or future indicative; sometimes the imperative

Cf. Mt. 12:29; Jn. 8:52; Acts 27:31; 1 Cor. 4:15; 1 Jn. 5:16

Future Less Probable Condition

Protasis	*Apodosis*
εἰ + optative mood	ἄv + optative mood

Cf. Lk. 1:62; Acts 27:39; 17:27

GREEK-ENGLISH VOCABULARY

The following list includes all terms introduced in the vocabularies. Principal parts of verbs will be found in those lists where the terms are introduced. Numbers after Greek words refer to the chapter where the words are introduced.

A

ἀγαθός, -ή, -όν (3) good
ἀγαπάω (15) I love
ἀγάπη, -ης, ἡ (4) love
ἀγαπητός, -ή, -όν (6) beloved, dear
ἄγγελος, -ου, ὁ (3) angel, messenger
ἅγιος, -α, -ον (3) holy
ἀγοράζω (9) I buy
ἀγρός, -οῦ, ὁ (22) field
ἄγω (2, 9) I lead, bring
ἀδελφός, -οῦ, ὁ (3) brother
αἷμα, αἵματος, τό (14) blood
αἴρω, (18) I lift, take or pick up, take away
αἰτέω (17) I ask, ask for, request
αἰών, -αἰῶνος, ὁ (13) eternity, age
αἰώνιος, -ον (10) eternal
ἀκάθαρτος, -ον (20) unclean
ἀκολουθέω (17) I follow, accompany
ἀκούω (2, 9) I hear
ἀλήθεια, -ας, ἡ (4) truth
ἀληθής, (M. and F.); -ές (N.) (14) true
ἀλλά (4) but, yet, rather
ἀλλήλων (11) of one another
ἄλλος, -η, -ο (3) other, another
ἁμαρτάνω (9, 15) I sin, do wrong
ἁμαρτία, –ας, ἡ (4) sin
ἁμαρτωλός, -όν (20) sinful; as a noun: sinner
ἀμήν (7) so let it be, amen, truly, verily
ἄν (7) An untranslated postpositive bit whose presence in a clause introduces an element of contingency.
ἀναβαίνω (15) I go up, ascend
ἀναγινώσκω (9) I read
ἀνάστασις, -εως, ἡ (13) resurrection
ἄνεμος, -ου, ὁ (22) wind
ἀνήρ, ἀνδρός, ὁ (13) man
ἄνθρωπος, -ου, ὁ (3) human being, man
ἀνίστημι (16) I raise, raise up; rise, stand up
ἀνοίγω (2, 9) I open
ἄξιος, -α, -ον (20) worthy

ἀπαγγέλλω (15) I report, announce, proclaim
ἅπας (14) whole, all, everybody
ἀπέρχομαι (11) I go away, depart
ἀπό (7); (Gen.) from
ἀποδίδωμι (16) I give away, pay, return, give back
ἀποθνήσκω (9) I die
ἀποκρίνομαι (11) I answer, reply
ἀποκτείνω (15) I kill
ἀπόλλυμι (16) I ruin, destroy, lose; Mid./Pass. I perish, die, am ruined
ἀπολύω (7) I release, let go, set free, dismiss, send away
ἀποστέλλω (15) I send away, send out
ἀπόστολος, -ου, ὁ (8) apostle
ἅπτω (11) I light, kindle; Mid. I touch, take hold of
ἄρα (21) so, then, consequently
ἀρνέομαι (18) I deny, repudiate
ἀρνίον, -ου, τό (22) lamb
ἄρτι (19) now, just now
ἄρτος, -ου, ὁ (7) bread
ἀρχή, ῆς, ἡ (10) beginning, ruler
ἀρχιερεύς, -έως, ὁ (13) high priest
ἄρχομαι (21) I begin
ἄρχων, ἄρχοντος, ὁ (13) ruler
ἀσθενέω (17) I am weak, sick
ἀσπάζομαι (11) I greet, welcome
αὐτός, -ή, -ό (5) he, she, it (oblique cases only); self (predicate position); the same (attributive position)
ἀφίημι (16) I send away, cancel, pardon, leave
ἄχρι (or ἄχρις) (7); (Gen.) as far as, until

B

βάλλω (15) I throw, put, place
βαπτίζω (2, 9) I baptize
βασιλεία, -ας, ἡ (4) kingdom, realm, reign
βασιλεύς, -έως, ὁ (13) king

209

βιβλίον, -ου, τό (22) book
βλασφημέω (17) I blaspheme, revile
βλέπω (2, 9) I see
βούλομαι (11, 21) I wish, am willing

Γ

γάρ (5) for
γέ (10) indeed, at least, really, even
γενεά, -ᾶς, ἡ (22) generation
γεννάω (15) I beget
γένος, γένους, τό (14) race, descendants
γῆ, -ῆς, ἡ (4) earth
γίνομαι (11) I come to be, become, happen
γινώσκω (2, 9) I know, learn, perceive
γλῶσσα, -ης, ἡ (4) tongue, language
γραμματεύς, γραμματέως, ὁ (13) scribe, expert in the law
γραφή, -ῆς, ἡ (7) writing, scripture
γράφω (2, 9) I write
γυνή, γυναικός, ἡ (13) woman

Δ

δαιμόνιον, -ου, τό (5) demon
δέ (5) but, and
δεῖ (21) it is necessary, one must, one ought
δείκνυμι (or δεικνύω) (16) I show
δεξιός, -ά, -όν (10) right
δεύτερος, -α, -ον (20) second
δέχομαι (11) I receive, take
δέω (17) I bind, tie
διά (8); (Gen.) through
(Acc.) on account of
διάβολος, -ον, (16) slanderous; as a noun: slanderer, devil
διαθήκη, -ης, -ἡ (22) covenant, will
διακονέω (17) I wait upon, serve, care for
διακονία, -ας, ἡ (22) waiting at tables, service, ministry
διδάσκαλος, -ου, ὁ (8) teacher
διδάσκω (2, 9) I teach
διδαχή, -ῆς, ἡ (22) teaching
δίδωμι (16) I give, yield, hand over, give up
διέρχομαι (11) I go, pass through
δίκαιος, -α, -ον (4) righteous
δικαιοσύνη, -ης, ἡ (5) righteousness
δικαιόω (15) I justify, pronounce righteous
διό (21) therefore, for this reason
διώκω (9) I pursue, persecute
δοκέω (17) I think, believe; seem
δόξα, -ης, ἡ (4) glory
δοξάζω (6, 9) I glorify

δοῦλος, -ου, ὁ (5) slave, servant
δύναμαι (21) I can, am able
δύναμις, δυνάμεως, ἡ (13) power, might; ability
δυνατός, -ή, -όν (20) powerful, possible
δύο (14) two
δώδεκα (20) twelve
δῶρον, ου, τό (5) gift

Ε

ἐάν (20) if
ἑαυτοῦ, -ῆς, -οῦ (6) of himself, of herself, of itself
ἐγγίζω (9) I come near, approach
ἐγγύς (19) near
ἐγείρω (18) I wake, raise or raise up, rise
ἐγώ (5) I
ἔθνος, ἔθνους, τό (14) nation, gentile
εἰ (4) if, whether
εἰμί (3, 9) I am, exist
εἰρήνη, -ης, ἡ (5) peace
εἰς (7); (Acc.) into, against, in order to
εἷς, μία, ἕν (14) one
εἰσέρχομαι (11) I enter, come into, go into
ἐκ (ἐξ before an initial vowel) (7); (Gen.) out of
ἕκαστος, -η, -ον (6) each, every
ἐκβάλλω (7, 9) I throw out, send out, expel
ἐκεῖ (19) there, in that place, to that place
ἐκεῖνος, -η, -ο (6) that
ἐκκλησία, -ας, ἡ (5) church, assembly
ἐκπορεύομαι (11) I go out
ἐλεέω (17) I have mercy, pity
ἐλπίζω (9) I hope
ἐλπίς, ἐλπίδος, ἡ (13) hope
ἐμαυτοῦ, -ῆς (6) of myself
ἐμός, -ή, -όν (10) my
ἔμπροσθεν (21); (Gen.) in front of, before
(Acc.) in front of, ahead
ἐν (7); (Dat.) in
ἐντολή, -ῆς, ἡ (7) commandment, order
ἐνώπιον (7); (Gen.) before
ἐξέρχομαι (11) I come out, go out
ἔξεστι(ν) (21) It is permitted, is possible, proper
ἐξουσία, -ας, ἡ (5) power, authority
ἔξω (7); (Gen.) outside
ἐπαγγελία, -ας, ἡ (10) promise
ἐπερωτάω (15) I ask
ἐπί (10); (Gen.) on, over
(Dat.) on the basis of, at
(Acc.) on, at, to

ἐπιγινώσκω (9) I come to know, recognize

ἐπιθυμία, -ας, ἡ (22) desire, passion

ἐπικαλέω (15) I call, name; I invoke, appeal to

ἐπιστρέφω (9) I return, turn around, turn back

ἐπιτίθημι (16) I lay upon, put upon

ἐπιτιμάω (18) I rebuke, reprove, warn

ἑπτά (20) seven

ἐργάζομαι (11) I work, do, accomplish

ἔργον, -ου, τό (3) work

ἔρημος, -ου, ἡ (4) wilderness, desert

ἔρχομαι (11) I come, go

ἐρωτάω (15) I ask, ask a question, request

ἐσθίω (9) I eat

ἔσχατος, -η, -ον (4) last

ἕτερος, -α, -ον (4) other

ἔτι (8) still, yet

ἑτοιμάζω (9) I prepare

ἔτος, ἔτους, τό (14) year

εὐαγγελίζω (6, 9) I evangelize, proclaim the gospel

εὐαγγέλιον, -ου, τό (3) gospel

εὐθύς, εὐθέως (19) immediately, at once

εὐλογέω (17) I bless, praise, speak well of

εὑρίσκω (2, 9) I find

εὐχαριστέω (17) I give thanks

ἐχθρός, -ά, -όν (20) hating; as a noun: enemy

ἔχω (2, 9) I have

ἕως (7); (Gen.) as far as, until

Z

ζάω (15) I live

ζητέω (15) I seek, look for

ζωή, -ῆς, ἡ (4) life

H

ἡ (4) the

ἤ (20, 23) or; than

ἥ (5) who, which, what

ἤδη (19) now, already, by this time

ἥλιος, -ου, ὁ (22) sun

ἡμέρα, -ας, ἡ (4) day

Θ

θάλασσα, -ης, ἡ (4) sea

θάνατος, -ου, ὁ (7) death

θαυμάζω (9) I marvel, wonder at

θέλημα, θελήματος, τό (14) will

θέλω (21) I wish, want, will

θεός, -οῦ, ὁ (3) God

θεραπεύω (9) I heal, care for, serve

θεωρέω (17) I behold, look at, perceive

θηρίον, -ου, τό (22) wild beast

θλῖψις, θλῖψεως, ἡ (13) tribulation, affliction

θρόνος, -ου, ὁ (8) throne

θύρα, -ας, ἡ (22) door, entrance

I

ἴδιος, -α, -ον (4) one's own

ἰδού (16) See! Behold!

ἱερεύς, ἱερέως, ὁ (13) priest

ἱερόν, -οῦ, τό (3) temple

'Ιησοῦς, -οῦ, ὁ (6) Jesus

ἱκανός, -ή, -όν (20) sufficient, able, considerable

ἱμάτιον, -ου, τό (11) garment

ἵνα (20) in order that, that

'Ιουδαῖος, -α, -ον (6) Jewish; as a noun: Jew

ἵστημι (16) I put, place, set; I stand, appear, stand still

'Ιωάν(ν)ης, -ου, ὁ (4) John

K

καθαρίζω (9) I cleanse

κάθημαι (11) I sit, stay, reside

καθίζω (9) I seat, sit

καθώς (8) just as

καί (4) and, even, also

καί ... καί (4) both ... and

καινός, -ή, -όν (20) new

καιρός, -οῦ, ὁ (11) time

κακός, -ή, -όν (20) bad, evil

καλέω (15) I call

καλός, -ή, -όν (3) beautiful

καλῶς (19) well, beautifully

καρδία, -ας, ἡ (4) heart

καρπός, -οῦ, ὁ (8) fruit

κατά (8); (Gen.) down from, against (Acc.) according to, throughout, during

καταβαίνω (15) I come down, go down

κατοικέω (17) I inhabit, dwell, live

καυχάομαι (18) I boast, glory, pride oneself in

κεφαλή, -ῆς, ἡ (7) head

κηρύσσω (2, 9) I preach, proclaim

κλαίω (9) I weep, cry out

κόσμος, ου, ὁ (3) world

κράζω (6, 9) I cry out
κρατέω (17) I hold, take into my possession, grasp
κρίνω (15) I judge, consider, decide
κρίσις, κρίσεως, ἡ (13) judgment
κύριος, -ου, ὁ (3) lord

Λ

λαλέω (15) I speak, give forth a sound
λαμβάνω (15) I take, receive
λαός, -οῦ, ὁ (5) people
λέγω (2, 9) I say, utter, express with words
λείπω (9) I leave
λίθος, -ου, ὁ (8) stone
λογίζομαι (11) I reckon, consider, count
λόγος, -ου, ὁ (3) word
λοιπός, -ή, -όν (4) remaining, other
λύω (2, 9) I loose, set free, untie, abolish

M

μαθητής, -οῦ, ὁ (4) disciple
μακάριος, -α, -ον (4) blessed
μᾶλλον (21) more, rather
μαρτυρέω (17) I bear witness, confirm, testify
μαρτυρία, -ας, ἡ (22) testimony, evidence
μάρτυς, μάρτυρος, ὁ (13) witness, martyr
μέγας, μεγάλη, μέγα (14) great, large
μείζων, -ονος, (21) larger, greater
μέλλω (21) I am about to, am on the point of; intend, propose
μέλος, μέλους, τό (14) member, part, limb
μέν (20) on the one hand, in fact, indeed
μένω (15) I remain, stay, abide
μέρος, μέρους, τό (14) part
μέσος, -η, -ον (10) middle, in the midst of
μετά (8); (Gen.) with
            (Acc.) after
μετανοέω (17) I change my mind, repent
μή (20) not, lest
μηδέ (21) and not, but not, nor, not even
μηδείς, μηδεμία, μηδέν (14) no, no one, nobody, nothing
μητέ (20) and not
μήτε ... μήτε (20) neither ... nor
μήτηρ, μητρός, ἡ (13) mother
μικρός, -ά, -όν (20) small, little
μισέω (17) I hate, abhor
μνημεῖον, -ου, τό (22) tomb, monument
μόνος, -η, -ον (10) only

N

ναί (5) yes, certainly
ναός, -οῦ, ὁ (22) temple
νεκρός, -ά, -όν (3) dead
νόμος, -ου, ὁ (3) law
νῦν (8) now
νύξ, νυκτός, ἡ (13) night

O

ὁ, ἡ, τό (3, 4) the
ὁδός, -οῦ, ἡ (4) way, road, way of life
οἶδα (10) I know
οἰκία, -ας, ἡ (10) house
οἰκοδομέω (17) I build, edify
οἶκος, -ου, ὁ (6) house
οἶνος, -ου, ὁ (22) wine
ὀλίγος, -η, -ον (20) little, few
ὅλος, -η, -ον (4) whole, all
ὅμοιος, -α, -ον (23) like
ὁμοίως (19) likewise, so, similarly, in the same way
ὄνομα, ὀνόματος, τό (14) name
ὀπίσω (19); (Gen.) behind, after
            (Adv.) behind
ὅπου (19) where, whither
ὅπως (20) in order that, that
ὁράω (15) I see
ὀργή, -ῆς, ἡ (22) anger, wrath, indignation
ὄρος, ὄρους, τό (14) mountain
ὅς, ἥ, ὅ (5) who, which, what
ὅσος, -η, -ον (4) as great as, as much as, all who
ὅστις, ἥτις, ὅ τι (20) whoever, whichever, whatever
ὅταν (20) whenever
ὅτε (8) when, while, as long as
ὅτι (7) that, because
οὐ, οὐκ, οὐχ (5) no, not
οὐαί (20) Woe! Alas!
οὐδέ (5) and not, nor, neither, not even
  οὐδέ ... οὐδέ (5) neither ... nor
οὐδείς, οὐδεμία, οὐδέν (14) no, no one, nobody, nothing
οὐκέτι (19) no longer
οὖν (5) therefore
οὐρανός, -οῦ, ὁ (3) heaven
οὖς, ὠτός, τό (14) ear
οὔτε (11) and not
  οὔτε ... οὔτε (11) neither ... nor

οὗτος, αὕτη, τοῦτο (6) this
οὕτως (8) thus
οὐχί (21) not, no
ὀφείλω (15) I owe, am indebted, ought, must, am obligated
ὀφθαλμός, -οῦ, ὁ (7) eye
ὄχλος, -ου, ὁ (5) crowd

Π

παιδίον, -ου, τό (10) child
πάλιν (8) again, back
πάντοτε (19) always, at all times
παρά (10); (Gen.) from alongside
(Dat.) beside, in the presence of
(Acc.) alongside of
παραβολή, -ῆς, ἡ (10) parable
παραγγέλλω (15) I give orders, command
παραγίνομαι (11) I come, arrive
παραδίδωμι (16) I hand over, deliver, pass on, hand down
παρακαλέω (15) I beseech, exhort, console
παραλαμβάνω (9) I receive, take along or with
παρέρχομαι (11) I pass away, pass by
παρθένος, -ου, ἡ (4) virgin
παρίστημι (16) I place beside, present, offer; stand
παρρησία, -ας, ἡ (22) boldness, confidence
πᾶς, πᾶσα, πᾶν (14) all, every, whole
πάσχω (9) I suffer, endure
πατήρ, πατρός, ὁ (13) father
πείθω (9) I persuade
πειράζω (9) I try, atempt, put to the test, tempt
πέμπω (2, 9) I send
πέντε (20) five
περί (8); (Gen.) concerning, about
(Acc.) around
περιπατέω (17) I walk around, go about, walk
περισσεύω (9) I abound, am rich
περιτομή, -ῆς, ἡ (22) circumcision
πίνω (9) I drink
πίπτω (9) I fall
πιστεύω (2, 9) I believe
πίστις, πίστεως, ἡ (13) faith
πιστός, -ή, -όν (3) faithful
πλανάω (18) I lead astray, deceive, wander about
πλείων, -ονος (21) more
πλῆθος, πλήθους, τό (14) multitude, crowd

πλήν (19); (Gen.) except
(Adv.) but, however, only
πληρόω (15) I fulfill, fill
πλοῖον, -ου, τό (10) boat
πνεῦμα, πνεύματος, τό (14) spirit, breath, wind
ποιέω (15) I do, make, practice
ποῖος, -α, -ον (21) of what kind? which? what?
πόλις, πόλεως, ἡ (13) city
πολύς, πολλή, πολύ (14) much, many
πονηρός, -ά, -όν (6) evil
πορεύομαι (11) I go, proceed, travel
ποτήριον, -ου, τό (22) cup
ποῦ (19) where?
πούς, ποδός, ὁ (13) foot
πράσσω (9) I do, accomplish
πρεσβύτερος, -α, -ον (4) elder
πρό (7); (Gen.) before
πρόβατον, -ου, τό (22) sheep
πρός (7); (Acc.) to, toward, with
προσέρχομαι (11) I come to, go to
προσευχή, -ῆς, ἡ (22) prayer
προσεύχομαι (11) I pray
προσκυνέω (17) I worship, prostrate myself before
προσφέρω (18) I bring (to), offer, present
πρόσωπον, -ου, τό (3) face, presence
προφήτης, ου, ὁ (4) prophet
πρῶτος, -η, -ον (4) first, earlier, earliest
πτωχός, -ή, -όν (20) poor; as a noun: a poor man or woman
πῦρ, πυρός, τό (14) fire
πῶς (8) how? in what way?

Ρ

ῥῆμα, ῥήματος, τό (14) word, saying

Σ

σάββατον, -ου, τό (11) Sabbath
σάρξ, σαρκός, ἡ (13) flesh
σεαυτοῦ, -ῆς (6) of yourself
σημεῖον, -ου, τό (5) sign
σήμερον (19) today
Σίμων, Σίμονος, ὁ (13) Simon
σκανδαλίζω (9) I cause to sin, cause to fall; give offense to
σκότος, σκότους, τό (14) darkness
σοφία, -ας, ἡ (10) wisdom
σπείρω (18) I sow, scatter

σπέρμα, σπέρματος, τό (14) seed, descendant(s)
σταυρόω (15) I crucify
στόμα, στόματος, τό (14) mouth
στρέφω (9) I turn
σύ (5) you
σύν (7); (Dat.) with
συνάγω (7) I gather, bring, lead together
συναγωγή, -ῆς, ἡ (10) synagogue
συνείδησις, συνειδήσεως, ἡ (13) consciousness, conscience
συνέρχομαι (11) I come together
σῴζω (2, 9) I save
σῶμα, σώματος, τό (14) body
σωτηρία, -ας, ἡ (22) salvation

Τ

τε (13) and
τε καί (13) and
τε . . . τε (13) as . . . so; not only . . . but also
τέκνον, -ου, τό (3) child
τέλος, τέλους, τό (14) end
τέσσαρες (M. and F.); τέσσαρα (N. may occur as τέσσερα); (14) four
τηρέω (15) I keep, observe, fulfill
τίθημι (16) I put, place, lay
τιμή, -ῆς, ἡ (22) honor, price
τίς (M. and F.); τί (N.); (14) who? which? what?
　τί as an adverb: why?
τις (M. and F.); τι (N.); (14) someone, a certain one, something
τό (3) the
τοιοῦτος, τοιαύτη, τοιοῦτον (or τοιοῦτο) (10) such
τόπος, -ου, ὁ (11) place
τότε (8) then, at that time
τρεῖς (M. and F.); τρία (N.); (14) three
τρίτος, -η, -ον (20) third
τυφλός, -ή, -όν (20) blind

Υ

ὕδωρ, ὕδατος, τό (14) water
υἱός, -οῦ, ὁ (3) son
ὑπάγω (8, 9) I depart, go, go away
ὑπάρχω (8, 9) I am, exist
ὑπέρ (8); (Gen.) in behalf of
　(Acc.) above

ὑπό (8); (Gen.) by
　(Acc.) under
ὑπομονή, -ῆς, ἡ (22) steadfast endurance
ὑποστρέφω (9) I return, turn back
ὑποτάσσω (9) I subject, subordinate; pass. subject oneself, be subjected

Φ

φαίνω (15) I shine, give light, become visible
φανερόω (15) I manifest, reveal
φέρω (18) I bear, carry, bring
φεύγω (9) I flee, escape
φημί (16) I say, affirm
φιλέω (17) I love, like
φοβέομαι (17) I am afraid, fear, am frightened
φόβος, -ου, ὁ (22) fear, terror
φυλακή, -ῆς, ἡ (22) guard, prison, watch
φυλάσσω (9) I watch, guard, keep
φυλή, -ῆς, ἡ (22) tribe
φωνέω (17) I call, cry out, summon
φωνή, -ῆς, ἡ (4) voice
φῶς, φωτός, τό (14) light

Χ

χαίρω (18) I rejoice, am glad
χαρά, -ᾶς, ἡ (4) joy
χάρις, χάριτος, ἡ (13) grace, favor
χείρ, χειρός, ἡ (13) hand
χρεία, -ας, ἡ (22) need
Χριστός, -οῦ, ὁ (6) the Anointed One, Messiah, Christ
χρόνος, -ου, ὁ (8) time
χωρίς (21); (Gen) without, apart from

Ψ

ψυχή, -ῆς, ἡ (4) soul, life, living creature

Ω

ὧδε (19) here, in this place; in this case
ὥρα, -ας, ἡ (5) hour
ὡς (8) as, about
ὥσπερ (23) just as, even as
ὥστε (21) so that; for this reason, therefore

ENGLISH-GREEK VOCABULARY

(Numbers indicate chapters)

A

abandon (9)   λείπω
abhor (17)   μισέω
abide (15)   μένω
ability (13)   δύναμις, -εως, ἡ
able (20, 21)   δύναμαι; ἱκανός, -ή, -όν
abound (9)   περισσεύω
about (8, 9)   περί; ὡς
above (8)   ὑπέρ
accompany (17)   ἀκολουθέω
accomplish (9, 11)   ἐργάζομαι; πράσσω
according to (8)   κατά
affirm (15)   φημί
affliction (13)   θλῖψις, θλίψεως, ἡ
afraid (17)   φοβέομαι
after (8, 19)   μετά; ὀπίσω
again (8)   πάλιν
against (8)   κατά
age (13)   αἰών, αἰῶνος, ὁ
ahead (21)   ἔμπροσθεν
alas (20)   οὐαί
all (4, 14)   πᾶς, πᾶσα, πᾶν; ὅλος, -η, -ον
alongside (10)   παρά
already (19)   ἤδη
also (4)   καί
always (19)   πάντοτε
am (3, 11)   γίνομαι; εἰμί; ὑπάρχω
am about to (21)   μέλλω
amen (7)   ἀμήν
am on the point of (21)   μέλλω
and (4, 5, 13)   δέ; καί; τε; τε καί
and not (5, 11, 20, 21)   μήδε; μήτε; οὐδέ; οὔτε
angel (3)   ἄγγελος, -ου, ὁ
anger (22)   ὀργή, -ης, ἡ
announce (15)   ἀπαγγέλλω
anointed one (6)   Χριστός, -οῦ, ὁ
another, of one (11)   ἀλλήλων
answer (11)   ἀποκρίνομαι
apart from (21)   χωρίς
apostle (8)   ἀπόστολος, -ου, ὁ
appeal to (15)   ἐπικαλέω
approach (9)   ἐγγίζω

around (8)   περί
arrive (11)   παραγίνομαι
as (8)   ὡς
as far as (7)   ἕως
as great as (4)   ὅσος, -η, -ον
as long as (8)   ὅτε
as much as (4)   ὅσος, -η, -ον
as . . . so (13)   τὲ . . . τέ
ascend (15)   ἀναβαίνω
ask, ask for (15, 17)   αἰτέω; ἐπερωτάω; ἐρωτάω
assembly (5)   ἐκκλησία, -ας, ἡ
at (10)   ἐπί
at all times (19)   πάντοτε
at least (20)   γέ
at once (19)   εὐθύς; εὐθέως
at that time (8)   τότε
attempt (9)   πειράζω
authority (5)   ἐξουσία, -ας, ἡ

B

bad (20)   κακός, -ή, -όν
back (8)   πάλιν
baptize (2, 9)   βαπτίζω
bear (18)   φέρω
bear witness (17)   μαρτυρέω
beautiful (3)   καλός, -ή, -όν
beautifully (19)   καλῶς
because (7)   ὅτι
become (11)   γίνομαι
become visible (15)   φαίνω
before (7, 21)   ἐνώπιον; ἔμπροσθεν; πρό
beget (15)   γεννάω
begin (21)   ἄρχομαι
beginning (10)   ἀρχή, -ῆς, -ἡ
behind (19)   ὀπίσω
behold (16, 17)   θεωρέω; ἰδού
believe (2, 9, 17)   δοκέω; πιστεύω
beloved (6)   ἀγαπητός, -ή, -όν
beseech (15)   παρακαλέω
beside (10)   παρά
bind (17)   δέω
blaspheme (17)   βλασφημέω

215

bless (17)　εὐλογέω
blessed (4)　μακάριος, -α, -ον
blind (20)　τυφλός, -ή, -όν
blood (14)　αἷμα, αἵματος, -τό
boast (18)　καυχάομαι
boat (10)　πλοῖον, -ου, τό
body (14)　σῶμα, σώματος, τό
boldness (22)　παρρησία, -ας, ἡ
book (22)　βίβλιον, -ου, τό
both . . . and (4)　καὶ . . . καί
bread (7)　ἄρτος, -ου, ὁ
breath (14)　πνεῦμα, πνεύματος, τό
bring (7, 18)　προσφέρω; συνάγω; φέρω
bring good news (9)　εὐαγγελίζω
brother (3)　ἀδελφός, -οῦ, ὁ
build (17)　οἰκοδομέω
but (4, 19)　δέ; ἀλλά; πλήν
but not (21)　μηδέ
buy (8)　ἀγοράζω
by (8)　ὑπό
by this time (19)　ἤδη

C

call (15, 17)　ἐπικαλέω; καλέω; φωνέω
can (21)　δύναμαι
cancel (16)　ἀφίημι
care for (17)　διακονέω
carry (18)　φέρω
cause to fall; cause to sin (9)　σκανδαλίζω
certain one (14)　τις, τι
certainly (5)　ναί
change my mind (17)　μετανοέω
child (3, 10)　παιδίον, -ου, τό; τέκνον, -ου, τό
Christ (6)　Χριστός, -οῦ, ὁ
church (5)　ἐκκλησία, -ας, ἡ
circumcision (22)　περιτομή, -ῆς, ἡ
city (13)　πόλις, πόλεως, ἡ
cleanse (9)　καθαρίζω
come (11)　ἔρχομαι; παραγίνομαι
come down (15)　καταβαίνω
come into (11)　εἰσέρχομαι
come near (9)　ἐγγίζω
come out (11)　ἐξέρχομαι
come to (11)　προσέρχομαι
come to be (11)　γίνομαι
come together (11)　συνέρχομαι
command (15)　παραγγέλλω
commandment (7)　ἐντολή, -ῆς, ἡ
concerning (8)　περί
confidence (22)　παρρησία, -ας, ἡ
confirm (17)　μαρτυρέω

conscience (13)　συνείδησις, συνειδήσεως, ἡ
consciousness (13)　συνείδησις, συνειδήσεως, ἡ
consequently (21)　ἄρα
consider (11, 15)　κρίνω; λογίζομαι
considerable (20)　ἱκανός, -ή, -όν
console (15)　παρακαλέω
count (11)　λογίζομαι
covenant (22)　διαθήκη, -ης, ἡ
crowd (5, 14)　ὄχλος, -ου, ὁ; πλῆθος, πλήθους, τό
crucify (15)　σταυρόω
cry out (6, 9, 17)　κλαίω; κράζω; φωνέω
cup (22)　ποτήριον, -ου, τό

D

darkness (14)　σκότος, σκότους, τό
day (4)　ἡμέρα, -ας, ἡ
dead (3)　νεκρός, -ά, -όν
dear (6)　ἀγαπητός, -ή, -όν
death (7)　θάνατος, -ου, ὁ
deceive (18)　πλανάω
decide (15)　κρίνω
deliver (16)　παραδίδωμι
demon (5)　δαιμόνιον, -ου, τό
deny (18)　ἀρνέομαι
depart (8, 9)　ὑπάγω
descendant(s) (14)　γένος, γένους, τό; σπέρμα, σπέρματος, τό
desert (4)　ἔρημος, -ου, ἡ
desolate (4)　ἔρημος, -ον
destroy (16)　ἀπόλλυμι
devil (16)　διάβολος, -ου, ὁ
die (9, 16)　ἀποθνήσκω; ἀπόλλυμι
disciple (4)　μαθητής, -οῦ, ὁ
do (9, 11, 15)　ἐργάζομαι; ποιέω; πράσσω
door (22)　θύρα, -ας, ἡ
down from (8)　κατά
do wrong (15)　ἁμαρτάνω
drink (9)　πίνω
during (8)　κατά
dwell (17)　κατοικέω

E

each (6)　ἕκαστος, -η, -ον
eager desire (22)　ἐπιθυμία, -ας, ἡ
ear (14)　οὖς, ὠτός, τό
earlier, earliest (4)　πρῶτος, -η, -ον
earth (4)　γῆ, -ῆς, ἡ
eat (9)　ἐσθίω
edify (17)　οἰκοδομέω

elder (4) πρεσβύτερος, -α, -ον
empty (4) ἔρημος, -ον
end (14) τέλος, τέλους, τό
endure (9) πάσχω
enemy (20) ἐχθρός, -ά, -όν
enter (11) εἰσέρχομαι
entrance (22) θύρα, -ας, ἡ
escape (9) φεύγω
eternal (10) αἰώνιος
eternity (13) αἰών, αἰῶνος, ὁ
evangelize (6, 9) εὐαγγελλίζω
even (4, 8, 20) ἔτι; καί; γέ
even as (23) ὥσπερ
every (6, 14) ἕκαστος, -η, -ον; πᾶς, πᾶσα, πᾶν
everybody (14) ἅπας, ἅπασα, ἅπαν
evidence (22) μαρτυρία, -ας, ἡ
evil (6, 20) κακός, -ή, -όν; πονηρός, -ά, -όν
except (19) πλήν
exhort (15) παρακαλέω
exist (3, 8, 9) εἰμί; ὑπάρχω
expel (9) ἐκβάλλω
expert in the law (13) γραμματεύς, γραμματέως, ὁ
eye (7) ὀφθαλμός, -οῦ, ὁ

F

face (3) πρόσωπον, -ου, τό
faith (13) πίστις, πίστεως, ἡ
faithful (3) πιστός, -ή, -όν
fall (9) πίπτω
father (13) πατήρ, πατρός, ὁ
favor (13) χάρις, χάριτος, ἡ
fear (17, 22) φοβέομαι; φόβος, -ου, ὁ
few (20) ὀλίγος, -η, -ον
field (22) ἀγρός, -οῦ, ὁ
fill (15) πληρόω
find (2, 9) εὑρίσκω
fire (14) πῦρ, πυρός, τό
first (4) πρῶτος, -η, -ον
five (20) πέντε
flee (9) φεύγω
flesh (13) σάρξ, σαρκός, ἡ
follow (17) ἀκολουθέω
foot (13) πούς, ποδός, ὁ
for (5) γάρ
for this reason (21) διό; ὥστε
four (14) τέσσαρες, τέσσαρα
frightened, I am (17) φοβέομαι
from (7) ἀπό
fruit (8) καρπός, -οῦ, ὁ
fulfill (15) πληρόω; τηρέω

G

garment (11) ἱμάτιον, -ου, τό
gather (7) συνάγω
gather together (9) συνάγω
generation (22) γενεά, -άς, ἡ
Gentile (14) ἔθνος, ἔθνους, τό
give (16) δίδωμι
give away (16) ἀποδίδωμι
give back (16) ἀποδίδωμι
give light (15) φαίνω
give offense to (9) σκανδαλίζω
give orders (15) παραγγέλλω
give thanks (17) εὐχαριστέω
give up (16) δίδωμι
glad, I am (18) χαίρω
glorify (6, 9) δοξάζω
glory (4, 18) δόξα, -ης, ἡ; καυχάομαι
go (8, 9, 11) ὑπάγω; διέρχομαι; ἔρχομαι; πορεύομαι
go about (17) περιπατέω
go away (8, 9) ὑπάγω
go down (15) καταβαίνω
go into (11) εἰσέρχομαι
go out (11) ἐκπορεύομαι; ἐξέρχομαι
go to (11) προσέρχομαι
go up (15) ἀναβαίνω
God, god (3) θεός, -οῦ, ὁ
good (3) ἀγαθός, -ή, -όν
gospel (3) εὐαγγέλιον, -ου, τό
grace (13) χάρις, χάριτος, ἡ
grasp (17) κρατέω
great (14) μέγας, μεγάλη, μέγα
greater (15) μείζων, μείζονος

H

hand (13) χείρ, χειρός, ἡ
hand down (16, 17) παραδίδωμι
hand over (16) δίδωμι; παραδίδωμι
happen (11) γίνομαι
hate (17) μισέω
hating (20) ἐχθρός, -ά, -όν
have (2, 9) ἔχω
he (5) αὐτός
head (7) κεφαλή, -ῆς, ἡ
heal (9) θεραπεύω
hear (2, 9) ἀκούω
heart (4) καρδία, -ας, ἡ
heaven (3) οὐρανός, -οῦ, ὁ
here (19) ὧδε
herself, of (6) ἑαυτῆς
high priest (13) ἀρχιερεύς, ἀρχιερέως, ὁ

himself, of (6)   ἑαυτοῦ
hold (17)   κρατέω
honor (22)   τιμή, -ῆς, ἡ
hope (9, 13)   ἐλπίζω; ἐλπίς, ἐλπίδος, ἡ
hour (5)   ὥρα, -ας, ἡ
house (6, 10)   οἰκία, -ας, ἡ; οἶκος, -ου, ὁ
how? (8)   πῶς
however (19)   πλήν

I

I (5)   ἐγώ
if (4, 20)   εἰ; ἐάν
immediately (19)   εὐθύς; εὐθέως
in (7)   ἐν
indebted, I am (15)   ὀφείλω
indeed (20)   γέ; μέν
indignation (22)   ὀργή, -ῆς, ἡ
in behalf of (8)   ὑπέρ
in fact (20)   μέν
in front of (21)   ἔμπροσθεν
inhabit (17)   κατοικέω
in order that (20)   ἵνα; ὅπως
intend (21)   μέλλω
in that place (19)   ἐκεῖ
in the presence of (10)   παρά
in this case, in this place (19)   ὧδε
in what way? (8)   πῶς
into (7)   εἰς
invoke (15)   ἐπικαλέω
it (5)   αὐτό
itself, of (6)   ἑαυτοῦ

J

Jesus (6)   Ἰησοῦς, -οῦ, ὁ
Jew (6)   Ἰουδαῖος, -ου, ὁ
Jewish (6)   Ἰουδαῖος, -α, -ον
John (4)   Ἰωάν(ν)ης, -ου, ὁ
joy (4)   χαρά, -ᾶς, ἡ
judge (15)   κρίνω
judgment (13)   κρίσις, κρίσεως, ἡ
just (4)   δίκαιος, -α, -ον
just as (8, 23)   καθώς; ὥσπερ
justify (15)   δικαιόω
just now (19)   ἄρτι

K

keep (9, 15)   τηρέω; φυλάσσω
kill (15)   ἀποκτείνω
king (13)   βασιλεύς, βασιλέως, ὁ
kingdom (4)   βασιλεία, -ας, ἡ

know (9, 10)   γινώσκω; οἶδα
know, come to (9)   ἐπιγινώσκω

L

lamb (22)   ἀρνίον, -ου, τό
language (4)   γλῶσσα, -ης, ἡ
large (14)   μέγας, μεγάλη, μέγα
larger (15)   μείζων, μείζονος
last (4)   ἔσχατος, -η, -ον
law (3)   νόμος, -ου, ὁ
lay (16)   τίθημι
lay upon (16)   ἐπιτίθημι
lead (2, 9)   ἄγω
lead astray (18)   πλανάω
lead together (7)   συνάγω
leave (9, 16)   λείπω; ἀφίημι
lest (20)   μή
let go (7)   ἀπολύω
life (4)   ζωή, -ῆς, ἡ; ψυχή, -ῆς, ἡ
lift (18)   αἴρω
light a fire (9, 11)   ἅπτω
light (14)   φῶς, φωτός, τό
like (17, 23)   ὅμοιος, -α, -ον; φιλέω
likewise (19)   ὁμοίως
limb (14)   μέλος, μέλους, τό
little (20)   μικρός, -ά, -όν; ὀλίγος, -η, -ον
live (15, 17)   ζάω; κατοικέω
living creature (4)   ψυχή, -ῆς, ἡ
look at (17)   θεωρέω
look for (15)   ζητέω
loose (2)   λύω
Lord, lord (3)   κύριος, -ου, ὁ
lose (16)   ἀπόλλυμι
love (4, 15, 17)   ἀγάπη, -ης, ἡ; ἀγαπάω; φιλέω

M

make (15)   ποιέω
make manifest (15)   φανερόω
man (3, 13)   ἄνθρωπος, -ου, ὁ; ἀνήρ, ἀνδρός, ὁ
many (14)   πολύς, πολλή, πολύ
martyr (13)   μάρτυς, μάρτυρος, ὁ
marvel (9)   θαυμάζω
member (14)   μέλος, μέλους, τό
mercy, to have (17)   ἐλεέω
Messiah (6)   Χριστός, -οῦ, ὁ
middle (10)   μέσος, -η, -ον
midst of (10)   μέσος, -η, -ον
might (13)   δύναμις, δυναμέως, ἡ
ministry (22)   διακονία, -ας, ἡ

monument (22) μνημεῖον, -ου, τό
more (21) μᾶλλον; πλείων, πλείονος
mother (13) μήτηρ, μητρός, ἡ
mountain (14) ὄρος, ὄρους, τό
mouth (14) στόμα, στόματος, τό
much (14) πολύς, πολλή, πολύ
multitude (14) πλῆθος, πλήθους, τό
must (21) δεῖ
my (10) ἐμός, -ή, -όν
myself, of (6) ἐμαυτοῦ, -ῆς

N

name (14) ὄνομα, ὀνόματος, τό
name, I give a (15) ἐπικαλέω
nation (14) ἔθνος, ἔθνους, τό
near (19) ἐγγύς
necessary (21) δεῖ
need (22) χρεία, -ας, ἡ
neither (5, 11) μήτε; οὐδέ; οὔτε
nevertheless (19) πλήν
new (20) καινός, -ή, -όν
night (13) νύξ, νυκτός, ἡ
no (5, 14, 21) μηδείς; οὐδείς; οὐ; οὐχί
nobody (14) μηδείς; οὐδείς
no longer (19) οὐκέτι
no one (14) οὐδείς; μηδείς
nor (5, 11, 21) μήδε; οὐδέ; οὔτε
not (5, 20, 21) μή; οὐ; οὐκ; οὐχ; οὐχί
not even (21) μήδε
not only . . . but also (13) τὲ . . . τέ
nothing (14) μηδείς; οὐδείς
now (8, 19) ἤδη; νῦν; ἄρτι

O

observe (15) τηρέω
of what kind? (21) ποῖος, -α, -ον
offense, give (9) σκανδαλίζω
offer (16) παρίστημι; προσφέρω
on (10) ἐπί
on account of (18) διά
on the basis of (10) ἐπί
on the one hand (20) μέν
one (14) εἷς, μία, ἕν
one's own (4) ἴδιος, -α, -ον
only (10) μόνος, -η, -ον; πλήν
open (2, 9) ἀνοίγω
or (20) ἤ
order (7) ἐντολή, -ῆς, ἡ
other (4) ἕτερος, -α, -ον; λοιπός, -ή, -όν
ought (21) δεῖ
out of (7) ἐκ

outside (7) ἔξω
over (10) ἐπί
owe (15) ὀφείλω

P

parable (10) παραβολή, -ῆς, ἡ
pardon (16) ἀφίημι
part (14) μέλος, μέλους, τό; μέρος, μέρους, τό
pass away (11) παρέρχομαι
pass by (11) παρέρχομαι
pass on (16) παραδίδωμι
pass through (11) διέρχομαι
passion (22) ἐπιθυμία, -ας, ἡ
pay (16) ἀποδίδωμι
peace (5) εἰρήνη, -ης, ἡ
people (5) λαός, -οῦ, ὁ
perceive (17) θεωρέω
perish (16) ἀπόλλυμι
permitted, it is (21) ἔξεστι
persecute (9) διώκω
persuade (9) πείθω
pick up (18) αἴρω
pity (17) ἐλεέω
place (15, 16) βάλλω; ἵστημι; τίθημι
place (noun: 10) τόπος, -ου, ὁ
place beside (16) παρίστημι
poor (20) πτωχός, -ή, -όν
possible (20) δυνατός, -ή, -όν
possible, it is (21) ἔξεστι
possession, take into (17) κρατέω
power (5, 13) δύναμις, δυνάμεως, ἡ; ἐξουσία, -ας, ἡ
powerful (20) δυνατός, -ή, -όν
practice (15) ποιέω
praise (17) εὐλογέω
pray (11) προσεύχομαι
prayer (22) προσευχή, -ῆς, ἡ
preach (2, 9) κηρύσσω
prepare (9) ἑτοιμάζω
present (16) παρίστημι; προσφέρω
price (22) τιμή, -ῆς, ἡ
pride oneself in (18) καυχάομαι
priest (13) ἱερεύς, ἱερέως, ὁ
prison (22) φυλακή, -ῆς, ἡ
proceed (11) πορεύομαι
proclaim (9, 15) κηρύσσω; ἀπαγγέλλω
promise (10) ἐπαγγελία, -ας, ἡ
pronounce righteous (15) δικαιόω
proper, it is (21) ἔξεστι
prophet (4) προφήτης, -ου, ὁ
propose (21) μέλλω

prostrate oneself before (17)   προσκυνέω
pursue (9)   διώκω
put (15, 16)   βάλλω; ἵστημι; τίθημι
put upon (16)   ἐπιτίθημι

R

race (14)   γένος, γένους, τό
raise (up) (16, 18)   ἀνίστημι; ἐγείρω
rather (4, 21)   μᾶλλον
read (9)   ἀναγινώσκω
really (20)   γέ
realm (4)   βασιλεία, -ας, ἡ
rebuke (18)   ἐπιτιμάω
receive (9, 11)   δέχομαι; λαμβάνω; παραλαμβάνω
reckon (11)   λογίζομαι
recognize (9)   ἐπιγινώσκω
reign (4)   βασιλεία, -ας, ἡ
rejoice (18)   χαίρω
release (7, 9,)   ἀπολύω
remain (15)   μένω
remaining (4)   λοιπός, -ή, -όν
repent (17)   μετανοέω
reply (11)   ἀποκρίνομαι
report (15)   ἀπαγγέλλω
reprove (18)   ἐπιτιμάω
repudiate (18)   ἀρνέομαι
request (15, 17)   ἐρωτάω; αἰτέω
reside (11)   κάθημαι
resurrection (13)   ἀνάστασις, ἀναστάσεως, ἡ
return (9)   ἐπιστρέφω; ὑποστρέφω
revile (7)   βλασφημέω
rich, I am (9)   περισσεύω
right (10)   δεξιός, -ά, -όν
righteous (4)   δίκαιος, -α, -ον
righteousness (5)   δικαιοσύνη, -ης, ἡ
rise (16, 18)   ἐγείρω; ἀνίστημι
road (4)   ὁδός, -οῦ, ἡ
ruin (16)   ἀπόλλυμι
ruler (10, 13)   ἀρχή, -ῆς, ἡ; ἄρχων, ἄρχοντος, ὁ

S

Sabbath (11)   σάββατον, -ου, τό
salvation (22)   σωτηρία, -ας, ἡ
same way, in the (19)   ὁμοίως
save (2, 9)   σῴζω
say (2, 9, 16)   λέγω; φημί
saying (14)   ῥῆμα, ῥήματος, τό
scatter (18)   σπείρω
scribe (13)   γραμματεύς, γραμματέως, ἡ

Scripture (7)   γραφή, -ῆς, ἡ
sea (4)   θάλασσα, -ης, ἡ
season (11)   καιρός, -οῦ, ὁ
seat (9)   καθίζω
second (20)   δεύτερος, -α, -ον
see (2, 9, 15, 16)   βλέπω; ἰδού; ὁράω
seed (14)   σπέρμα, σπέρματος, τό
seek (15)   ζητέω
seem (17)   δοκέω
send (2, 9)   πέμπω
send away (15, 16)   ἀποστέλλω; ἀφίημι
send out (7)   ἐκβάλλω
servant (5)   δοῦλος, -ου, ὁ
serve (17)   διακονέω
service (22)   διακονία, -ας, ἡ
set (16)   ἵστημι
seven (20)   ἑπτά
she (5)   αὐτή
sheep (22)   πρόβατον, -ου, τό
shine (15)   φαίνω
show (16)   δείκνυμι
sick, I am (17)   ἀσθενέω
sign (5)   σημεῖον, -ου, τό
similarly (19)   ὁμοίως
Simon (3)   Σίμων, Σίμονος, ὁ
sin (4, 9, 15)   ἁμαρτία, -ας, ἡ; ἁμαρτάνω
sinful (20)   ἁμαρτωλός, -όν
sinner (20)   ἁμαρτωλός, -οῦ, ὁ
sit (9, 11)   κάθημαι; καθίζω
slanderous (16)   διάβολος, -ον
slave (5)   δοῦλος, -ου, ὁ
small (20)   μικρός, -ά, -όν
so (19)   ὁμοίως
so let it be (7)   ἀμήν
so that (21)   ὥστε
so then (21)   ἄρα
someone (14)   τις, τι
something (14)   τις, τι
son (3)   υἱός, -οῦ, ὁ
soul (4)   ψυχή, -ῆς, ἡ
sound (give forth) (15)   λαλέω
sow (18)   σπείρω
speak (15)   λαλέω
speak well of (17)   εὐλογέω
spirit (14)   πνεῦμα, πνεύματος, τό
stand (16)   ἵστημι; παρίστημι
stand up (16)   ἀνίστημι
stay (11, 15)   κάθημαι; μένω
steadfast endurance (22)   ὑπομονή, -ῆς, ἡ
still (8)   ἔτι
stone (8)   λίθος, -ου, ὁ
subject; subject oneself; be subjected (9)   ὑποτάσσω

subordinate (9) ὑποτάσσω
such (10) τοιοῦτος, τοιαύτη, τοιοῦτον
suffer (9) πάσχω
sufficient (20) ἱκανός, -ή, -όν
summon (17) φωνέω
sun (22) ἥλιος, -ου, ὁ
synagogue (10) συναγωγή, ῆς, ἡ

T

take (9, 11) λαμβάνω; δέχομαι
take away (18) αἴρω
take hold of (11) ἅπτομαι
take up (18) αἴρω
teach (2, 9) διδάσκω
teacher (8) διδάσκαλος, -ου, ὁ
teaching (22) διδαχή, -ῆς, ἡ
temple (3, 22) ἱερόν, -οῦ, τό; ναός, -οῦ, ὁ
tempt (9) πειράζω
terror (22) φόβος, -ου, ὁ
test, I put to (9) πειράζω
testify (17) μαρτυρέω
testimony (22) μαρτυρία, -ας, ἡ
than (23) ἤ
that (6, 7, 20) ἐκεῖνος, -η, -ον; ἵνα; ὅπως;
    ὅτι
the (3) ὁ, ἡ, τό
then (5, 8) οὖν; τότε
there (19) ἐκεῖ
therefore (5, 21) οὖν; διό; ὥστε
think (17) δοκέω
third (20) τρίτος, -η, -ον
this, this one (6) οὗτος, αὕτη, τοῦτο
three (14) τρεῖς, τρία
throne (8) θρόνος, -ου, ὁ
through (8) διά
throughout (8) κατά
throw (15) βάλλω
throw out (7, 9) ἐκβάλλω
thus (8) οὕτως
tie (17) δέω
time (8, 11) καιρός, -οῦ, ὁ; χρόνος, -ου, ὁ
to (7, 10) ἐπί; πρός
to that place (19) ἐκεῖ
to this place (19) ὧδε
today (19) σήμερον
tomb (22) μνημεῖον, -ου, τό
tongue (4) γλῶσσα, -ης, ἡ
touch (11) ἅπτομαι
toward (7) πρός
travel (11) πορεύομαι
tribe (22) φυλή, -ῆς, ἡ
tribulation (13) θλῖψις, θλίψεως, ἡ

true (14) ἀληθής, -ές
truly (7) ἀμήν
trust (13) πίστις, πίστεως, ἡ
truth (4) ἀλήθεια, -ας, ἡ
try (9) πειράζω
turn (9) στρέφω
turn around (9) ἐπιστρέφω
turn back (9) ἐπιστρέφω
twelve (20) δώδεκα
two (14) δύο

U

unclean (20) ἀκάθαρτος, -ον
under (8) ὑπό
until (7) ἕως
utter (2, 9) λέγω

V

virgin (4) παρθένος, -ου, ὁ
visible, become (15) φαίνω
voice (4) φωνή, -ῆς, ἡ

W

waiting (at tables) (22) διακονία, -ας, ἡ
wait upon (17) διακονέω
wake (18) ἐγείρω
walk, walk around (17) περιπατέω
wander about (18) πλανάω
want (21) θέλω
warn (18) ἐπιτιμάω
watch (9, 22) φυλακή, -ῆς, ἡ; φυλάσσω
water (14) ὕδωρ, ὕδατος, τό
way (4) ὁδός, -οῦ, ἡ
weak (17) ἀσθενέω
weep (9) κλαίω
welcome (11) ἀσπάζομαι
well (19) καλῶς
what (5) ὅς, ἥ, ὅ
what? (14) ποῖος, -α, -ον; τίς, τί
whatever (20) ὅστις, ἥτις, ὅ τι
when (8) ὅτε
whenever (20) ὅταν
where (19) ὅπου; ποῦ
whether (4) εἰ
which (5, 14) ὅς, ἥ, ὅ
which? (14, 21) ποῖος, -α, -ον; τίς, τί
whichever (20) ὅστις, ἥτις, ὅ τι
while (8) ὅτε
whither (19) ὅπου
who (5) ὅς, ἥ, ὅ
who? (14) τίς, τί

whoever (20) ὅστις, ἥτις, ὅ τι
whole (4, 14) ὅλος, -η, -ον; πᾶς, πᾶσα, πᾶν
wicked (6) πονηρός, -ά, -όν
wild beast (22) θηρίον, -ου, τό
wilderness (4) ἔρημος, -ου, ἡ
will (14, 21, 22) θέλημα, θελήματος, τό; θέλω; διαθήκη, -ης, ἡ
willing (11, 21) βούλομαι
wind (14, 22) πνεῦμα, πνεύματος, τό; ἄνεμος, -ου, ὁ
wine (22) οἶνος, -ου, ὁ
wisdom (10) σοφία, -ας, ἡ
wish (11,21) θέλω; βούλομαι
with (7, 8) μετά; πρός; σύν
without (21) χωρίς
witness (13) μάρτυς, μάρτυρος, ὁ
woe (20) οὐαί
woman (13) γυνή, γυναικός, ἡ
wonder at (9) θαυμάζω

word (3, 14) λόγος, -ου, ὁ; ῥῆμα, ῥήματος, τό
work (3, 11) ἔργον, -ου, τό; ἐργάζομαι
world (3) κόσμος, -ου, ὁ
worship (17) προσκυνέω
worthy (20) ἄξιος, -α, -ον
wrath (22) ὀργή, -ῆς, ἡ
write (2, 9) γράφω
writing (7) γραφή, -ῆς, ἡ
wrong, do (9) ἁμαρτάνω

Y

year (14) ἔτος, ἔτους, τό
yes (5) ναί
yet (4, 8) ἀλλά; ἔτι
yield (16) δίδωμι
you (5) σύ
yourself, of (6) σεαυτοῦ, -ῆς

Index of Subjects

Ablative   17

Accents
    acute, grave, and circumflex   4
    contract verbs   117
    enclitics   23, 37, 112
    general rules   4f.
    imperative mood   189
    infinitives   176 nn. 4 and 5
    liquid verbs   121
    nouns   6f.
    optative mood   193 n. 3
    participles   136f., 139f.
    proclitics   21
    subjunctive mood   165
    third declension   99, 103, 109, 112
    verbs   6

Accusative
    defined   18
    forms of—see each declension
    function
        as object of the preposition   50
        cognate accusative   203
        direct object   18 and n. 5
        double accusative   203
        expressing extent or time   18, n. 5,
        203
        subject of the infinitive   178f.

Active Voice   11 n. 4; see also specific tenses

Adjective
    defined   16
    agreement   21
    and the article   21f., 24
    as a substantive   22
    comparative and superlative   122f.
    declensions (first 28–32, second 19f.,
        third 108–111)
    participle as   134, 148–152
    position (attributive and predicate)   21f.

Adverb
    defined   60f.
    comparative and superlative   122f.
    formation   61
    function   60f.

Aktionsarten
    aorist tense   66f.; also see Unitary
        Action
    defined   13

future tense   13
imperfect tense   57–59
perfect tense   74–76
present tense   13

Alphabet 1
    breathing marks   3f.
    diphthongs   2
    formation   1–3
    syllabification   4
    vowels   2

Anticipated Answers to Questions   171

Aorist Tense
    Aktionsart of   66f.
    defined   66
    formations: indicative mood
        first aorist active   67
        first aorist middle   92
        first aorist passive   71
        second aorist active   68
        second aorist middle   92
        second aorist passive   71f.
    formations: dependent moods
        imperative   189f.
        infinitive   176f.
        optative   193f.
        participles   137–140
        subjunctive   164f.
    functions
        constative   68f.
        culminative   69
        inceptive   69

Apodosis   33

Article
    anarthrous constructions   24, 149
    articular construction   24
    as demonstrative   113 n. 3, 179
    attributive position   21f., 32, 38f.
    formation of: masculine   20f.; neuter
        20f.; feminine   31f.
    predicate position   22, 38f.
    Sharpe's Rule   150 n. 6

Attraction of the Relative   40

Attributive
    adjective   21f.
    participle   148–150
    position—see Article

Augment   57f., 67, 138, 165f., 176, 188, 193

Breathing Marks   3f.

Cases—see specific case

Causal Clauses
   διὰ τό and the infinitive   182
   instrumental dative as   202
   participles   156f.
   with ὅτι   51, 182

Circumstantial Participle—see Participle

Comparisons
   comparative and superlative degrees
      of adjective   122f.
      of adverb   122f.

Complements
   infinitive as   179f.
   nouns used as object complements   41
      n. 5, 200f.
   participle as   150f.

Compound Verbs   50, 58

Conditions
   apodosis and protasis   33
   four classes
      future less probable   195
      future more probable   169, 171
      simple or logical   32f.
      unreal or contrary to fact   59f., 78
   indefinite relative to express   170f.
   participle to express   157

Consonantal Changes and Contractions
   dentals, labials, and palatals (gutturals)
      12, 99, 101 n. 2
   elision for euphony   7, 53 n. 2
   with aorist and future tenses   12, 67
   with aorist passives   71
   with perfect reduplication   74

Copulative Verb   23, 56, 82

Crasis   96

Dative
   defined   18, 201
   expressing personal interest
      advantage or disadvantage   201
      indirect object   201
      possession   201

      reference or sphere   201
   forms of—see each declension
   instrumental dative   17
      association   202
      direct object   203
      cause   202
      manner   202
      means   87
   locative dative   17
      place where   202
      time when   202

Declensions   16–18; see also First, Second,
   or Third Declension

Demonstrative Pronouns
   formation   44
   function   44f.

Dental Consonants   12, 67, 85, 87, 100

Deponent Verbs   81 nn. 1 and 2, 88

Diaeresis Mark   7

Diphthongs—see Alphabet

Direct Discourse   1, 52

Εἰμί   22–24

Emphasis   37

Enclitics—see Accents

Endings
   noun
      first declension   29
      second declension   19f.
      third declension   99, 106

   verb
      imperative mood   189
      optative mood   193f.
      primary active   11
      primary middle   83
      secondary active   57
      secondary middle   91
      subjunctive mood   163
   verbals
      infinitive   176
      participle   135

Epexegetic Infinitive   180

Euphony 7, 93, 101

Feminine Nouns of Second Declension 32

Final Consonants
  movable ν 13
  only ν, σ, or ρ used 106

First Declension
  feminine 28–31
  masculine 31

Future Tense
  formation: active 11, middle 84,
    passive 85
  liquid 121
  periphrastic 151
  significance 13, 151

Future Perfect Tense 152

Gender of Nominal Forms 17

Genitive
  absolute 158f.
  adjectival
    apposition 198
    comparison 199
    contents 198
    description (qualitative, attributive,
      reference) 197
    objective 199
    partitive 199
    possession 198
    relationship 198
    subjective 198

  adverbial
    kind of time 199
    object complement of certain verbs
      200f.
    source, authorship, or
      separation 200
  definition 18
  forms of—see each declension

Imperative Mood
  formation
    regular -ω conjugation 189
    present tense contract verbs 190
    -μι verbs 190f.
    liquid verbs 191
  functions
    command or entreaty 191
    prohibition 192

in English 188
  significance of tenses 191f.
  subjunctive instead of 193

Imperfect Tense
  definition 57
  formation
    active 57f.
    middle/passive 91f.
    contract verbs 118f.
    -μι verbs 127f.
  function
    conative 58
    continuous 58
    inceptive 59
    in conditional clauses 59f.
    iterative 58

Impersonal Verbs 174, 178

Indefinite Pronoun 111f., 170f.

Indirect Discourse 183f.

Infinitives
  definition 174
  formation of tenses 176f.
  functions
    as object 179f.
    as subject 178f.
    expressing cause 182
    expressing indirect discourse 183f.
    expressing purpose 181
    expressing result 182
    expressing time 181f.
    with impersonal verbs 178
  noun characteristics of 175f.
  significance of tenses 174f.

Inflectional Forms 17f.

Instrumental Dative 17; see also Dative

Intensive Pronoun 38

Interrogative Pronoun 111f.

Intransitive Verb 129

Iota Subscript 3

Labial Consonants 12, 67, 85f.

Linear Action 13

Liquid Consonants 87, 116, 121

Liquid Verbs 121f.

Locative Dative 17; see also Dative

Masculine Nouns of First Declension 31

-μι Verbs Chapter 16

Middle Voice 82f.; see also specific tenses

Mode—see Mood 11 n. 5

Mood
    definition 11, n. 5
    imperative 188
    indicative 11 n. 5
    optative 194
    subjunctive 162

Negative Particles 132 n. 2, 167, 171, 192

Nominative
    definition 18
    forms of—see each declension
    function
        absolute 122
        complement 23f.
        predicate 18
        subject 18
        to name someone 122

Noun
    see entries under first, second, or third
        declension
    definition 16
    gender 17
    number 17

Number
    agreement between subject and verb 103
    of nominal forms 17
    of verb forms 10

Numerals 109–111

Object Clauses 51f., 179f., 183f.

Oblique Cases 38, 171

Optative Mood
    formation 193f.
    functions
        future less probable condition 195
        potential 195
        wishing 194

Palatal (Guttural) Consonants 12, 67, 85f.

Participle
    concerning translation 145f.
    definition 134
    formation
        two sets of endings 135
        present: active 136; middle 137;
            passive 137
        aorist: active 137f.; middle 139;
            passive 139f.
        perfect: active 140f.; middle 140;
            passive 140f.
        contract verbs 141f.
        liquid verbs 142
        -μι verbs 143f.
    function
        adjectival 148–150
        circumstantial (adverbial)—see Chap-
            ter 19
        supplementary 150–152
    kind of action 138, 146–148
    temporal value 146–148

Passive Voice 70; see also specific tenses

Past Perfect Tense—see Pluperfect Tense

(Present) Perfect Tense
    Aktionsart of 74
    formation 74f.
    function 76

Periphrasis with Participles
    present 151, imperfect 151, future
        151
    perfect 151f., pluperfect 152, future
        perfect 152

Personal Endings—see Endings

Personal Pronouns
    formation 36f.
    function 37–39

Pluperfect Tense
    formation 76f.
    function 76

Plural—see Number

Possessive Pronouns 37, 39, 46, 73

Postpositive Position 35

Predicate Position—see Article

Preformative (prefix) 10, 57f., 67, 74, 85

Prepositions
 definition 50
 function as substantive 51

Present Tense
 definition 13
 formation
  indicative mood: -ω conjugation 11;
   contract verbs 117–119; -μι verbs
   126f., 129–131; imperative mood
   189f.; infinitive 174–177; optative
   mood 193; participle 136f., subjunctive mood 164–166

Primary Endings
 active 11
 middle 83

Primary Tenses 11

Principal Parts of Verbs 10 n. 3

Proclitics 21

Prohibition 167, 192f.

Pronouns—see specific type

Pronunciation 1–3

Protasis 33

Punctuation 7

Purpose Clauses
 ἵνα and the subjunctive 168
 infinitive 181
 ὅπως and the subjunctive 168
 participle 158

Questions
 deliberative 167
 direct 7, 168, 171, 178, 183
 indirect 183
 punctuation mark 7

Reciprocal Pronoun 88f.

Reduplication 74

Reflexive Pronoun 45f.

Relative Pronoun 39f.

Result Clauses 182f.

Second Declension
 masculine 19
 neuter 19f.

Secondary Endings
 active 56f.
 middle 91

Secondary Tenses 11

Singular-see Number

Subject
 articular 24
 definition and case of 16, 18, 23f.
 infinitive as 178f.
 neuter plural subject and singular verb
  103
 participle as 149f.

Subjunctive Mood
 definition 162f.
 formation
  -ω verbs: present 164, aorist 164
  contract verbs 166
  liquid verbs 166
  -μι verbs 165f.
 function
  deliberative 167f.
  future more probable
   condition 169f.
  hortatory 166f.
  indefinite relative clauses 170f.
  indefinite time, with ὅταν 169
  prohibition 167
  purpose 168
 future orientation 162f.
 significance of tense 163, 167–170

Substantive 22, 51, 149, 178

Sufformative 10

Superlative 122f.

Supplementary—see Participle

Syllabification 4

Tenses-see specific tense

Third Declension
 accent of 99, 103, 109, 112
 consonantal contractions 99
 description of 97

formation of
  adjectives   109–111
  feminine nouns   101f.
  indefinite and interrogative pronouns
    111f.
  masculine nouns   100f., 103
  neuter nouns   106–108
  numerals   109–111
  summary chart   108

Transitive Verbs   18, 129

Uncials   1f.

Unitary Action   13 n. 9, 66f., 68–70, 138,
157f., 163, 167–171, 175, 188, 191–194

Verbal Adjective—see Participle

Verbal Noun—see Infinitive

Verbs
  definition   9
  formation—see specific tense
  mood   10, 11 n. 5
  number   10
  person   10

preformative   10
stem   9f.
sufformative   10
tables:
  λύω, a regular verb of the -ω
    conjugation, indicative mood
    (organized by endings)   94
  λύω, a regular verb of the -ω conju-
    gation, indicative mood (orga-
    nized by principal parts) 94f.
  ἄγω, a regular verb of the -ω conju-
    gation, indicative mood (show-
    ing a vowel initial letter and a
    consonantal stem ending;
    organized by endings)   95f.
  εἰμί Table 5   207
tense—see specific tense
voice   11 n. 4

Vocative
  direct address   18
  formation—see each declension

Voice—see Active, Middle, or Passive

Vowels   2

Index of Scriptures
(* indicates citation only)

Matthew	*Page*
1:1ff.	1*
1:2, 6f., 12, 19f.	1*
1:22	1*, 87, 168
1:23	1*, 13*
2:7	134
2:10	203*
2:13	177*, 181
2:23	168
3:14	58
4:6	33
5:3-10	51*
5:3, 8	201
5:16	51
5:24	191*
5:42	190*
5:45	22
6:1	181
6:2, 5, 16	169
7:6	167
7:24	149
8:2	38
9:6	177*
10:8	190*
10:29	120
12:6, 12	199
12:10	178
12:25	134
12:31	199
12:32	171
13:2, 32	123
13:16	51
13:19-23	45*
13:30	191*
13:38	24
14:4	174f.
14:5, 16	175
14:7	183*
14:24, 26, 27-30	191
14:28, 29, 30	192
14:36	168f.
15:14	120
15:30f.	182
16:13-17	183
16:16	24
16:19	152
16:21	177*, 178*
17:5	44f.
18:8, 13	199*

18:18	152
18:26	38
19:6	182
19:27	76
21:8	123
21:45	184
22:11, 43	203
23:23	177*
23:31	201
24:46	147
25:6	202*
25:20	147f., 150, 158
25:24	147 n. 3, 148
26:6	159
26:7	149, 158f.
26:8	151*, 158
26:25	146
26:34	182*
26:39	192
27:4	148
27:5	83
27:11	37
28:5	134

Mark	
1:4	197
1:9	70
2:7, 10	177*
2:10	180
3:4	178
4:1	123
4:15	169
4:16, 29, 31f.	169*
5:4	175, 182*
5:14	183*
5:29	157
5:33	156f.
5:35, 39	69
5:36	149 n. 5
6:49	184
7:14	38
8:31	178
9:5, 35	179
10:17	24
10:38	179
10:45	181
11:8	123
11:14	194 and n. 4

11:22	199	15:30	201
11:24	191	16:3	179, 181
11:44	194*	18:11	199
12:7	167	21:14	190*
12:14	168	21:24	151
12:18	183*	21:37	58
12:41	58	22:23	195*
13:26	147	22:35	201*
14:3	198	22:69	151
14:4	151*	23:40	38
14:30	202*	24:13	203*
14:35	203		
14:39	38	*John*	
15:29, 30	157	1:1	24
15:47	198	1:6	122
		1:50	183*
		2:19	192
Luke		2:20	69
1:15	201*	2:24	182
1:29, 61f.	195*	2:25	182*
2:15	167	3:21, 24	152
2:26	152	3:28	151f.
3:7-10	168	3:29	202
3:15	195*	4:7, 17	39*
4:29, 30	182	5:5, 9, 16	59
5:4	151	5:10, 12	148
5:5	147	5:14	39*
5:21	177	5:31	170
5:24	177*	5:46	60
6:8, 30, 38	190*	6:6	39
6:11	193*, 195*	6:27	18, 168
6:33	38*	6:28	168f.
6:47	149, 150 n. 6	6:50, 58	51
6:48	149	6:58	69
7:9	148	6:60, 64	134
7:12	202	6:70	171
7:39	60	7:9	134
7:40	180	8:16	170
8:9	195*	8:21, 24	120
8:49	159	8:36	170
8:49, 50, 52	193	9:25	157
8:54	192*	9:31, 32	184
9:22	178*	9:41	184*
9:44	191*	10:4f.	184*
9:46	195*	10:18	69
10:2	201*	10:25, 27	103
10:8	171	10:36	52
11:1	180, 181f.	10:37f.	168f.
12:2	88	11:6	203
12:43	44	11:19	76*
13:33	177*	11:31	202
15:7	199*	11:36	58
15:17	202	13:5	87
15:26	195*		

13:17	170	**Romans**	
13:23	151	1:4	200
13:35	201	3:25	199
14:20	45*	4:11	198
14:21	45	5:7	120
14:26	44, 203	5:9	87
14:28	199	5:17	146
14:31	166f.	6:2	202
15:12	13*	6:2, 15	195*
15:13	199	6:3f.	70
15:20	38 n. 2, 40,	6:9	147 and n. 2
	201*	6:13	146
15:22	60*	7:7	24, 195*
17:2	199	7:25	39*
18:16, 18	76*	8:8	203
19:25	198	8:24	149 n. 5
21:13	88	9:14	194*
21:15	198	9:25f.	134
		10:9	170
Acts		10:12	38*
1:3	182*	11:20	202
3:26	158	11:23	180
5:24	195*	14:9	69
7:5	158*	14:13	180
7:40	122	15:5	194*
8:20	193*, 194 and	15:13	194
	n. 4	15:26	199
8:22	201*		
8:31	193*, 195,	**1 Corinthians**	
	195*	1:10	38*
9:17	134	1:12	198
10:17	195*	1:18	199
13:11	158	2:7-8	78
14:31	166f.	3:1-2	88
14:36	168f.	5:8	183*
15:29	201*	6:11	83
15:36	167*	7:11	177*
17:18	193*, 195*	10:13	40
17:22	18	10:32	201f.
17:27	193*, 194*	11:22	201
18:20	159*	12:19	60
18:25	58	12:29f.	171
20:34	39*	14:2	87
21:33	195*	14:20	191
24:19	193*	14:33	197f.
25:16, 16	195*	15:10	39*
25:20	193*	15:13f.	70
26:7	202*	15:14	74
26:10, 12	200		
26:14	159	**2 Corinthians**	
26:16	190*	2:7	202
26:29	194f.*	2:11	18
27:39	193	2:17	151

5:5	198	**Philemon**	
10:1	38	20	194
11:14	83		
		Hebrews	
Galatians		1:3	197f.
1:10	60	1:10	198
1:23	151	1:12	38
2:17	195*	2:3	157
		2:8	150
Ephesians		2:14	70, 201*
1:15	51*	2:17	70
2:5	202	5:12	198
2:20	159*	5:13	201*
4:27	190*	6:4, 5	201*
6:14	190*	9:12	83
		10:17	201*
Philippians		10:36	83
1:6	24	11:13, 39	83*
1:18	202	12:11	198
1:21	179	12:22	202
2:12	183*	13:13	157
2:13	179		
2:24	76	**James**	
4:15	201*	2:16	198
		4:12	177*
Colossians		5:12	18
1:3	158		
1:5	148	**1 Peter**	
1:6	151	1:2	194
1:8	149	1:14	197
3:9, 10	134, 157	3:4	32
		3:14	193*, 195
1 Thessalonians		3:17	195
1:2f., 3	198		
1:6	200	**2 Peter**	
2:9	199	3:9	177*
4:3f.	180		
4:6	68	**1 John**	
4:9	181	1:1	76*
5:23	194	1:5	24
		2:12-14	76*
2 Thessalonians		2:16	198
2:16	38	4:8	22
2:17	24, 193*	4:10, 13	52
3:5	194	5:16	203*
1 Timothy		**Revelation**	
4:1	201*	1:17	150 n. 6
		11:17	18
2 Timothy		18:2f., 5, 14	70
1:8	167, 193	18:10	70, 202
4:7	203	22:3	203
4:16	194		

List of Scriptures Used as Exercises
[Numbers within ( ) refer to page]

Matthew 1:1–8 cited only (8); 2:22b–23 (172); 3:13 (184); 4:7–9a (132); 5:8, 9 (124); 6:14 modified (132), 9, 10 (195); 10:22 modified (153); 11:11 (203); 12:2–4 (185), 18, 20 cited only (8); 14:34, 35 (160), 24, 25 (203); 19:28 modified (96), 19, 21 (196); 20:18, 19 (185); 22:45 (124), 23, 24, 29 (172), 46 (185); 24:35 (96), 9 modified (153); 26:43 (159), 44 (160), 60b, 61 (184), 9, 10 (204); 27:8 (124), 49 (195).

Mark 10:31 modified (96); 11:25 modified (132), 17–19 (172); 13:21 (196); 14:35 modified (96); 15:46 (171).

Luke 1:32, 33 (131), 28, 29, 30 (196); 2:15 modified (96); 5:17 (184); 7:33 (160); 11:29 (132); 16:10 (124); 17:26, 27 modified (96).

John 1:10 modified (53); 3:2 modified (79), 1 (124); 5:22 (132), 37, 38 (153), 10, 11 (196); 6:32 (132), 41 (153), 59, 45 (160), 29–31 (171); 8:19 (103), 39–42 (124); 9:22 (204); 11:31 modified (78), 34a (132), 2, 17, 44 (204); 12:29–31 (104); 14:10 modified (52), 20 (104); 15:20 (123), 15 (124); 17:4, 5 modified (78), 12 (132), 18, 19 (172); 20:30 (152), 26, 29 (159), 31 (172), 27 (196).

Acts 1:8 (104); 2:3, 5 (153), 6–8, 13 (159); 3:17 (104), 25 (132); 4:14–16 (184); 5:32 (112), 27 modified, 28 (132); 7:17 modified (96); 8:13 (104), 16, 25 (152), 14 (160); 9:2, 17 (172), 16 (185), 11, 15 (196); 16:3 (113); 20:16 (196); 24:24 (104); 28:21 modified (96).

Romans 3:19a modified (72); 5:12 modified (96); 6:12, 13 (195); 7:25 (204); 8:38, 39 (96); 11:11 (204).

1 Corinthians 2:8, 11 (112); 6, 7 (153); 3:8 (153); 6:15, 19, 20 (113); 7:14 (104), 4 (113), 16 (114); 8:3 (124); 9:1 (104); 11:8, 9 (104), 5a (204); 12:15, 18, 19 (172); 14:20 (196); 15:10 (104), 35, 38 (132), 12 (153); 16:10 modified (96).

2 Corinthians 4:13, 14 (153), 5, 6 (204); 5:16 (104), 14 (113); 6:14 (204); 9:3 (172).

Galatians 1:17 modified (89); 3:27, 28 (113); 5:14 (124); 6:14 (204).

Ephesians 2:5 (204).

Colossians 2:10, 11 (204); 3:9, 10 (196).

1 Thessalonians 4:10 (185).

Hebrews 1:10 (104), 12 (113); 5:14 (204).

James 1:20 (104); 2:18a (104), 26 (113), 18a, 19, 21a (124), 22, 23, 25 (159), 18 (195).

1 Peter 1:16 (89).

1 John 1:7 (172); 2:18 modified (89); 3:17, 18 (172); 4:1 (196).

Revelation 11:16, 17 (152); 21:5 (196); 22:17 (196).

λύω, A REGULAR VERB OF THE OMEGA CONJUGATION

Principal Parts   λύω   λύσω   ἔλυσα

	Present A.	Present M./P.	Imperfect A.	Imperfect M./P.	Future A.	Future M.	Aorist A.	Aorist M.
Indic. Mood								
Sg.								
1.	λύω	λύομαι	ἔλυον	ἐλυόμην	λύσω	λύσομαι	ἔλυσα	ἐλυσάμην
2.	λύεις	λύῃ	ἔλυες	ἐλύου	λύσεις	λύσῃ	ἔλυσας	ἐλύσω
3.	λύει	λύεται	ἔλυε	ἐλύετο	λύσει	λύσεται	ἔλυσε	ἐλύσατο
Pl.								
1.	λύομεν	λυόμεθα	ἐλύομεν	ἐλυόμεθα	λύσομεν	λυσόμεθα	ἐλύσαμεν	ἐλυσάμεθα
2.	λύετε	λύεσθε	ἐλύετε	ἐλύεσθε	λύσετε	λύσεσθε	ἐλύσατε	ἐλύσασθε
3.	λύουσι	λύονται	ἔλυον	ἐλύοντο	λύσουσι	λύσονται	ἔλυσαν	ἐλύσαντο
Subj. Mood								
Sg.								
1.	λύω	λύωμαι					λύσω	λύσωμαι
2.	λύῃς	λύῃ					λύσῃς	λύσῃ
3.	λύῃ	λύηται					λύσῃ	λύσηται
Pl.								
1.	λύωμεν	λυώμεθα					λύσωμεν	λυσώμεθα
2.	λύητε	λύησθε					λύσητε	λύσησθε
3.	λύωσι(ω)	λύωνται					λύσωσι(ν)	λύσωνται
Imv. Mood								
Sg.								
2.	λῦε	λύου					λῦσον	λῦσαι
3.	λυέτω	λυέσθω					λυσάτω	λυσάσθω
Pl.								
2.	λύετε	λύεσθε					λύσατε	λύσασθε
3.	λυέτωσαν	λυέσθωσαν					λυσάτωσαν	λυσάσθως
Infin.	λύειν	λύεσθαι			λύσειν	λύσεσθαι	λῦσαι	λύσασθαι
Part.								
M.	λύων	λυόμενος			λύσων	λυσόμενος	λύσας	λυσάμενο
F.	λύουσα	λυομένη			λύσουσα	λυσομένη	λύσασα	λυσαμένη
N.	λῦον	λυόμενον			λύσον	λυσόμενον	λύσαν	λυσάμενο